Healing
Plots

Healing Plots

The Narrative Basis of Psychotherapy

Edited by
Amia Lieblich, Dan P. McAdams,
and Ruthellen Josselson

American Psychological Association
Washington, DC

Published by
American Psychological Association
750 First Street, NE
Washington, DC 20002
www.apa.org

To order
APA Order Department
P.O. Box 92984
Washington, DC 20090-2984
Tel: (800) 374-2721
Direct: (202) 336-5510
Fax: (202) 336-5502
TDD/TTY: (202) 336-6123
Online: www.apa.org/books/
E-mail: order@apa.org

In the U.K., Europe, Africa, and the Middle
East, copies may be ordered from
American Psychological Association
3 Henrietta Street
Covent Garden, London
WC2E 8LU England

Typeset in Goudy by World Composition Services, Inc., Sterling, VA

Printer: Port City Press, Inc., Baltimore, MD
Cover Designer: Naylor Design, Washington, DC
Project Manager: Debbie Hardin, Carlsbad, CA

The opinions and statements published are the responsibility of the authors, and such
opinions and statements do not necessarily represent the policies of the American
Psychological Association.

Library of Congress Cataloging-in-Publication Data

Healing plots : the narrative basis of psychotherapy / edited by Amia Lieblich,
Dan P. McAdams, and Ruthellen Josselson.—1st ed.
    p. cm.—(The narrative study of lives)
Includes bibliographical references and index.
ISBN 1-59147-100-1 (alk. paper)
1. Psychotherapy. 2. Storytelling. 3. Narrative therapy. I. Lieblich, Amia, 1939–
II. McAdams, Dan P. III. Josselson, Ruthellen. IV. Series.

RC489.S74H418 2004
616.89′165—dc22   2003017997

British Library Cataloguing-in-Publication Data
A CIP record is available from the British Library.

Printed in the United States of America
First Edition

CONTENTS

Contributors .... *vii*

Acknowledgments .... *ix*

Introduction 3

Chapter 1. The Significance of Narrative and Storytelling in
            Postpsychological Counseling and Psychotherapy 11
            John McLeod

Chapter 2. Demonic and Tragic Narratives in Psychotherapy 29
            Nahi Alon and Haim Omer

Chapter 3. The Paradigm of Tragedy as Meta-Narrative:
            A Window to Understanding the Life Story of a
            Woman in Economic and Social Deprivation 49
            Michal Krumer-Nevo

Chapter 4. Between Abstract Individualism and Gendered Lives:
            Negotiating Abused Women's Agency and Identity
            in Therapy 67
            Suvi Keskinen

Chapter 5. Echoes of Silence: Remembering and Repeating
            Childhood Trauma 89
            Lynn Sorsoli

Chapter 6. On Becoming the Narrator of One's Own Life 111
            Ruthellen Josselson

Chapter 7.   Living to Tell the Tale: Redemption Narratives,
              Shame Management, and Offender Rehabilitation ... 129
              Shadd Maruna and Derek Ramsden

Chapter 8.   The Core Conflictual Relationship Theme
              Approach to Relational Narratives: Interpersonal
              Themes in the Context of Intergenerational
              Communication of Trauma 151
              Hadas Wiseman and Jacques P. Barber

Chapter 9.   The Place of Psychotherapy in the Life Stories of
              Women in Households Without Men 171
              Amia Lieblich

Chapter 10.   A Love Story: Self-Defining Memories in
              Couples Therapy 189
              Jefferson A. Singer

Author Index 209

Subject Index 213

About the Editors 221

CONTRIBUTORS

Nahi Alon, private practice, Tel Aviv, Israel

Jacques P. Barber, University of Pennsylvania, Philadelphia

Ruthellen Josselson, Hebrew University of Jerusalem, Israel; Fielding
  Graduate Institute, Baltimore, MD

Suvi Keskinen, University of Tampere, Tampere, Finland

Michal Krumer-Nevo, Ben-Gurion University, Beer-Sheva, Israel

Amia Lieblich, Hebrew University of Jerusalem, Israel

Shadd Maruna, University of Cambridge, Cambridge, England

Dan P. McAdams, Northwestern University, Evanston, IL

John McLeod, University of Abertay, Dundee, Scotland

Haim Omer, Tel Aviv University, Israel

Derek Ramsden, Her Majesty's Prison Service, London, England

Jefferson A. Singer, Connecticut College, New London

Lynn Sorsoli, Wellesley College, Wellesley, MA

Hadas Wiseman, University of Haifa, Israel

ACKNOWLEDGMENTS

The editors would like to thank the many people who reviewed manuscripts and provided substantive input for this volume. In particular, we offer our thanks to Irving Alexander, Dan Bar-On, Yoram Bilu, Susan Chase, Bert Cohler, Ravenna Helson, Mary Ann Machado, Jim Marcia, Sam Osherson, Jennifer Pals, Monisha Pasupathi, Peter Raggatt, Cheryl Rampage, Annie Rogers, George Rosenwald, Kjell Ruderstam, and Richard Stuart for their hard work in reviewing manuscripts. Finally, we wish to thank Jeanne M. Foley and the Foley Center for the Study of Lives for their generous support of our book series and for establishing the Foley Center for the Study of Lives at Northwestern University.

THE NARRATIVE STUDY OF LIVES ADVISORY BOARD

James E. Marcia, Psychology, *Simon Fraser University*
Jean Baker Miller, Psychoanalysis, *Stone Center, Wellesley College*
Elliot Mishler, Psychiatry, *Cambridge Hospital*
Richard L. Ochberg, *Boston, MA*
June H. Price, Nursing, *Farleigh Dickinson University*
Gabriele Rosenthal, Sociology, *Gesamthochschule Kassel, Germany*
George C. Rosenwald, Psychology, *University of Michigan*
William McKinley Runyan, School of Social Service, *University of California, Berkeley*
Abigail J. Stewart, Psychology and Women's Studies, *University of Michigan*
George E. Vaillant, Psychiatry, *Dartmouth Medical Center*
Guy Widdershoven, Philosophy, *University of Limburg, The Netherlands*

Healing
Plots

INTRODUCTION

Although many therapeutic case studies may be read as literary works, the process of psychotherapy can only be described in the form of narration. What therapists do and how they think about their work is infused with narrative principles.

Tales of mental illness, treatment, and healing—from Sigmund Freud's cases to contemporary novels about mental illness and recovery—have always attracted a wide readership. Our fascination with these stories may stem from many sources. The suffering of others may evoke our curiosity, empathy, or fear. We may identify with the story's protagonist, seeing parallels to our own struggles and finding hope for recovery, healing, or growth. What typically goes on in therapy is shrouded in mystery for many of us, so we may look to these stories to enlighten us and give us an intriguing glimpse into the unknown.

Freud was perhaps the first to recognize the intimate connection between narrative and therapy. His case studies set out his understanding of the therapeutic principles that he was discovering and have become classics in the psychoanalytical and psychotherapeutic literature. Each of Freud's major case histories can be seen as a story of great interest as well as a condensed course in the technique of psychoanalytical therapy. For example, his case of Dora (1905/1963), still read by analysts and students today, provides a compelling narrative of therapeutic process and psychoanalytical interpretation. Literary theorists have noted, furthermore, how Freud used a number of devices in the Dora case—dramatic flashbacks, warnings to the reader, and deviations from chronology—to construct a narrative that resembles in some ways the 20th-century novels of Marcel Proust or Henry James and the plays of Henrik Ibsen (Marcus, 1977). Although some therapeutic case studies, therefore, may be viewed as literary works themselves, the process of psychotherapy has also been viewed as a literary affair. We believe that this is true for all sorts of therapy in current use, and not only in the case of psychoanalytical treatments. Therapists and clients coconstruct stories, create and revise narratives with the hope of finding solutions to personal problems, better coping strategies to meet life's challenges, enhanced growth and development, and greater psychological insight (Schafer, 1981; White & Epston, 1990). Many forms of psychotherapy—from psychoanalysis to cognitive–behavioral therapy—involve life storytelling and retelling; in other words, they are based on narrative. The construction of a story in some form or shape is part of the intake or diagnostic procedures, as well as of the final report every therapist creates, whether for herself, her peer practitioners, students, or the agencies toward which she is responsible. It is also part of how the therapist mentally records each session with every patient as he or she makes note of "what happened" in the meeting.

This is the third volume in the American Psychological Association series, *The Narrative Study of Lives* (see Josselson, Lieblich, & McAdams, 2003; McAdams, Josselson, & Lieblich, 2001). Each volume in the series examines how psychologists, sociologists, anthropologists, historians, and other scholars examine and conceptualize human lives in narrative terms. The current volume focuses on the relationship between therapy and narrative. The chapter authors will address questions such as these: In what ways is therapy shaped by narrative assumptions about human life? How do therapists and their clients negotiate narrative conflict and complexity? What kinds of stories animate the psychotherapeutic process? Are some stories better than others in therapy? How do life stories change through and as a result of therapy? And what might we learn about narratives themselves from studying the process of therapy?

All of the authors in this volume share a general belief that therapeutic interventions of many kinds often involve the coconstruction of healing narratives in the face of personal, moral, and social adversity. Therapy is a process of developing a narrative that brings integration and some degree of coherence to a chaotic life. The transformation of life narrative in therapy—and in life more generally—is what fundamental *identity* change is all about. The construction and reconstruction of narrative identity takes place in a complex social and cultural context, within a community of shared values and morality.

The chapters collected in this volume describe and analyze the process of therapy from a variety of perspectives, contexts, and cultural settings, using examples from research in the United States, Europe, and Israel. They collectively demonstrate how narratives shape and humanize our work as therapists, on the one hand, and how, on the other, the process of therapy enriches our understanding of narratives and their place in contemporary studies of human identity.

ORGANIZATION OF THE VOLUME

Chapter 1 provides a historical–social context for understanding why and how therapists focus on clients narratives. John McLeod provides a critique of psychotherapy as a modern cultural invention. In the past, the social significance of psychotherapy relied on its accommodation to modernity with its central values of rationality, progress, consumption, and safety. Its main thrust was to lead the individual to look inward, to find his or her harmony within. The new look or postpsychological approach, as proposed by McLeod, invites the individual to look outward toward the social–cultural world with its language and symbols. Although narratives have their role and function in both psychological and postpsychological perspectives, the meaning of the concept is quite different. Among other things, in the latter, the client is regarded as a member of his or her culture, and difficulties stem from the interface of society and the individual. The basis of postpsychological therapy, then, is its appreciation of the central role of the narrative in the transmission of cultural values and in all human interaction and meaning-making endeavors (Bruner, 2002).

In chapter 2, Nahi Alon and Haim Omer join McLeod in claiming that narratives in therapy and in popular beliefs illuminate the historical–cultural sources of influence on current ideologies and practices. Master narratives, which have evolved through the ages, influence all our thoughts and actions, as well as clinical theory and practice. In this chapter, two such master narratives are explored and contrasted. The demonic narrative is based on an extreme split between good and evil, and the attribution of all suffering to conspiring wickedness, which is often hidden. The tragic narrative, which is presented as an antidote to the former, reads as a call for modesty in approaching human ability to control life in its vicissitudes. It emphasizes the nonpersonal and unintentional sources of suffering and advocates compassion toward sufferers rather than eradication of evil. The authors argue that the demonic and tragic are not essential attributes of psychological theories but are rather interpretive styles that infiltrate the work of therapy.

The influence of the concept and tradition of literary tragedy also underlies Michal Krumer-Nevo's chapter 3. As therapists, asks the author, how do we talk about our clients? In social science discourse, women who live in economic and social deprivation tend to be rendered, both in research and in therapy, either as victims, casualties of circumstance, or as blame-worthy and responsible for their circumstances. The chapter points out the problems of these conceptualizations and suggests an alternative view using three basic components of the dramatic tragedy: the impossible choice of the hero, the contest with fate, and the ironic reversal of fortune. This alternative narrative interpretation is exemplified through the life story of a woman who lives in deep and long-term economic and social deprivation. Krumer-Nevo's interpretation paves the way for an empathic and original approach to this woman as a protagonist agent, responsible and doomed at the same time.

Suvi Keskinen's chapter 4 also explores the implicit narratives used for the construction of women's plight and recovery, emphasizing the role of policy-makers and counselors in supporting one or another script for people in transition. In therapy, according to the author, some of the clients' narratives receive recognition and are reinforced, whereas others are judged detrimental to the healing process. Keskinen described how social workers and their female clients who frequent domestic abuse counseling centers negotiate the discrepancy between the desired narrative of abstract individ-ual agency and the more traditional gendered narrative of women as care-givers for their families. Emphasizing cultural setting as influencing both personal and professional life stories, Keskinen analyzes conversations be-tween therapists and their clients to demonstrate how therapists use implicit and explicit narratives to construct their clients' identity.

Although the former chapters weigh different therapeutic narratives against each other, Lynn Sorsoli's chapter 5 problematizes the importance of disclosure as effecting psychological recovery. Working with women survi-vors of sexual abuse, the author concludes that narrating their past traumas does not always lead to healing, security, or relief. In her work with the four survivors whose stories this chapter comprises, Sorsoli was interested in the manner of their telling or not telling. Her main finding is that the narrators' words, silences, and emotions can be taken as manifesting essential elements of the traumatic experiences that persistently repeat in their lives. A good therapist, according to Sorsoli, would not only honor these survivors' struggles but also move beyond words and develop a way to listen to what remains unsaid.

A different kind of silence is perhaps present when words are used but no personal story emerges from them. How do we construct our own autobiography? We all borrow stories from each other to construct it. Ruth-ellen Josselson's chapter 6 explores the costs and limits of this phenomenon. Starting with the question of what it might mean not to be the narrator of one's life, the chapter describes a young woman who seemed to have delegated the function of narrating her life story to her mother. In therapy, to which she had been referred by her mother, she could report about events but never tell stories in which she was the heroine, the agent. Gradually her therapist realized that the young woman was a protagonist in a story narrated by her mother. What Josselson stresses is how easy and tempting it may be for a therapist to take the role of creating a coherent story for one's client, thus perpetuating the condition of narrating another's life.

That stories are at the core of recovery processes, and that some scripts are preferred by the social system over others, are also the basic assumptions of Shadd Maruna and Derek Ramsden's chapter 7. In Alcoholics Anonymous, for more than 60 years people have managed, by sharing their stories, to overcome addiction and encourage others to do so. The authors determine how the story and its telling helps recovery. Based on their study of the life stories of 30 chronic offenders in Britain, the authors propose that narrative reconstruction of the offender life story can be understood as a form of shame management. This involves a social process of autobiographical reconstruction, whereby outcast groups or individuals overcome their stigmatization and find their way back into mainstream society. The authors offer an analysis of the elements of such justificatory narratives.

By studying a variety of special groups of women or men, this volume demonstrates how informed attention to the shape and processes of narrative opens new vistas in the understanding, communicating, and healing of human suffering. Exploring the relational themes among sons and daughters of Holocaust survivors is the topic of Hadas Wiseman and Jacques Barber's chapter 8. The Core Conflictual Relationship Theme (CCRT) method was adapted by the authors for a study of a nonclinical sample of second-generation Holocaust survivors' offspring, as a means to explore the intergenerational transmission or communication of their parents' traumas. What may be seen as some form of distorted communication between the generations is in fact a particular style of "know-not-knowing," of a wordless interpersonal space that characterizes many of the relational stories collected in this study. Thus, this chapter joins Sorsoli's work about the silent gaps in the self-disclosure of traumatized women, indicating some important generality in the discourse of traumas, whether in the therapy context or in the framework of narrative research.

Many writers on psychotherapy stress the interpersonal core of both symptoms and healing. While collecting life stories of women who live in a variety of unconventional households, Amia Lieblich discovered a high frequency of spontaneous references to psychotherapy or counseling in the narratives. In chapter 9, she documents the way in which the central theme of therapy as constructed in her participants' narratives is the narrators' present and absent relationships. In spite of the participants' independence and agency as manifested in their entire self-presentation, concerns about motherhood, couple relationships, and relationships with parents were dominant reasons for seeking therapy. Rather than a means for overcoming symptoms, therapy gets integrated into the narrators' life stories primarily as a means to cope with relational problems. On a broader level, it is perhaps the narrative discourse itself that leads people to construct their life plots within relational spaces.

Stories of individuals in their social–cultural world are always at the core of narrative scholarship. The volume closes with Jefferson Singer's chapter 10. Through the life story of a couple and a detailed analysis of a single self-defining remembered episode, Singer's account opens for the reader an unusual landscape of love in fantasy and reality as it unfolds in memory and therapy. Demonstrating how an analysis of this episode was used to produce change in the couple relationship, Singer boldly expresses what the editors of this volume consider to be basic for all therapy processes: Life is constructed and reconstructed through the stories we tell about ourselves and our relationships. What makes us suffer or remain hopeful are the narratives we create out of the facts of our lives.

Taken together, these chapters provide a landscape of psychotherapy as viewed through the lens of narrative, painted by sensitive therapists and scholars who make the concepts of story, telling, and silence integral to their practice and thinking. In doing so, these contributions enrich the scholarly interest in stories, their construction, coconstruction, and communication. As a group, they demonstrate the immense power of stories, and therefore their creators, in making meanings and changing lives on the one hand, and the input of language, culture and society in providing a menu of good and bad stories to their consumers, on the other hand. In the following case studies, identifying characteristics have been altered to disguise the identity of patients.

Amia Lieblich
In collaboration with Dan P. McAdams and Ruthellen Josselson

REFERENCES

Bruner, J. (2002). *Making stories: Law, literature' life*. New York: Farrar, Straus & Giroux.

Freud, S. (1963). *Dora: An analysis of a case of hysteria (With an introduction by P. Rieff)*. New York: Macmillan. (Original published 1905)

Josselson, R., Lieblich, A., & McAdams, D. P. (Eds.). (2003). *Up close and personal: The teaching and learning of narrative research*. Washington, DC: American Psychological Association.

Marcus, S. (1977). Freud and Dora: Story, history, case history. In T. Shapiro (Ed.), *Psychoanalysis and contemporary science* (pp. 389–442). New York: International Universities Press.

McAdams, D. P., Josselson, R., & Lieblich, A. (Eds.). (2001). *Turns in the road: Narrative studies of lives in transition*. Washington, DC: American Psychological Association.

Schafer, R. (1981). Narration in the psychoanalytic dialogue. In W. J. J. Mitchell (Ed.), *On narrative* (pp. 25–49). Chicago: University of Chicago Press.

White, M., & Epston, D. (1990). *Narrative means to therapeutic ends*. New York: Norton.

1

THE SIGNIFICANCE OF NARRATIVE AND STORYTELLING IN POSTPSYCHOLOGICAL COUNSELING AND PSYCHOTHERAPY

JOHN McLEOD

When the social history of the 20th century is written, psychotherapy and counseling will come to be seen as a unique and distinctively modern cultural invention. What came to be known as therapy grew out of religion, opening a cultural space anchored in the scientific legitimacy of medicine and psychology, yet drawing on old ideas from drama, rhetoric, and art. It eventually expanded to fill the gaps left behind as traditional forms of personal problem-solving and meaning-making dissolved. Therapy provided meaning bridges between the compartments of increasingly fragmented modern lives. The reach and credibility of therapy grew throughout the 20th century. At the same time, and at the same pace, there was growth in the level of multiplicity of life in modern industrialized societies (van den Berg, 1974). Therapy provided a place where individuals could seek resolution and understanding of the problems in living generated by an ever-expanding menu of choices. Therapy was the place to go to achieve some balance between reason and emotion, self and other, tradition and progress. And therapy itself was required constantly to reinvent itself to reflect demands of a changing social landscape (Cushman, 1995; McLeod, 2001).

The social significance of therapy relied on its accommodation to the key values of modern culture: rationality, progress, consumption, and safety. The great achievements of modern civilization were built on science and technology, which promote a rational, detached approach to the world. The actual day-to-day operation of modern society depended on bureaucratic forms of administration that are grounded in rational (or pseudorational) procedures. There was therefore great pressure on people in modern cultures to be rational and to control the expression of feeling. This control was necessarily internal and psychological, rather than external and collective, because of the breakdown of communal forms of life and the anonymity of mass society. Modern culture was also built on an assumption of progress— the future will be better than the past because of the advancement of science, technology, and general knowledge. The notion of progress was also applied to the person. Each of us could become a better person. The concept of the person as *consumer* was integral to the advanced capitalist economies of the modern world. The economic system needed (apparently) a steady expansion in markets and production. One way of achieving this economic growth was to give people choice in the objects they buy and use. At the same time, the exercise of choice reinforced the value of rationality and provided opportunities for identity construction (Giddens, 1991). Finally, as a social system based on rationality, control, progress, and consumption expanded, it came to resemble a self-contained perfect world, clean and safe, much like Disneyland or MacDonalds. Outside of this bubble were tragic human realities such as catastrophe, war, famine, and disease. Increasing effort was devoted to fending off these risks.

Therapy became a central and necessary element of modern cultural life because it provided a space in which the implications of modernity could be explored at a personal level, in response to the unique dilemmas and situations faced by the individual client.

In the closing years of the 20th century, it became apparent that questions were beginning to be asked in therapy about the relationship between therapy and society and between therapy and the knowledges that had, up until then, sustained that relationship. As Peavy (1996) put it, the time had come for a "new look."

POSTPSYCHOLOGICAL THERAPY

A form of therapy evolved that did not operate by inviting the person to look inward at the self or at his or her repertoire of behavior but to look outward, at the ways in which he or she engages with the social world through language, dialogue, and action: "The notion of language as a social phenomenon can lead us to perceive the therapeutic process as an outer journey into the language and symbols of a culture, rather than as an inner journey into one's true self" (Lynch, 1997, p. 128). There are several distinct approaches within this new look. The best known of these approaches is probably the narrative therapy of Michael White and David Epston (1990), which has been further developed in the work of Parry and Doan (1994), Monk, Winslade, Crocket, and Epston (1996), and Speedy (2000). A central theme in narrative therapy is that of enabling the person to reauthor his or her life story as a means of resisting the control or subjugation of dominant cultural narratives. Another important recent movement within therapy has been the growth of philosophical counseling (Lahav & Tillmanns, 1995; Schuster, 1999), which helps people to overcome problems in living by exploring their worldviews and engaging in dialogue around the basic assumptions that guide their actions. The method of philosophical counseling usually involves inviting the client to read selected philosophical texts and find meaning through exploration and application of this cultural resource. The sociodynamic therapy created by Vance Peavy (1996, 1997, 1999) is a constructivist therapy that encourages clients to use cultural tools to enable them to participate more successfully in social life. The ecological therapy developed by Willi (1999) uses the idea that each person constructs a social niche for him- or herself and may develop emotional difficulties either when this niche has been disrupted by external events or when his or her own maturation as a person makes it necessary to build a new niche.

A common strand in these approaches to therapy is that, to a greater or lesser extent, they define therapy as primarily a *social* process rather than a psychological one. The term *postpsychological therapy* provides an appropriate way to describe these therapies (McLeod, 1999). The history of counseling and psychotherapy, and the overwhelming mass of theory, research and training, are rooted in psychological models. Anyone practicing as a therapist today (with the exception, perhaps, of some philosophical counselors) has inevitably assimilated psychological notions of what therapy is and how it should be carried out. The postpsychological therapies map out an approach in which psychology functions as a contributory discipline with no greater status than sociology, anthropology, linguistic, philosophy, and the humanities. *Postpsychological* can be read in similar fashion to *postmodern*. The concept of postmodernism has come to serve as a cohering principle in contemporary philosophy, art, and social science. It is readily apparent that we live in a world that is dominated by modern ways of thinking, feeling, and organizing. Yet at the same time, there can be glimpsed an emergence of something different, of whatever it is that will come *after* the modern. In a similar way, postpsychological therapy can be seen as foreshadowing whatever it is that will come *after* the psychological therapies.

The implication is that we are seeing a historical and cultural shift in relation to the meaning and practice of therapy.

In the second half of the 19th century, psychological therapy began to emerge as the mode of dealing with individual problems in living that would eventually replace the various forms of spiritual and religious support and healing that were widely available at that time. These religious and spiritual practices continue to be available, even now, despite the greater popularity of therapy and psychologically based self-help. It seems unlikely that the development of postpsychological therapy, whatever it eventually comes to be called, will result in the disappearance of the current mainstream forms of therapy. But just as with the case of the rapid growth of psychological therapy in the latter half of the 20th century, the emergence of postpsychological approaches can be understood as signifying a significant cultural moment. Despite the many different theoretical models and systems that have been developed, it is possible to regard 20th-century psychological therapy as centered on the application within individual lives of the concept of *self*. The various theoretical orientations can be viewed as providing contrasting ideas about the characteristics of the self, how it develops, and how it changes. But there has existed an underlying common focus in the assumption that therapy is concerned with enabling people to acquire an accurate appreciation of their unique self and how it interacts with the world. By contrast, the key point of convergence for practitioners and theorists seeking to reconstruct therapy in a postpsychological direction has turned out to be the concept of narrative. The importance of the concept of narrative within postpsychological therapies has not been sufficiently acknowledged because of the wide range of uses of narrative within the recent psychotherapy literature (McLeod, 1997). Therapists from virtually every theoretical orientation have written about the role that narrative plays in their work. The complex and multifaceted professional and theoretical discourse that has grown up around the concept of narrative conceals an underlying split in the way that the term is understood. On the one hand are theorists such as Luborsky and Crits-Christoph (1990) and Bucci (1995), who have discovered that a sensitivity to the way that therapy clients tell stories or narrate their experience is of great value in opening up access to psychological processes that may be otherwise hidden. The classic example of this kind of psychological approach to narrative can be found in the work of Lester Luborsky on core conflictual relationship themes. Luborsky has developed a method for identifying client narratives within therapy discourse and then analyzing them in terms of a model of narrative structure (wish; response of other; response of self), which allows the therapist to observe significant psychodynamic phenomena, for example around unconscious desires and transference patterns. This is an example of how a concept of narrative can be used to enhance the effectiveness of a therapy that takes as its aim the exploration of a self that is understood in psychodynamic, psychological terms.

By contrast, those writing and practicing from a postpsychological perspective do not make use of a concept of self to theorize the therapeutic process. The person seeking help is primarily regarded as a member of a culture, and his or her difficulties are understood in terms of his or her relationship with that culture. The concept of narrative is central to a postpsychological perspective because it brings together crucial aspects of the therapeutic process. The person seeking help is a narrator and actively tells and reauthors stories that enable him or her to convey a sense of identity and to make sense of problematic experiences by integrating them into a coherent and complete story. The idea of narrative therefore includes within it a *personal* dimension in terms of the unique life stories that make up the teller's autobiography. Narrative also implies an *interpersonal* process. Telling a story is a performance, shaped by the responses of the audience. Finally, the concept of narrative brings with it an appreciation of the *cultural* resources from which individual stories are constructed.

The key point is that, although the idea of narrative has proved interesting and useful to therapists from all approaches, it has different meanings when applied from a psychological or postpsychological perspective. It may be helpful to define approaches to therapy that are fundamentally psychological but that draw on narrative ideas as *narrative-informed*. Postpsychological therapies are perhaps better understood as representing forms of *narrative therapy*, in recognition of the central role of narrative in the way they operate.

The following sections of this chapter seek to bring the distinctive characteristics of the postpsychological use of narrative into clearer focus by first locating narrative within a social and historical context, and then by considering an example of how it works in practice.

THE SOCIOCULTURAL CONTEXT POSTPSYCHOLOGICAL INTEREST IN NARRATIVE

Familiar though his name may be to us, the storyteller in his living immediacy is by no means a living force. He has already become something remote from us and something that is getting even more distant . . . the art of storytelling is coming to an end. Less and less frequently do we encounter people with the capacity to tell a tale properly. More and more often there is embarrassment all round when the wish to hear a story is expressed. It is as if something that seemed inalienable to us, the securest among our possessions, were taken from us: the ability to exchange experiences. . . . One reason for this phenomenon is obvious:

experience has fallen in value.... With the World War a process began to become apparent which has not halted since then. Was it not noticeable that at the end of the war that men returned from the battlefield grown silent—not richer, but poorer in communicable experience? What ten years later was poured out in the flood of war books was anything but experience that goes from mouth to mouth. And there was nothing remarkable about that. For never has experience been contradicted more thoroughly.... A generation that had gone to school on a horse-drawn streetcar now stood under the open sky in a countryside in which nothing remained unchanged but the clouds; and beneath these clouds, in a field of force of destructive torrents and explosions, was the tiny, fragile human body. (Benjamin, 1936/1970, pp. 83–84)

This passage from the European social philosopher Walter Benjamin captures a key factor in the importance of the concept of narrative in the new postpsychological therapies: the erosion and transformation of storytelling, or oral narrative, in everyday life. Although it is certainly true that postpsychological theorists have explicitly positioned their work within contemporary intellectual movements such as postmodernism, poststructuralism, constructivism, and social constructionism, it can be argued that these movements have not been the driving force for narrative-based therapies but have merely offered frameworks for understanding and explaining what needed to be done. The driving force for postpsychological or sociocultural therapy has been the gradual loss, in modern, industrialized societies, of the oral tradition in which personal storytelling took place within small family or community groups and its replacement by a range of literary and media products.

As Sarbin (1986) has pointed out, we live in a storied world. In the past, virtually all of the stories that a person heard would have been performed in person, whether by friends or family members or a priest at a pulpit. This kind of oral narrative is guided by the quality of contact between teller and audience, and involves bodily, physical presence. It is an intrinsically relational experience. It is also an experience that is memorable and relies on memory (individual or collective) for its existence through time. Many oral narratives are repeated and ritualized through being told on special occasions. In contemporary society, although oral narrative certainly exists, it has been overlaid by many new and different types of narration that are recorded, transmitted remotely, received passively, and are commercial products of one kind or another. Television, cinema, popular music, the news media, and novels represent vast narrative industries that surround and saturate the self with stories (Gergen, 1991). In addition, many people who have undergone university education in science or social science-based subjects have been socialized into what Bruner (1986, 1990) has described as *paradigmatic*, rather than narrative, ways of representing and knowing the world. Psychotherapy itself has contributed to this process of undermining oral narrative. Although all forms of therapy invite the client or patient to tell his or her story, most therapies move quickly into a next stage of analyzing the story in terms of underlying psychological processes and factors (object relations, schemas, the self-concept, etc.). So, although the opportunity to talk and to be "heard" represents a major element in the appeal of therapy for most people (Howe, 1993), the reality for many clients is that their stories all too soon come to be redefined in terms of the theoretical constructs of their therapists, in this way becoming a formulation.

It is difficult to know what effect the narrative industries have had on the identities and ways of being that are available to people in modern societies. Some of the possible dimensions of impact are outlined in Exhibit 1.1. It is important to keep in mind that the significance of technological and cultural change on individual lives is seldom clear-cut. Most people live in worlds in which traditional, modern, and postmodern realities coexist as layers of a historical consciousness. In addition, the impact of the narrative industries cannot easily be disentangled from the effects of the invention of photography, mechanical reproduction of works of art, global travel, the expansion of leisure, and, indeed, literacy itself (Ong, 1982).

In relation to the role of counseling and psychotherapy in providing arenas in which individuals can engage in resolving and understanding problems in living that arise in their lives, there are perhaps two key points of difference between oral narratives and the consumption of stories provided through sources such as novels and television dramas. First, personal oral narratives usually position the teller as hero, or main protagonist of the story. Second, personally performed stories access and convey emotion in an embodied fashion. The teller of a personal story is aware of what he or she is feeling and how the story takes him or her closer to, or further away from, areas of feeling. The listener or audience, in such a situation, resonate to the emotions that are expressed by the teller. Neither of these processes occurs with anything like the same intensity in media-based narratives. The experience of reading a novel or watching a film is primarily one of being an observer. Although the reader of a novel may be caught up, for a while, in the agency of the protagonist, he or she can never step in to the narrative and tell his or her story, or even interrupt: Relatively little personal agency is involved in being a reader or viewer. Similarly, novels, television, and movies convey only a limited appreciation of the inner experience of emotion and feeling of characters. These media provide an external view of the surface of the person as *actor*. Some elements of contemporary psychotherapy, reflecting these dimensions of cultural life, have become attuned to an image of the person as a flat character, one who is only observed at a distance.

EXHIBIT 1.1
Narrative in Traditional, Modern, and Postmodern Periods

Traditional	Modern	Postmodern
Oral culture	Literary, print culture	Television, Internet, and computer games culture
Participatory, communal storytelling	Passive, individualized story-reading	Possibility of pseudointeraction with electronic media
Narrative embedded in a collective moral–religious framework	Narrative located in secularized everyday reality and autonomous self	Globalized everyday reality: multiple, disputed moral frameworks
Relatively limited stock of mythic–religious stories	Wide range of stories available (novels, newspapers)	Seemingly limitless narrative choice (global narrative industries)
Heroic themes: honor, loyalty, sacrifice	Romantic themes—ordinary person as hero	Ironic themes—reflexivity, rejection of possibility of hero
Circular, repetitive story structure: use of musicality and poetry to reinforce memorability	Linear, logical story structure (e.g., adventure or detective novel)	Disruption, experimentation, and deconstruction in relation to narrative structures
Stories embedded in a culture	Stories explore cultural difference but characterize other cultures as dangerous or primitive	Celebration of diversity of voices: assimilation of stories from other cultures
Personal or family stories shared in community arena (group confession)	Problem stories told in confidence to one other person	Public disclosure of problem stories: testimony, survivors speak out, Oprah Winfrey and Jerry Springer
Problem stories understood in moral–religious terms	Problem stories conceptualized in scientific (psychological–psychiatric) terms	Range of different ways of making sense of problem stories
Narrative unity and coherence sought at communal level	Narrative unity and coherence sought at individual level	Questioning of possibility of narrative unity

Note. From *Narrative and psychotherapy* (p. 24), by J. McLeod, 1997, London: Sage. Copyright 1997 by Sage Publications. Adapted with permission.

Writing about the representation of the client in managed care, Cushman and Gilford (1999, p. 25) observed that "the self begins to appear flat, unnuanced, uncomplex . . . emotions seems to be located on the surface of this thin self." And McAdams (1996, p. 303), discussing the types of self-report questionnaires that are increasingly used to monitor the effectiveness of managed care, suggested that these scales yield "little more than a systematic psychology of the stranger . . . the kind of information that strangers quickly glean from one another as they size one another up and anticipate future interactions. . . . " In opposition to cultural forces that reinforce an external perspective on the self, one of the significant trends in contemporary psychotherapy has been the increasing salience of the notion of personal *agency* (Bohart, 2000; Rennie, 2000). This can be regarded, in part, as a return to a more traditional concept of the person. The image of the person in 18th-century society is of someone who is always busy, always doing something. The image of the late-20th-century person, by contrast, is that of someone who is a consumer, choosing products, or a spectator who is watching other people doing things, often on television.

These sociocultural themes come together in the image of the person as storyteller. There is a double agency implied in the concept of storytelling. The person telling a story is engaged in purposeful social action. The performance of the story creates a live drama in which teller and audience are involved and which they remember in terms of their personal participation. But more than this, the story itself conveys an account in which the person is portrayed as overcoming obstacles and challenges. The agency that is expressed in and through narrative can be seen as reflecting the assumptions of an everyday folk psychology, in which people are viewed as having purposes and intentions rather than the objectifying assumptions implicit in modern psychological theories founded on notions of internal states (White, 2001).

Walter Benjamin evoked the image of the "storyteller in his living immediacy." Postpsychological therapy embraces this image and provides a cultural arena in which it can be enacted. The extent to which the act of reclaiming an "ability to exchange experiences" can be viewed as an act of resistance, in the face of the narrative industries, is illustrated in the story of Tom (Madigan, 1999).

RESISTING DOMINANT NARRATIVES: THE STORY OF TOM

The account of his work with Tom that has been provided by the narrative therapist Stephen Madigan illustrates some of the ways in which a postpsychological approach can operate, and exemplifies the central role of narrative within such an approach (Madigan, 1999). Tom had been a psychiatric in-patient for more than 12 months. A 66-year-old married, middle-class White man, he had been diagnosed with a chronic depressive personality and had received massive amounts of psychological and medical therapy: 30 ECT sessions, 6 different types of medication, and a year of group and individual psychodynamic therapy. The staff in the psychiatric unit believed that nothing seemed to work with Tom and drafted in Madigan as a last resort.

The institutional narrative of Tom's condition was documented in a 6-pound file. This file defined Tom as an individual marked by a self characterised by deficit (Gergen, 1990): a depressive personality. The story of Tom inscribed in this file was also performed, on an everyday basis, by the staff of the in-patient unit, through the ways in which they talked about and treated him. The severity and hopelessness of his condition was emphasised by the use of the term *chronic*. These factors are central to a postpsychological understanding of Tom at this point in his life. The social world within which Tom was living was one in which some very definite structures of power and knowledge could be seen to exist. The purpose of the psychiatric unit was to identify the causes of psychological disorder, through detailed assessment, and then to deliver appropriate treatment. Within this knowledge system, staff could draw on a sophisticated set of patient narratives, reinforced by evidence from research and clinical experience and codified in the *DSM* manual (American Psychiatric Association, 1994). Madigan (1999, p. 153) referred to these narratives as "discursive constraints used to inscribe and privatize Tom's body as chronic."

In their therapy sessions over three months, Madigan met with Tom and his wife Jane and on two occasions with two of their adult children. At the first session, Tom reported that he had been "depressed" since his retirement 18 months earlier. On being asked if the word *depressed* was a word of his own or whether it belonged to someone else, Tom stated that it was a "hospital word" and that what he was really feeling was bored and unaccomplished. The conversation moved into an exploration of how bored and unaccomplished feelings were situated within "men's culture and training, expectations, economics and love" (pp. 18–19). In reflecting on this process, Madigan described himself as seeking to "undermine hospital certainties" and "open space" for other possibilities based on alternative other knowledges, and initiating conversations that represented a form of resistance and transformation. For example, Tom talked about a passion for gardening that stood in sharp contrast to his state of medicated, depressed hopelessness.

Three weeks into therapy, Tom, his wife, and therapist initiated a therapeutic letter campaign. The letter read as follows:

Dear friends of Tom and Jane,
My name is Stephen Madigan and I have been working alongside Tom and Jane for the last three weeks. As Tom sees it, he has been taken over by a "great sense of boredom" and feeling like he never quite "accomplished enough" throughout his life as a father, friend, husband, worker, neighbour. Tom's feelings of boredom accompanied by an unaccomplished life seemed to have "boxed him into a corner" to the point where it twice convinced him that he was not worthy of living. Tom says that being confined in the hospital for so long made him feel like giving up, but lately, Tom says that he "might have a chance."

Tom, Jane and I are writing to ask if you would write a letter on Tom's behalf that might add an alternative description to the story that the boredom, the feelings of living and unaccomplished life, and a few of the hospital staff, are telling about Tom.

In the letter could you relay an experience that you have had with Tom that you see as neither boring or unaccomplished, and indicate what kind of future you would like to enjoy alongside Tom.

Tom, Jane and I thank you for your help in this matter, and Tom wants all of you to know that he is feeling a "bit better" these past few weeks.

Warm regards.

Tom, Jane and Stephen.

(Madigan, 1999, p. 158)

Tom and Jane received 41 letters supporting them with hope and counter-stories. These letters helped Tom to become able to draw on an alternative knowledge of himself, as a person with resources and a great deal to give. Following a celebration party, Tom walked away from the hospital and began to create a different life for himself.

The case of Tom conveys some of the key aspects of a postpsychological approach to therapy and the way that the concept of narrative is used within such an approach. The problem is understood not to reside *within* a person but within the relationship between the person and the culture in which he or she lives his or her life. More specifically, the influence of the dominant culture is seen to operate primarily through talk: language, discourse, and narrative. For Tom, the discourse of the clinic, and the discourse associated with being a middle-class man, combined to create, at a key transition point in his life course, a highly powerful story of himself as chronically depressed. The aim of therapy was to find spaces and interstices in this dominant narrative through which alternative knowledges might be allowed to generate other stories. The therapist achieved this by drawing on everyday cultural resources. Some of the cultural resources and practices that Tom was encouraged to apply to his situation were his own ability to use everyday language ("bored and unaccomplished" rather than "depressed"); his familiarity with the knowledge and skills associated with being a gardener; the use of letter writing; creating a ritual (a party) to announce a change in social identity. Nowhere in the therapy was there any focus on individual psychological processes. The consistent goal of the therapy was to create possibilities for *re-membering*, for Tom to connect with others and to become an active and valued member of communities and networks that would afford him meaning and satisfaction. Ideas of narrative and story underpin all of this work: Tom's retirement as a disruption of his life narrative, the contrasting stories told about Tom by hospital staff and by his friends, the background cultural narratives expressed both in the *DSM* and in Tom's assumptions about what it means to be a man.

CONCLUSION

The basis of postpsychological therapy lies in an appreciation of the central role of narrative in human interaction: Stories are the essential way in which people make sense of their experience (Bruner, 2002). Relating a story about an event conveys the intentionality and purpose of the teller and his or her understanding of relationships and the social world, expresses feelings, and communicates a moral evaluation of what has happened (Bruner, 1990; McLeod, 1997). In narrative therapy, particular attention is paid to the stories told by the client. These stories are taken to reflect not only the individual experience of the teller but also to place him or her within a cultural time and place: We tell our own personal tales but do so by drawing on a cultural stock of narrative forms (Rapport & Overing, 2000). We are born into the story of our family and community and the story of who we are (e.g., the birth story, the story behind our name), and as we grow up we adopt narrative templates provided by myths, films, novels, and other cultural resources to give shape and meaning to our individual life narrative (Sarbin, 1986). In narrative therapy, the person's relationship with the stories of his or her culture can provide a rich source of meaning making (Dwivedi, 1997).

Underpinning this approach is an assumption of sociality. People are social beings and have a basic need to tell their stories. Holding back on telling the story involves a process of physiological inhibition that can have negative effects on health (Pennebaker, 1997). Telling one's story promotes a sense of knowing and being known and leads to social inclusion (Epston & White, 1995; McLeod, 1999).

The stories that we tell are always coconstructed, are told in the presence of a real or implied audience (Bakhtin, 1986; Langellier, 1989). There is a dialogical aspect to stories. Constructing a story is a situated performance, a version of events created at a particular time and place to have a specific effect. A story is something that is created *between* people rather than existing in one person's mind. The narrativization of experience is an open-ended process. There are always other stories that can be told about the same events or experiences.

The concept of *voice* refers to the way in which a story is told. The life narrative represents a weaving together of multiple voices (Stiles, 1999). For example, the story of someone's life, or episodes in that life, can be narrated through an official, psychiatric–medical voice; a personal and vulnerable voice; or the harsh critical voice of an angry parent. One of the tasks of therapy is to disentangle these voices (Penn & Frankfurt, 1994). The concept of voice also conveys something of the embodied nature of storytelling, by drawing attention to the physical qualities of *how* the story is told, in terms of volume, tone, rhythm, and the use of speech forms such as metaphor, repetition, and contrast.

It is possible to identify different types of stories (Polanyi, 1982, 1985; Riessman, 1993). *Habitual narratives* are accounts of what usually happened. *Personal stories* are vivid, concrete accounts of specific events. *Chronicles* or *reports* are like empty stories, which give information about what happened but no sense of drama, purpose, or meaning. The *macronarrative* is a generalized story of the "good life" that may be implicit in habitual and personal narratives and that acts as a kind of organizing principle for everyday stories by providing a narrative framework (the story of how things *should* be or ideally *can* be) for evaluating action (McLeod & Lynch, 2000). In therapy, the person seeking help, collaboratively with the therapist, constructs a "storyworld" (McLeod & Balamoutsou, 2000) that represents the landscapes of action and consciousness that are most salient for him or her at that time. Typically, the narratives that constitute a storyworld convey the drama of the person's relationships with others (Boothe, von Wyl, & Wepfer, 1999).

The spaces between words are also of significance for narrative therapists (Cornforth, 2001). The experience of being *silenced* is emotionally painful and problematic for most people. Silencing can be a consequence of the social isolation that can result in many situations, such as bereavement, emigration–exile, illness, and disability. Silencing can also be produced through purposeful oppression of persons, for example those who may have been sexually, physically, or emotionally abused by family members or those who are members of political, ethnic, religious, or sexual-orientation minority categories. A life story that is silenced or that is habitual minimizes the possibility of dialogical engagement with other persons. Problems can be understood as being those areas of personal experience around which the person is not able, or willing, to engage in conversation.

People find it helpful to have an opportunity to tell their stories in a setting in which what they have to say is accepted and valued by others. The basic experience of another person becoming an empathic witness to one's account of troubles is meaningful and worthwhile (Kleinman, 1988). The role of the counselor or psychotherapist includes being both witness to, and coeditor of, the stories told by the person seeking help.

In therapy, it can be useful to be given the opportunity to generate different versions of a story concerning life issues (Russell, 1991). Usually, the telling and retelling of the story produces at least some heroic and success narratives ("unique outcomes") alongside the more habitual problem-saturated accounts of troubles that people bring into therapy. The contrast between these alternative stories also initiates a search for a more satisfactory integrating or overarching narrative (the macronarrative) through which they can be understood. The ritual of therapy makes it possible for the person to articulate his or her life narrative (or parts of it) with support and without interruption or competition. This gives the person a chance to reflect on his or her story and to consider whether there are any parts of it that he or she might want to update, reconstruct, or repair. The metaphor of re-authoring (White & Epston, 1990) captures this sense of deepening and expanding the types of story that a person can tell about him- or herself.

The skills of the narrative-informed therapist are built on a sensitivity and awareness in relation to language use and narrative forms. For example, it is useful for therapists to be familiar with different models of how stories are structured and to the quality of the story that is told in respect to its coherence and poetic flow. There is a rhythm to storytelling within a therapy session. A typical pattern is that the person talks about what generally happens (habitual narratives), then shifts into an actual story that exemplifies, dramatizes, and makes concrete and specific what is being talked about. In doing so the person draws the listener (therapist) into his or her subjective, emotional, and moral world. Following the story, there may often be a period of reflection, evaluation, and interpretation where the meaning of the story is explored (Angus, Levitt, & Hardtke, 1999; Bucci, 1995). This process of sense-making helps to develop a perspective on the problem. There is also a rhythm and poetics associated with the telling of a story, expressed through repetition, contrast, reported speech dialogue, pace, and voice quality (Gee, 1991).

Although not given particular prominence within its literatures, post-psychological therapy is built on a moral and political stance that emphasizes notions of common humanity and the common good. Interdependence, equality, caring, and the construction of meaningful community are key values within this approach.

REFERENCES

American Psychiatric Association. (1994). *Diagnostic and statistical manual of mental disorders* (4th ed.). Washington, DC: Author.

Angus, L., Levitt, H., & Hardtke, K. (1999). The Narrative Process Coding System: Research applications and implications for psychotherapy practice. *Journal of Clinical Psychology, 55,* 1255–1270.

Bakhtin, M. M. (1986). *Speech genres and other late essays.* Austin: University of Texas Press.

Benjamin, W. (1970). The storyteller. Reflections on the works of Nikolai Leskov. In H. Arendt (Ed.), *Illuminations* (pp. 87–107). London: Jonathan Cape. (Original published 1936)

Bohart, A. C. (2000). The client is the most important common factor: Clients' self-healing capacities and psychotherapy. *Journal of Psychotherapy Integration*, *10*, 127–148.

Boothe, B., von Wyl, A., & Wepfer, R. (1999). Narrative dynamics and psychodynamics. *Psychotherapy Research*, *9*, 258–273.

Bruner, J. (1986). *Actual minds, possible worlds*. Cambridge, MA: Harvard University Press.

Bruner, J. (1990). *Acts of meaning*. Cambridge, MA: Harvard University Press.

Bruner, J. (2002). *Making stories. Law, literature, life*. New York: Farrar, Straus & Giroux.

Bucci, W. (1995). The power of the narrative: A multiple code account. In J. W. Pennebaker (Ed.), *Emotion, disclosure and health* (pp. 93–104). Washington, DC: American Psychological Association.

Cornforth, S. (2001). Culture: The song without words. *Counselling and Psychotherapy Research*, *1*, 194–199.

Cushman, P. (1995). *Constructing the self, constructing America: A cultural history of psychotherapy*. Reading, MA: Addison-Wesley.

Cushman, P., & Gilford, P. (1999). From emptiness to multiplicity: The self at the year 2000. *Psychohistory Review*, *27*, 15–31.

Dwivedi, K. N. (Ed.). (1997). *The therapeutic use of stories*. London: Routledge.

Epston, D., & White, M. (1995). Termination as a rite of passage: Questioning strategies for a therapy of inclusion. In R. A. Neimeyer & M. J. Mahoney (Eds.), *Constructivism in psychotherapy* (pp. 339–354). Washington, DC: American Psychological Association.

Gee, J. P. (1991). A linguistic approach to narrative. *Journal of Narrative and Life History*, *1*, 15–39.

Gergen, K. J. (1990). Therapeutic professions and the diffusion of deficit. *Journal of Mind and Behavior*, *11*, 353–368.

Gergen, K. J. (1991). *The saturated self: Dilemmas of identity in modern life*. New York: Basic Books.

Giddens, A. (1991). *Modernity and self-identity: Self and society in the late modern age*. Cambridge: Polity Press.

Howe, D. (1993). *On being a client: Understanding the process of counselling and psychotherapy*. London: Sage.

Kleinman, A. (1988). *The illness narratives: Suffering, healing and the human condition*. New York: Basic Books.

Lahav, R., & da Venza Tillmanns, M. (Eds.). (1995). *Essays on philosophical counselling*. Lanham, MD: University Press of America.

Langellier, K. M. (1989). Personal narratives: Perspectives on theory and research. *Text and Performance Quarterly*, *9*, 243–276.

Luborsky, L., & Crits-Christoph, P. (Eds.). (1990). *Understanding transference: The CCRT method*. New York: Basic Books.

Lynch, G. 'A. (1997). Words and silence: Counselling and psychotherapy after Wittgenstein. *Counselling, 8*(2), 126–128.

Madigan, S. (1999). Inscription, description and deciphering chronic identities. In I. Parker (Ed.), *Deconstructing psychotherapy* (pp. 150–163). London: Sage.

McAdams, D. P. (1996). Personality, modernity, and the storied self: A contemporary framework for studying persons. *Psychological Inquiry, 7,* 295–321.

McLeod, J. (1997). *Narrative and psychotherapy.* London: Sage.

McLeod, J. (1999). Counselling as a social process. *Counseling, 10,* 217–226.

McLeod, J. (2001). *Qualitative research in counselling and psychotherapy.* London: Sage.

McLeod, J., & Balamoutsou, S. (2000). Narrative process in the assimilation of a problematic experience: Qualitative analysis of a single case. *Zeitschrift für qualitative Bildungs–Beratungs–und Sozialforshung, 2,* 283–302.

McLeod, J., & Lynch, G. (2000). This is our life: Strong evaluation in psychotherapy narrative. *European Journal of Psychotherapy, Counselling and Health, 3,* 389–406.

Monk, G., Winslade, J., Crocket, K., & Epston, D. (Eds.). (1996). *Narrative therapy in practice: The archeology of hope.* San Francisco: Jossey-Bass.

Ong, W. J. (1982). *Orality and literacy: The technologizing of the word.* London: Routledge.

Parry, A., & Doan, R. E. (1994). *Story re-visions. Narrative therapy in the postmodern world.* New York: Guilford Press.

Peavy, R. V. (1996). Counselling as a culture of healing. *British Journal of Guidance and Counselling, 24,* 141–150.

Peavy, R. V. (1997). A constructive framework for career counseling. In T. L. Sexton & B. L. Griffin (Eds.), *Constructivist thinking in counseling practice, research and training* (pp. 122–140). New York: Teachers College Press.

Peavy, R. V. (1999). *An essay on cultural tools and the sociodynamic perspective for counselling.* Unpublished manuscript, Victoria, BC, Canada.

Penn, P., & Frankfurt, M. (1994). Creating a participant text: Writing, multiple voices, narrative multiplicity. *Family Process, 33,* 217–232.

Pennebaker, J. W. (1997). *Opening up: The healing power of expressing emotions.* New York: Guilford Press.

Polanyi, L. (1982). Linguistic and social constraints on storytelling. *Journal of Pragmatics, 6,* 509–524.

Polanyi, L. (1985). *Telling the American story: A structural and cultural analysis of converstational storytelling.* New York: Ablex.

Rapport, N., & Overing, J. (2000). *Key concepts for social and cultural anthropology.* London: Routledge.

Rennie, D. L. (2000). Aspects of the client's control of the psychotherapeutic process. *Journal of Psychotherapy Integration, 10,* 151–167.

Riessman, C. K. (1993). *Narrative analysis.* London: Sage.

Russell, R. L. (1991). Narrative views of humanity: Science and action: Lessons for cognitive therapy. *Journal of Cognitive Psychotherapy, 5*, 241–256.

Sarbin, T. R. (1986). The narrative as a root metaphor for psychology. In T. R. Sarbin (Ed.), *Narrative psychology: The storied nature of human conduct* (pp. 1–37). New York: Praeger.

Schuster, S. (1999). *Philosophy practice: An alternative to counseling and psychotherapy.* Westport, CT: Praeger.

Speedy, J. (2000). The "storied" helper: Narrative ideas and practices in counselling and psychotherapy. *European Journal of Psychotherapy, Counselling and Health, 3*, 361–374.

Stiles, W. B. (1999). Signs and voices in psychotherapy. *Psychotherapy Research, 9*, 1–21.

Van den Berg, J. H. (1974). *Divided existence and complex society.* Pittsburgh: Duquesne University Press.

White, M. (2001). Folk psychology. *Dulwich Centre Journal, 2*, 4–17.

White, M., & Epston, D. (1990). *Narrative means to therapeutic ends.* New York: Norton.

Willi, J. (1999). *Ecological psychotherapy: Developing by shaping the personal niche.* Seattle, WA: Hogrefe & Huber.

2

DEMONIC AND TRAGIC NARRATIVES IN PSYCHOTHERAPY

NAHI ALON AND HAIM OMER

It is a truism that the way psychotherapists perceive and understand their clients is greatly influenced by the guiding narratives provided by their theories. Over and beyond these theoretical narratives, however, our thinking, perceiving, and doing, both as laypersons and professionals, are also conditioned by cultural master narratives that have evolved through the ages. In this chapter we first describe one such master narrative, the demonic narrative, which has greatly influenced clinical theory and practice and, perhaps more than any other, determined the impact of psychotherapeutic thinking on the general public. We believe that the psychological version of this demonic narrative leads psychotherapists and consumers of popular psychology to engage in habits of thought that in the past involved the belief in witches, possession, demons, and Satan. We shall also describe another master-narrative, the tragic narrative, which may serve as an antidote to the demonic one.

Although we cannot do justice to the cultural richness of the two narratives because of the length of the chapter, some of the high points in their respective manifestations may be highlighted. The demonic narrative comes to the fore whenever a dualistic split between good and evil is a cultural ruling theme. Some well-known examples of this dualism are the

God–Satan conflict in Christianity, the light and darkness conflict in the Zoroasthrian religion, and the polarity of spirit and matter in neo-Platonic and gnostic worldviews. There are also fully secular versions of the demonic narrative, such as the Nazi split between pure and impure races, the communist division of the world into exploiters and exploited, or the Cold War mentality of total suspicion. Extreme dualistic worldviews have a tendency to evolve conspiracy theories, which illustrate the demonic narrative to perfection. As a rule, one might say that demonic explanations gain in power in situations of social upheaval and distress. The demonic narrative then serves the purpose of providing clarity and channeling frustration.

In the tragic narrative, by contrast, suffering is not seen as the result of an evil conspiracy but as the outcome of an interplay of factors whose endstage often reflects a paradoxical reversal of some of its contributing forces. One of our chief sources of inspiration for the tragic outlook is Buddhist philosophy, which views suffering as an inevitable part of life and not as a result of "evil" forces. The Buddhist emphasis on compassion is also a powerful antidote against demonization. We also drew from Western sources of inspiration, such as the tragedy as an artistic and cultural form (in classical Greece, Elizabethan England, and 18th-century France) and the work of philosophers such as Epicurus, Epictetus, Marcus Aurelius, Montaigne, Spinoza, and Schopenhauer. Our chief contemporary source is the French thinker André Compte-Sponville, whose work (1984) can be viewed as a modern primer of the tragic narrative. Compte-Sponville has perhaps more than any other modern writer emphasized the nonpersonal and unintentional sources of suffering.

THE DEMONIC NARRATIVE

Demonic assumptions:

1. *All suffering comes from evil.* This is the basic demonic postulate: It reflects the refusal to accept that suffering may be the result of chance. Blind accidental suffering is a cosmic scandal that the human mind feels bound to reject. In all cultures and ages, people have tried to depict human pain as stemming from an evil principle. Because psychologists reject "evil" as an explanatory concept (psychology is purportedly nonjudgemental), the psychological counterpart to this demonic assumption takes on a special form: Suffering is viewed as stemming from *trauma*, which leads to pathological growths, destructive drives, and negative feelings. Thus, if my suffering

is of the order of x, it must be that an x amount of traumatization lies at its origin. We might call this assumption *the law of conservation of evil*, because of its structural similarity to the physical laws of conservation of matter and of energy. This parallel helps us understand the attractiveness of this assumption to the mind: Just as in a problem in physics or chemistry we say that we have solved the equation once we have shown that the matter or energy at the end is the same as in beginning, in the human sphere we feel that suffering has been explained once we have identified a matching quantum of trauma at its origins. The mind comes to rest when it succeeds in establishing that what is present at the end was already present at the beginning. This assumption has a constraining quality: It is not that suffering *might* but that it *must* be due to a proportionate traumatization. If we ask why the person thinks so, we may get a surprised answer: "How could it be otherwise?" This self-evident nature lies at the root of the elusiveness and unyieldingness of the demonic view.

2. *The roots of evil lie hidden.* The demonic view posits a basic difference in the reality status of surface and depth. Acts are only the outward signs of the soul's condition and only what lies underneath is fully real. Bad intentions and evil forces always come masked. The full extent of the evil remains hidden not only from the victim but often also from the perpetrator. This assumption actually states that the mind is built out of independent elements, of which some are more "real" than others, and only some of which (usually the less real ones) are present to consciousness. Henceforth, the devil may conspire and take control without the person's knowing it.

   Conspiracies, be they individual, social, or cosmic, are everpresent. To detect them, one must learn to interpret their veiled signs and unwitting disclosures. True to this assumption, we think of people who can see through superficial positive appearances to the hidden badness underneath as endowed with special acuity. For those of us who are not so gifted, demon doctors in the past and some writers of popular psychology books in the present have offered lists of signs by which we may all be alarmed to the presence of evil forces or dangerous psychological phenomena in our surroundings.

3. *The conspiring other only purports to be like one of us.* This is clearest in group forms of demonization: Jews, witches, and

lepers were often viewed as the absolute other. Also, in close personal relations, the process of demonization evolves when the feeling takes hold of the mind that the intimate other is, in some negative way, essentially different from us. At these moments, empathy breaks down, giving way to suspicion and blaming. Thus, when bad things happen to us, it must be that the other secretly willed them. Or, in the process of self-demonization, we may become convinced that some alien principle within us is conspiring against us.

4. *The hidden evil can only be detected by specialists.* The demonic view requires an interpretive science whose role is to reveal the hidden forces underneath. This interpretative science was traditionally the preserve of the confessor and the exorcist. These soul-doctors were believed to be versed in the demonic languages, which they used to communicate with the demons in the procedure of exorcism.

   Psychology represents this interpretive science for the secular mind. Thus psychologists are often popularly viewed as the people from whom one can hide nothing and who are versed in the language of the unconscious. It is commonly accepted that the psychologist, with the help of his or her instruments, has priviledged access to mental contents that are unknown to the subject of therapy. In case of discrepancy between the client's experience and the psychologist's understanding, the latter is assumed to take precedence. The intuitive sign-reader, who interprets the true meaning of the slips of spouse, child, parent, boss, or employee, is thus inspired by a hallowed cultural model: He or she follows the psychological creed, according to which a critical attitude toward the purported good intentions of others and self is the hallmark of the insightful person.

5. *Acknowledgment and confession are the preconditions of cure.* In the traditional demonic view, confession lies at the center of the purification process. The tools of the soul-doctor's that help bring sinners or the possessed to their "right mind" are sign-reading ability and an appropriate balance between a benign paternalistic and a threatening inquisitorial stance. To the traditional demonic mind there is a deep difference between the confessed and the unconfessed sinner: The first can be saved, the second, only destroyed. Mere outward confession, however, is not enough: To be effective, confession must come from the heart.

In the psychological sphere, what is meant by *the achievement of insight* may be rather similar to a religious confession. It consists in the avowal (before the intimate other or the therapist) of one's previously denied negative tendencies. By this avowal the person becomes ripe for cure. The attempts of spouses, parents, and psychotherapists to get the other (spouse, child, or client) to acknowledge his or her negative feelings and attitudes are often guided by the belief that the other is not only negatively motivated but also, consciously or unconsciously, bent on denying these negative motives.

6. *Real cure consists in the eradication of the underlying evil.* In the traditional demonic view bad acts stem from evil roots whose ultimate source is the devil. The sinner or possessed person can only be cured by the removal of these roots. In the psychological counterpart to this view, the evil roots are transformed into pathogenes caused by trauma and deprivation whose source is almost invariably the destructive acts of others (mostly the parents). Again, real cure is only possible if the pathogene is correctly identified and psychologically uprooted. This view has long overstepped the boundaries of professional psychology: Many laypeople have come to assume that all their problems have traumatic roots that they hope to uncover and eradicate. In this belief, they become prey to *self-demonization*, which is the spilling over of the demonic view into the inner subjective sphere.

THE PSYCHODEMONIC NARRATIVE

Psychological narratives have, of course, nothing to do with witches, demons, or exorcism. If we consider, however, traditional demonic views, we may note some striking structural parallels to many influential psychological narratives. In the traditional demonic narrative, innocent people are conquered by dark powers and made into unwitting hosts who further disseminate the rule of these powers. This process is not just an individual matter: The spreading contagion is part of a cosmic conspiracy. The dark elements that host within the individual are the agents of this conspiracy. Therefore, they disguise themselves as best they can (sometimes even from the host), to escape detection and pursue their work undisturbed. This disguise is abetted by a generalized conspiracy of silence designed to provide a cover-up for the expansion of the dark forces. Many of the participants in this conspiracy of silence are not in themselves demonic hosts but rather have been duped by the satanic powers to disbelieve imputations of witchcraft and possession. Skepticism is thus one of Satan's mainstays. The demonic forces implanted within their hosts end, however, by revealing themselves to the demon-doctor's trained eye. This discovery is followed by the grim but holy work of accusation, confession, exorcism, punishment, and purification. When the tension between satanic and redemptive forces in the world reaches a climax, the apocalypse is near. The missionary zeal of the anti-demonic forces is thus not only corrective but millenarian in scope (Cohn, 1975; Ginzburg, 1991)

In the psychodemonic narrative, the counterpart of the demonic host is the victimized carrier of unconscious wounds. Some typical versions of psychodemonic implants are the traces of traumatic experiences, the parents' negative internalized voices, and the perpetrators' programmed instructions. The hidden wounds lead the victim, as he or she grows, to subject others to similar traumatization. Psychological evil thus perpetuates itself very much like its demonic counterpart. Also similar is the manner by which the psychodemonic implants hide themselves from view, by numbing the person's mind, disguising themselves into their opposites, and dissociating themselves from the flow of consciousness. The trained eye, however, can see through the disguises to the hidden traumata and destructive feelings. Professional and social skepticism, however, function as a conspiracy of silence, hindering the unmasking process. The efforts of the therapist may find an ally in the victim, who feels the need to break out from the imposed silence and to speak the truth. Often, the truth-speaking voice within the client is actually the child within the adult, who comes back from its repressed banishment and unmasks the culprits. The therapist, often a one-time skeptic who was overwhelmed by the revelations to which he or she was exposed, refuses to be taken in by the conspiracy of silence and provides the victim with the safety required to overcome inner repression and outer oppression. This is perforce an extremely painful process, because it is not enough that the person understands; she must also relive the original experiences to become free from them. This pain, like the one involved in real exorcism, is necessary, both at an individual and a social level: It is the only way to clean the individual and society from the self-perpetuating spread of psychological destructiveness.

The demonic narrative may also have positive value for the individual and the group: It gives meaning to suffering, channels frustration, gives hope, mobilizes action, fosters in-group cohesion, clarifies ambiguities, and reduces guilt. We should keep in mind that many a great achievement might not have been possible without a good dose of redemptive zeal. On the other hand, the price of the demonic narrative is no less considerable: It oversimplifies complex situations and constricts human relations by fostering suspicion, blame, and hostility.

The following quotes illustrate the chief elements in the psychodemonic narrative. The first come from a best-seller fittingly titled *Toxic Parents* (Forward, 1990).

> Our parents plant mental and emotional seeds in us—seeds that grow as we do. . . . As you grew into adulthood, these seeds grew into invisible weeds that invaded your life in ways you never dreamed of. Their tendrils may have harmed your relationships, your career, or your family; they have certainly undermined your self confidence and self esteem. (p. 5)

> As I searched for a phrase to describe the common ground that these harmful parents share, the word that kept running through my mind was *toxic*. Like a chemical toxin, the emotional damage inflicted by these parents spreads throughout a child's being, and as the child grows, so does the pain. (p. 6)

These psychodemonic descriptions might seem typical of mass-oriented works of popular psychology. The same elements, however, may be found in mainstream professional books such as Alice Millers's *The Drama of the Gifted Child* (1981) from which the following quotations are taken:

> Again and again, readers from a number of countries have told me with great relief that after reading "The Drama of the Gifted Child" they felt for the first time in their life something approaching sympathy for the neglected, abused, or even battered child they had once been . . . it was not the books I read, it was not my teachers or my study of philosophy, nor was it my training to become a psychoanalyst that provided me with this knowledge. On the contrary, all of these together, with their mystifying conceptualization and their rejection of reality, prevented me from recognizing the truth for years. Surprisingly it was the child in me—condemned to silence long ago, abused, exploited, and turned to stone—who finally found her feelings and along with them her speech and told me, in pain, her story. (pp. xi–xii)

This quote casts the inner child as the hero of the narrative: The child is the truth-speaking oracle who escapes from repression and overturns the conspiracy of silence by which the whole of society is tainted and that enables the perpetuation of evil.

> I was amazed to discover that I had been an abused child, that from the very beginning of my life I had no choice but to comply totally with the needs and feelings of my mother and to ignore my own. My discovery also showed me . . . the inadequacy of psychoanalysis, which even reinforced my repression by means of its deceptive theories. For I had completed two analyses as part of my psychoanalytic training, but both analysts had been unable to question my version of the happy childhood I supposedly had enjoyed . . . [only much later] I was

confronted with the terror that my mother, a brilliant pedagogue, had inflicted on me in my upbringing. I had been subjected to this terror for years because no one close to me, not even my kind and wise father, was capable of noticing or challenging this form of child abuse. (p. xii)

The conspiracy of silence is so insidious that the victim, the perpetrator (the mother), the alleged guardians of the truth (philosophers and psychoanalysts), and even the victims' loving caretaker (the father) unwittingly help in smothering the truth.

Had just one person understood what was happening and come to my defense, it might have changed my entire life. That person could have helped me to recognize my mother's cruelty for what it was. . . . This part of my story—this lack of enlightened witnesses—may have been responsible for the attempts I have made in my books to provide information that would reach potential witnesses who could be of help to the suffering child. . . . In our society, with its hostility toward children, such people are still hard to find, but their number is growing daily. (pp. xii–xiii)

The evil described is of a kind that only the specialist can detect (the victim and her father missed it). What is called for is no less than the development of a new caste of experts: that of enlightened witnesses.

It was thanks to the pain of the child in me that I fully grasped what so many adults must ward off all their life, and I also realized why they fail to confront their truth, preferring instead to plan self-destruction on a gigantic atomic scale, without even recognizing the absurdity of what they are doing. These are the same people who, like all of us, entered the world as innocent infants, with the primary goals of growing, living in peace, and loving—never of destroying life. I recognized the compelling logic of this absurdity after I found the missing piece of the puzzle: the secret of childhood, till then closely guarded. (pp. xiv–xv)

The full scope of the mission is disclosed: It ranges from the abolition of child suffering to the prevention of atomic destruction. The prophet's life trajectory runs from her infancy as a silenced victim, through her painstaking recognition of the truth, to her acceptance of the mission, the recruitment of truth-seeking disciples, and the cleansing of society. The goal is the discovery of the hidden corner of the past where the secret crime was once committed, from which all human suffering stems. Childhood, newly purified, may become again the garden and the source of blessings it was originally meant to be.

Psychodemonic descriptions are not, however, restricted to the evil done by parents. Trauma in general is often portrayed as the insidious factor by which the transmission of suffering is achieved. The redemptive potential of this insight is unfathomable: A procedure that did away with the hold of trauma in the mind might harbinger the solution of all social problems. The following passages from *EMDR: Eye Movement Desensitization and Reprocessing*[1] (Shapiro & Forrest, 1997) illustrated this trend:

> Almost every kind of suffering that we define and label a disorder—almost every type of psychological complaint—can be traced to earlier life experinces, which can also be healed. (p. 8)

> The problem many trauma victims face is that the upsetting experience from the past . . . is "stuck" in their nervous system. Like a puppet-master, this old experience governs the person's reactions to present-day situations. (p. 23)

> [However,] there is an "I" that feels locked up and knows that there is a better way . . . over the years I have come to see clearly that this "I" is intrinsically healthy. EMDR can remove the block that is preventing the natural movement towards health; can release you into the present you always wanted, a present where you can feel free and in control. (p. 11)

In terms of the demonic narrative we can recognize four major figures in this sequence: (a) the helpless host; (b) the hidden puppet-master (repressed trauma); (c) the basically healthy, but paralysed, "I"; and (d) the saving procedure (EMDR). From these four figures, the whole argument of the world-saving crusade against the dark elements that damage the healthy I can be derived. Shapiro and Forrest presented their world-renewal claims through EMDR in a series of rhetorical questions:

> Although the economic and social realities leading to criminal behavior and despair have to be adressed, how much of this pain can be treated by psychological interventions [EMDR] before violence erupts? . . . (p. 231)

> In many countries, females are considered second-class citizens—but does the fact that this is a centuries-old cultural belief mean that it is not potentially traumatizing? Can EMDR help cut through negative acculturation itself? . . . (p. 234)

> One of the other questions opened up by EMDR is how much impact can the resolution of personal trauma have on the causes of war [as a social phenomenon] itself? (p. 236)

---

[1] We are not arguing against the potential helpfulness of EMDR, which is a procedure of established clinical merit. Our focus is on the psycho-demonic narrative and world-saving rhetoric in which the model is couched.

THE TRAGIC NARRATIVE

Tragic assumptions :

1. *Suffering is an essential part of life.* This seeming truism is so much opposed to the basic demonic postulate (*all suffering comes from evil*) that all by itself it could innoculate us against most demonizing dangers. Viewing suffering as an essential part of life means that no guilty party can be made completely responsible for it. The assumption does not imply that one should sit passively: Improvements and self-protection are not only possible but mandatory. However, nothing can ever bring about the elimination of suffering, which is simply the feeling side of human limitation, fallibility, vulnerability, and mortality. This assumption is thus anti-utopic but not fatalistic. Or rather, it reflects a kind of *constructive fatalism.* Whereas one can see the demonic view as reflecting a millenariam outlook (extirpating evil will bring redemption), the attitude of constructive fatalism reflects a readiness to work for improvement while accepting the inherent limitations of the human condition.

   In classical tragedy suffering is depicted as the blind result of a confluence of factors. Circumstance and personality join hands to turn the protagonist's best intentions to naught. Macbeth's personality might, under different circumstances, have led to a positive career. Likewise, a man not so constituted as Macbeth (or with another wife) might have remained untainted under the same circumstances. The term *fate* designates the combination of personality and circumstances that may lead to disaster. Fate is not good and not bad and has no intentions whatsoever. Fate is not anybody. It is therefore as much the opposite of Satan as of God. We find that such age-old terms as *Fate*—or with less bombast *bad luck* or *accident*—could be used with profit in psychotherapy as an antidote to the client's demonizing tendencies.

2. *Bad acts may stem from positive human qualities.* This assumption states that even those of our acts that carry the most negative consequences may stem from qualities and attitudes that have been or are still of positive value. These qualities, however, may have become so rigidified that they become divorced from the present circumstances. This assumption is expressed by the concept of *hubris.* Hubris indicates the ironic twist by which the very qualities that brought us success may bring

about the uncritical attitude that leads to disaster. It was Oedipus's kingly goodness and responsibility, his love of truth, and his certainty that he could solve any riddle (after all, he had defeated the Sphynx) that brought him to push with all his might to find the secret that destroyed him.

Hubris is actually the refusal to accept human limitation. It is when we forget how limited is our power and how partial our view that we are in greatest danger. Precisely when our way seems most clear and our doubts most petty may we stand closest to disaster.

This tragic view of human failings as rigidified extensions of human strengths can be good medicine against the demonic outlook. We identify with the tragic hero and with the tragic fate of real persons precisely because we can see how they are unwittingly drawn to destruction by their all too human strivings. Viewing suffering as the result of hubris is thus the contrary of viewing it as the result of demonic forces.

3. *The other is not different from us.* Aristotle attributed the therapeutic and purifying (cathartic) value of tragedy to the fact that it aroused *pity and fear*: pity for the sufferings of the tragic figure and fear that a similar fate might be our own. Tragedy thus purifies through identification. To the extent that we view the tragic figure as essentially different from ourselves, we do not understand, do not participate, and are not purified. Whereas the process of demonization works through disidentification (the person that, in our initial ignorance, seemed similar to us is gradually seen as different), the catharsis of tragedy works through the transcendence of apparent otherness: We become Macbeth, Othello, Oedipus, and Medea.

To maintain our picture of the other as a hostile alien, we must assume that behind any seemingly positive or neutral acts there lie negative intentions, motives, and feelings. The hidden is thus more real than the manifest. For the tragic mind, however, thoughts, feelings, and acts are equally real. They are all the different facets of one and the same reality. Reducing any of them to the status of an accident or an epiphenomenon, or turning any of the three into the handmaid of the other is a degradation of human fullness.

4. *We do not know better than the other what the other "really" experiences.* This principle follows from the former: We could only know what went on in the other's mind better than him or her if the mind were built out of independent elements, some of which were more real than the others, and if these

elements were not present to the other's consciousness but present instead to our discerning eyes. This, as we saw, would make tragic identification impossible: Had Oedipus "really" wanted to marry his mother or Macbeth "really" wanted to murder everybody, we could not have identified with them and there would have been no tragedy. The assumption that the mind is built out of independent elements lies, on the other hand, at the heart of the demonic and psychodemonic outlook. Without this assumption, no external independent force could strike root in the mind and take control of it against the person's will and better wisdom.

To identify with the tragic protagonist, we must be willing to follow him or her step by step. Of course we know the story beforehand, but never do we know better than the tragic figure what his or her thoughts, wishes, and feelings are. If we knew better, identification and catharsis would break down. All of this is the opposite of the demonic or psychodemonic assumption that we, as observers, have a priviledged access to the other's soul. This is true for psychotherapists as well as for husbands, wives, parents, and children: We never know the other's inner experience better than the other. We may have a broader context in mind, more experience of life's circumstances, or better hunches about consequences: However, the assumption that we know better the other's inner experience leads perforce to the perversion of all dialogue.

5. *Attempts to totally eradicate evil often lead to more suffering.* The greatest tragedies often come from the greatest dreams. Both on an individual and a group level attempts to eradicate evil are often accompanied by the feeling that redemption is at hand. Paradoxically, the very attempt to achieve redemption may prove devastating. Tragedy as an artistic form gives expression to this fateful irony: It describes the protagonist's decisive venture that, instead of curing, destroys.

But are these processes at all similar to what happens in the quiet of intimate relations? Certainly not in terms of the sheer mass of misery involved. However, the splitting between good and bad, the suspicion of concealment, and the crusading zest are common to the witchhunt and to many an intimate tragedy. The demonic view in personal relations actually amounts to a conspiracy theory at the individual level. People are not very often killed by it, but the suffering it causes suffices to shatter innumerable individuals and families.

CASE: FROM A PSYCHODEMONIC
TO A TRAGIC NARRATIVE

After having concluded his second year in computer sciences with good marks, Rafi felt he had no energy or desire to continue studying. In the two therapies he previously had participated in, Rafi had felt accepted and understood; but he did not think he had been helped. After telling his disappointed mother that he would not go back to the university, he asked her for money for a new therapy. She agreed.

Rafi made no eye contact with his therapist, and his voice and posture gave the impression of someone who was talking to himself. He felt he was a fake devoid of all talent. He said he had an enormous need for approval, but at the same time he dismissed every encouragement as worthless. He said that his teachers and classmates, who thought he was smart, had no idea of the difficulties he had in fulfilling even the easiest of assignments. All the wit and talent in the family had fallen to his older sister: She was the brilliant academic that his mother had always wished him to be.

Rafi's parents had divorced when Rafi was 13, and the father had immediately remarried. Rafi described his mother as a controlling and critical person, despite her outward appearance of tolerance and goodwill; his father, in contrast, was generous and easygoing, although the relationship with his new wife kept these good qualities at bay. The mother had tried to warn Rafi that his continuing attachment to his father was a deep mistake. Rafi would yet see that the father had never really cared for him. She was sure he would not leave Rafi one cent after his death. Rafi felt that her hatred for his father blinded her and distorted also her relationship to himself. The truth of the matter, in his eyes, was that her negative feelings toward him (Rafi), which she totally denied, were the real cause of his problems.

[Both Rafi and his mother attributed their suffering to a guilty party: Rafi to his mother and the mother to Rafi's father. What gives this attribution its peculiar demonic tinge is the split between the other's show of good will and his or her "real" underlying ill will. The two demonic narratives create a mutual escalation: Each side attempts to convince the other to accept his or her view; when the other is not convinced, the efforts are doubled: the positive shades are eliminated and the negative ones underscored.]

Rafi said that in spite of his mother's declarations that she would accept him as he was, her behavior indicated otherwise. She would say she had no expectations from him but continued expecting the utmost. Because of Rafi's threats that he would stop studying altogether, she had learned to react as if a B mark was also an achievement. But he knew she did not really think so. Neither did he. Furthermore, he did not feel he deserved even the Bs that he was getting.

[In the psychodemonic interaction, nothing is really what it seems. Declared acceptance is no real acceptance, satisfaction with B marks is no real satisfaction, and even the B marks are not really what they seem.]

Rafi's explanation for his troubles was clear: He had no self-esteem because his mother had never loved or appreciated him. She had only wanted him to fulfill her dreams or to be a new edition of his sister. His earliest memories were of how she would become cold and withdrawn whenever he disappointed her. As he grew, her demands became more and more aggressive. She never encouraged him when he was in pain: On the contrary, she would then become most caustic.

[True to the first demonic assumption, Rafi believed there should be a clear cause to his suffering. The magnitude of the cause, in addition, had to be proportionate to the pain: The depth of his depression required an equally deep rejection on his mother's side.]

Rafi lived by himself but came to his mother's house every Friday. These weekly meetings were punctuated by bouts of mutual blaming. Rafi would blame her for her lack of love and she would reply that he picked on her to avenge himself for his imaginary ills. Recently, Rafi had told her that he would not come to the Passover meal. He told his mother it was useless for him to come because his sister would get all the positive attention, he would get depressed and destroy the family festivity anyhow. Nevertheless, he agreed to come. He arrived in a dark mood and, on noticing his mother's displeasure, he asked her whether she would not have liked it better if he had not come. She said, "Yes." This hurt him no end. Her denial had always infuriated him, but her acknowledgment was even worse.

[Rafi's demand for a "confession" poses a damned if you do, damned if you don't paradox: Whether the mother says yes or no to Rafi's baiting question at the Passover evening, she will be found guilty. In the terms of the demonic narrative, we would rename this "the witch's paradox": The option is given the "witch" to prove her innocence by the ordeal of water (being held under water for five minutes). If she refuses, her guilt is established and she is burnt at the stake; if she accepts, she drowns and her guilt is also established.]

Only in his earlier therapies had Rafi received the confirmation that he had been a rejected child. The last therapist had been so cogent in this view that Rafi had found himself arguing that the mother had not been that bad after all.

As the therapist inquired about the circumstances surrounding the mother's different reactions, it became clear that she behaved reasonably with him when he was feeling well but became totally rejecting when he felt depressed. The therapist wondered why this should be so. Rafi said the mother claimed to be only trying to shake him out of his depressive lethargy.

The therapist remarked that the mother seemed extremely threatened by his negative moods.

[The demonic way of thinking is dichotomous (good–bad) and essentialist (badness is a real characteristic of the soul). The tragic way of thinking is interactive and conjunctural (the tragic fate reflects a confluence of personal tendencies with accidental conditions). By his questions, the therapist tried to enable a shift from a demonic to a tragic way of thinking: The mother's reactions, though painful to Rafi, might be understandable when taken in context.]

Rafi's focus of attention changed: He started to talk about his mother's life. Her younger brother had dropped out from his studies and, later on, from work and remained depressed and dependent on his parents throughout life. In addition, his mother's father had gone through a number of depressive episodes and had been medicated for years. The therapist wondered whether Rafi had not also been touched by this melancholic family tendency. Rafi agreed: From early adolescence, he had always been sad and had even contemplated suicide. The therapist wondered whether this might not be the reason for the mother's panic. She might have felt an acute need to save him from sharing the fate of her father and brother.

Although intrigued by this possibility, Rafi was not ready to accept it: A tragic redescription of the mother would have to await more favorable circumstances. Later in the therapy, however, Rafi said that the therapist's "neutral" attitude of neither siding with the mother nor condemning her had been a relieving experience for him. [The therapist's attitude toward the mother, however, had been compassionate rather than neutral.]

Although Rafi did not want to have a conjoint session with his mother (in his previous therapies such sessions had proved disastrous), he agreed that the therapist meet with her alone. The following dialogue repeated itself in a number of variations in the three sessions the therapist had with the mother:

> *Mother:* He wants attention and he wants revenge. He assumes the martyr's position to revenge himself for the ills I supposedly inflicted on him. He sees only the negative side of things. That justifies him in blaming and in giving up. Whenever something good happens, he focuses so much on the negative, that in the end he must give up. He uses his pessimism to free himself from duties. There is nothing I can do to change this. He will shun all happiness, only for the right of blaming, complaining, and giving up. The moment he enters the house with his sour face, I know what is in stock for me. I am always the guilty one. He won't accept one drop of responsibility. Blaming me is his only kick in life.

Therapist: How do you react to his accusations?

    [As in his work with Rafi, the therapist tries to focus on the interaction, rather than on inner qualities.]

Mother: I try to show him that it is not so. That I love him just as much as I love his sister. But he won't accept that!

Therapist: I believe he is wrong in his conclusion, but maybe he discerns something true about the way you express your care for him. I can imagine that the interaction that developed between you two, given his constant sadness and your fears, should have been quite different from the one between you and your daughter. Maybe Rafi interpreted this as lack of love.

    [The therapist tries to offer an alternative to the mother's right–wrong dichotomy: The conclusion may be wrong, but the inner experience valid.]

Mother: What do you mean?

Therapist: I guess you had it easier with your daughter. He was a difficult child, often sad and hard to satisfy. You could not but react differently to him.

Mother: But he thinks I *caused* his depression!

Therapist: Yes, he thinks so, and may also think so in the future. However, we know that depression has many causes: Parenting may be one of them, and is often not the most important. Was he very different as a child than he is now?

    [The therapist tries to encourage an attitude of "constructive fatalism." If she could think less in terms of "who is to blame" and become somewhat tragically acceptant, the vicious circle might be lessened.]

Mother: No, he was always sad and dissatisfied. And always very sensitive to rejection from other kids, from the kindergarten teacher, from everyone. He was always unsure, even when he got high marks.

Therapist: So he was like this from a very early age. He was in pain and the interaction with you developed so that you became more and more helpless. With your family history you were bound to be frightened by Rafi's sadness. Under these conditions worry and frustration invariably arises. And how would such a child react to this? With frustration and anger! This cycle is perhaps the hardest thing for the mother of a sad and bitter child.

Mother: Does he understand this?

[The mother assumes that acknowledgment (confession) is the precondition of cure.]

Therapist: No, and I am afraid he won't, at least for a while. A depressed young man is incapable of seeing anything except for the pain. When a dentist drills your tooth you cannot think very much about others: Only the pain matters. So, there is little chance of Rafi's viewing things differently now.

Mother: What can be done?

Therapist: I don't know. It is clear that your attempts to convince him you love him the same as his sister don't help. Maybe you could say to him that you actually were tenser with him, which of course is true. Saying that he is right in his perception doesn't mean that you are to blame.

Mother: I am afraid of how he will react. He might become even more blaming.

Therapist: Maybe Rafi will find it hard to hear this, but at least he will get your confirmation that his feelings are not totally groundless.

The mother felt that she needed the therapist's presence to be able to say that. For the present, however, because of Rafi's opposition, a joint session was out of the question. Even so, the tension in her relationship with Rafi began to subside.

Rafi found a job in a supermarket. Initially the mother was furious because of Rafi's "new self-destructive" step. (The belief in a self-destructive drive that acts in opposition to the host's better interests is a psychodemonic construct.) The therapist said that Rafi's decision might be a reasonable one. His most acute present problem had to do with his giving up in situations of interpersonal conflicts. With the therapist's help, Rafi might use the new job to experiment with better interpersonal solutions. The therapist pledged himself before the mother to help Rafi make use of the new situation for this goal. The mother stopped nudging Rafi about his decision. This led to an additional drop in the tension, so that Rafi finally agreed to a joint therapy session.

At the beginning of the session Rafi sat gloomy and silent. With some encouragement from the therapist, the mother began to speak. She said she often felt like a failure as a mother. All her hopes that she would be able to help Rafi out of his troubles caused only more pain. Nothing she ever did seemed to help. She knew that she was doing something wrong. For years Rafi had said that her relation to her daughter had been a different one. She had always denied this. She had now thought it over, however:

In a sense, he had been right. It was not that she loved him less. But she was afraid of him. She did not mean this as an accusation but as an acknowledgment. She cared for him as much as for his sister, but the relationship was different. It was harder, tenser, less pleasant. It was true that she was angry. The anger came out of her sense of failure and frustration. It was true that she had always had high expectations from him. She could not stop her expectations, even though she knew they did not help. She would then grow tense and her tenseness would betray itself to Rafi. She had always felt that, with him, she was under a looking glass. Rafi laughed: He really looked at her as if through a looking glass. The mother started laughing, too.

The mother's description of the situation reflects an evolving tragic perspective: Out of legitimate intentions each had been unwittingly pouring oil on the other's fire. From this perspective it became possible for the mother to acknowledge her ineffective reactions without giving or taking blame. She also stopped trying to get a symmetrical acknowledgment on Rafi's part: Acknowledgment (confession) was no longer viewed as a condition of improvement.

At this time, a tragic event put the relationship under severe strain: Rafi's father died. By the end of the Shivah[2] for his father, Rafi seemed to be sinking into a depression. He did not go back to work, refused to leave the house, and was obsessed about the wrongs he had suffered. The mother tried to shake Rafi out of his lethargy, said she would not help him wallow in self-pity, and started pressuring him to pull himself together. She mentioned, once again, the taboo subject of the father's will: Rafi would soon find out what the father had left him. Rafi got furious and blocked her way out of his house. She pushed him, slapped him, and left. The demonic cycle had reasserted itself.

This episode ended in an ironic twist. A week after the clash with his mother, Rafi found out that she had been right: The father had in fact left him nothing in his will. At first Rafi could not believe it. Little by little he found a way to hold to the belief that the father had loved him, by coming to think of him as a weak man who had been unable to hold his own against the two strong women in his life. In Rafi's therapy, the mother's ill-timed mention of the father's will and her eventual loss of control were also restoried: Maybe the mother had wanted to prepare him for the bitter truth and then got into a panic when she saw him sinking into a depression.

At about this time, Rafi said that the therapist's refusal, from the beginning of the therapy, to join, as had other psychologists, in his criticisms

---

[2] *Shivah* is the traditional Jewish week of mourning.

of his mother had intrigued him in a positive way. Rafi added, "Who wants to have monstrous parents after all?"

Rafi's and his mother's mutual attitudes were considerably softened. Occasionally, the negative cycle would recur, but there was no cutting edge to it. Surprisingly, the mother could credit two achievements to herself: She succeeded in getting Rafi to take antidepressant medication (the therapist had failed to convince him) and succeeded in getting him to buy an apartment. Even Rafi admitted that his stubbornness would have blocked any softer approach. After two years Rafi even went back to the university and finished his studies.

CONCLUSION

Are tragic or demonic narratives inherent to different therapeutic approaches? In our view these are more interpretive styles than inherent attributes of theories. Any therapeutic approach may lend itself to a demonic or a tragic emphasis. We also do not think that *demonic* or *tragic* are personal traits. The same therapist may go from one attitude to the other at different life stages, with different clients or even at different stages of the same therapy.

Actually, to attempt an eradication of demonization is almost a contradiction in terms. The tragically inclined therapist might then try not so much to flip the client's outlook but rather to soften or to redirect his or her rigidly suspicious, blaming, or millenarian attitudes. We propose the following rules of thumb for this process: (a) It is better to demonize an abstract principle than the concrete people with whom one shares one's life—thus, it is generally a mistake to strengthen clients' tendencies to demonize their parents or spouses; on the other hand, demonizing "greed" or "authoritarianism" may be a good idea at times; (b) it is better to demonize the problem than the self; and (c) it is better to attribute the "demons'" work to fate than to evil intentions. Even demons can then be pitied.

REFERENCES

Cohn, N. (1975). *Europe's inner demons: The demonization of Christians in Medieval Christendom*. London: Chatto & Heinemann.

Comte-Sponville, A. (1984). *Traité du Desespoir et de la Béatitude*. Paris: Presses Universitaires de France.

Forward, S. (1990). *Toxic parents: Overcoming their hurtful legacy and reclaiming your life*. New York: Bantam Books.

Guinzburg, C. (1991). *Ecstasies: Deciphering the witches' sabbath*. London: Hutchinson.

Miller, A. (1981). *The drama of the gifted child*. New York: Basic Books.

Shapiro, F., & Forrest, M. S. (1997). *EMDR: Eye movement desensitization and reprocessing*. New York: Basic Books.

3

THE PARADIGM OF TRAGEDY AS META-NARRATIVE: A WINDOW TO UNDERSTANDING THE LIFE STORY OF A WOMAN IN ECONOMIC AND SOCIAL DEPRIVATION

MICHAL KRUMER-NEVO

This chapter addresses the problem of the discourse commonly used to describe women living in economic and social deprivation. Narratives concerning people living in extreme poverty have fluctuated, both in research and in therapy, between a judgmental attitude that views them as responsible for their situation on account of their own weaknesses or failures and a compassionate attitude that views them as victims of circumstance and an environment over which they have no control. (For a detailed account of the representations of poor women in academic discourse, see Krumer-Nevo, 2003a). The tension between these two approaches is pervasive in theory and practice and results in either anger at unsuccessful women or pity for unfortunate victims. Seeing these women as either victims or culprits makes them one-dimensional characters, alienated and "other" (Fine, 1994). What is ignored is their capacity for agency, their strength, and the practical means by which they resist deprivation (Krumer-Nevo,

2000). Feminist critiques also point to the need to conceptualize the social situation of these women as a multiple marginality. In other words, it is a marginality in which economic inferiority is intertwined with gender, race, and ethnicity, relating specific situations of social inequality (Crenshaw, 1994; Etter-Lewis, 1991; Glenn, 1985; Polatnick, 1996).

What is missing is a meta-narrative that could enable us to see these women as a human mix of strengths and weaknesses, achievements and failures. In this chapter I propose a possible meta-narrative based on three structural components of dramatic tragedy as developed in classical theory of the genre: the impossible choice of the protagonist agent, the contest with fate, and the ironic reversal of fortune, to project the image of these women as protagonists, responsible and doomed at the same time.

TRAGEDY AS A CONCEPTUALIZATION OF AGENCY AND FATE

In discussing with colleagues my thoughts about the relevance of the term *tragedy* for women living in poverty and social exclusion, I encountered reactions of astonishment and even anger. Because in tragedy the fate of the protagonist is inevitably disastrous, and to speak of the lives of these women in terms of tragic fate seemed to constitute an acceptance of finality and the abandonment of any possibility of change. Others resented the implication that the women be regarded as tragic heroines—or as heroines at all— and still others resisted the notion of an external controlling destiny contradicting normative rationalistic middle-class ideas of self-determination and responsible agency. Through the years of my work as both researcher and clinical social worker I was impressed by the use of the term *fate* in the narratives of poor women, and I sought to understand it with the help of the literary genre in which it holds the most prominent place: tragedy.

I do not intend to claim that all the women who live in poverty see their lives as tragedy and themselves as heroines (although some of them may do so). Nor am I suggesting that we should see their lives as moving toward a catastrophic ending. The view of tragedy that I present does not address the final phase of a tragic drama—that is, the catastrophe, the protagonist's "recognition" that precedes and heralds it, and the catharsis of pity and terror that ensues on the catastrophic finale. What I do borrow from the tragic paradigm is the question of fate and the structural and functional aspects of the relationship between fate and the protagonist. The tragic paradigm offers a metaphor that has explanatory power. It offers a mode of discourse through which I can resolve the antinomies between heroine and victim, strengths and weaknesses, inner and outer, the public and the private realms.

TRAGEDY AND PSYCHOTHERAPY

Insights have already been derived from theories of tragedy for therapeutic purposes. Omer (1994), who uses literary genres as a therapeutic approach to reframe people's attitudes, wrote, "Patients should be heroes, not bystanders, in their life stories. . . . Heroes are not necessarily triumphant, but even the tale of a tragic hero is preferable to that of an extra. Faced with inescapable fate, the tragic hero expresses feelings and values that are deeply human" (p. 56). Schafer (1976) used the four primary literary genres defined by Northrop Frye (1957) as alternative ways of structuring the form and the content of human situations, as modes of interpreting the world and of understanding reality. The modes are comic, tragic, ironic, and romantic. The tragic mode derives from a painful awareness of the great dilemmas, the paradoxes, the uncertainties, and the complexities that are bound up with human activity and subjective experience. The person whose reality mode is tragic will be alert to the dangers, the mysteries, and the absurdities of existence. In psychoanalytical terms, according to Shafer, this kind of person is subject to the immense power of fixation, repression, regression, and repetition and is influenced by a strong awareness of the possibility of loss—of self or object.

Schafer described the tragic character as one who, because of specific intrapsychic structures, reacts with great sensitivity to the painful and complex aspects of human existence. However, he does not deal with those cases in which the painful aspects of human existence dominate daily external reality. This is the situation of poverty and exclusion, in which pain, loss, stress, frustration, and helplessness are not primarily a function of subjective sensitivity but rather of external reality.

Omer, who wrote of "investing the patient as a hero" (p. 56), also wrote of adding the figure of fate to the consciousness of his patient to provide a scapegoat—a source of evil to be blamed. But I suggest that this will only aggravate the patient's sense of victimhood. What is required is to see the patient as a protagonist—an adversary against her fate, her poverty-stricken and demeaning circumstances—even though she may have no tangible victories to show for it, just as the heroine of a tragedy has no tangible victories.

Hamilton's (1940) concept of person in situation is useful in this connection. Hamilton described the relationship between the person and her environment as creating a new unit, a gestalt that combines both person and environment and that constitutes the interface between external reality and internal reality, between the objective and the subjective. This is indeed the predicament that the hero of tragedy faces at the outset of the plot. The person-in-situation framework correlates excellently with theory of tragedy because in tragedy *fate* (circumstances, contingency not under the control of the individual) and the *will of the heroine* exist side by side as two powerful and antagonistic forces.

LIFE HISTORY

In this chapter I analyze the narrative of Sara, a woman who lived in poverty in terms of its tragic components. The interview that I conducted with Sara was undertaken in the framework of a qualitative research evaluation of the "Yachdav" (Together) program (Novick & Krumer-Nevo, 1993)—a group therapy program that was donated by welfare agencies for mothers whose children's development was at risk as a result of neglect or abuse. (For additional description of Yachdav, see Rosenfeld, Schon, & Sykes, 1995).

Forty-seven narrative interviews were taken within this framework, using the intersubjective approach of the narrative interview (Corradi, 1991). The women were asked to talk about the Yachdav program and to tell about their lives.

I met Sara for the purpose of the interview after the social worker, who had known her for years, told me that she was "not suitable for an interview. She is not verbal. She cannot tell a story. She is almost retarded." However, I found Sara very cooperative, telling, in her own way, a very interesting story. I here reconstruct Sara's life story from the interview, arranging the biographical details in chronological order (Rosenthal, 1993).

Sara was 38 years old at the time of the interview. She was born in Israel, to a family of eight of North African origin. She did not once mention her mother in the interview, and of her sisters said simply, "They are all okay, they all know how to read and write."

After Sara was born, she was hospitalized; at one point she said it was for a year, at another point for two years. The reason for the hospitalization is also unclear—Sara mentioned that she was small (possibly premature), mute, and that she underwent an operation on her armpit, which apparently made it possible for her to speak. In describing the family's reaction to her birth, she said, "My father said that they wouldn't let him see me, only through the window, they didn't let him come in. . . . He would say: she'll die, she'll die the whole time, the whole time, and the nurses said: No, she'll be all right, it will be okay."

Describing her childhood, Sara spoke only of her failure as a pupil. She was placed in a number of parallel frameworks (her regular class, a class for slow learners, and a class for extra lessons) and, in her opinion, this is what held her back: "I would go to extra lessons, and from there to the special class, then I would be with my own class, with everyone. It's difficult, I didn't know where I stood with myself." In spite of all these efforts she did not succeed in learning to read and write. Her father saw her going to school as a waste of time: "My father treated me as if I was sick, as if I don't have to go to school."

When she was in the eighth grade, she took a selection examination used in Israel at that time to determine who would continue on to regular high school, vocational high school, and who would not continue at all. Sara described this event in great detail, conveying the feeling that she was reliving the experience in spite of the many years that had elapsed. "I didn't catch onto things, they even took me out of the class, there was an examination in eighth grade and they took me completely out of the lesson so that I wouldn't spoil the class for the other children. . . . for about an hour, hour and a half, and afterwards I came back. I didn't even understand why they took me out, was I really that bad? . . . a friend of mine told me: you know why they took you out? Cause you don't know anything. That's it."

Because she had not taken the test, she was unable to continue her schooling, and began working as a cleaner in a retirement home. "I was a working girl, going from work to home, don't know how to read and write. Not going out, not asking anything. I waited for the chance to get married from staying buried at home. Maybe things will be better for me." Her father did not let her go out and she did not disobey him. At work she met the man who was to become her husband. "My father was afraid that he [her boyfriend] would do something to me and would throw me out before the wedding; our parents protected us terribly . . . so I would say to him: If you want to get to know me, come to my home . . . I just sit around with my parents. . . . After three or four months my father said to him: Bring me half of your salary for three months and I'll make you the wedding. My father gave me away and my husband brought half the money. The truth is I wanted to get married 'cause sitting around like that all the time is hard, also no one else would have taken me 'till today."

Sara was married at 20. From her husband she hid the secret of her disability to read or write. He hid the secret of his drinking and the fact that two of his brothers. who were previously Torah students, were mentally ill. After the wedding they lived with his parents, "What a mess, even the devil couldn't have made it." Sara discovered that her life was becoming far worse than before. Life with her in-laws and the exposure and proximity to mental illness marked the beginning of a dead-end existence. It is unclear how long the young couple lived with his parents. On one occasion Sara mentioned that they lived there for two years, until after the birth of their second daughter; on another occasion she mentioned only four months. However, both these time periods—four months after the wedding and the birth of the second daughter—seem to be important for Sara, because she mentioned them as the time of the discovery of the mutual secrets. "Four months after the wedding my husband told me that his brother was in hospital and that there were another two mentally ill members of the family."

Sara said that only after the birth of the second daughter was the husband informed that she could not read or write. Sara said that since the birth of the second child, she required daily Valium. After this birth, she also underwent an operation for tubal ligation, without her husband's knowledge. However, after some time (it is not clear how long) she was unable to withstand his pressure for more children, and again she underwent, according to her report without his knowledge, an additional operation for reopening her Fallopian tubes.

Sara and her husband have six children. She found it difficult to state the ages of the children and, as in the case of her own date of birth, she appeared unable to confirm the children's ages. When she counted the number of children and described their births, she did this in conjunction with a description of the number of rooms in the home or in relation to the move from one home to another. She gave birth to her first daughter when they lived in her mother-in-law's home, but when the second daughter was born, "I couldn't live there any more, already half crazy I was, so they [the welfare] gave us a home here, with the two children. Afterwards I brought another child, then they moved me to the transit camp. After this I brought another two children, the place was already crowded."

Sara described her married life as filled with suffering: She did not mention any occasion of pleasure or satisfaction. Her husband was a civilian worker in the army, but from time to time he did not go to work and spent his time drinking. He oscillated between being sober, when he ignored Sara, and being drunk, when he became verbally and physically abusive. He told her that she is "no wife, just a servant . . . he will never just sit and talk to me . . . I don't ever feel that he's together with me, like a husband and a wife." He breaks things in the home, falls asleep while smoking, and burns the sheets. To prevent a disaster, Sara makes sure that she goes to sleep after him. Sara said that she feels alone and receives no help from him in any way. He also prevented her from obtaining assistance, prohibited her from visiting her sister, or participating in the Yachdav group organized by the social workers. (In fact, she did not comply with the latter prohibition.)

Just as in her father's home, she said she was again closed in "like an idiot between four walls." She has asked her husband not to swear in front of the children and not to break plates on the floor where the baby crawls, but all she can actually do is to flee to her room and shut herself inside, so that she can at least not see what he is doing.

The children suffer from a number of difficulties. The oldest, about 15 years old, is described as particularly bright. She gets very high grades, but she is "peculiar," makes strange gestures with her hands and does not communicate at all with her parents. Sara and her husband are anxious about her strange behavior, and in order to "correct" her, they have beaten her and thrown out her old school notebooks, which she jealously safeguards. The child reacted with more extreme withdrawal behavior. Their son was recently expelled from school. Since they were only informed about this at the end of the summer, they did not have time to find an alternative framework before the start of the new school year. The baby is sickly, suffers from breathing and ear problems, frequently develops a high temperature, and requires recurrent hospitalization. The young daughter attends a boarding school. Sara said, "It's hard for me. I run to the school, to the municipality, to the hospital. . . . I run all the time, I'm collapsing. Just so that people won't laugh at us [because of the strange behavior of the eldest girl] . . . People don't know, they think that there is an older girl who can help."

Sara does not see a better future. She cannot read or write, is unable to use the automatic bank teller, or to bake a cake from a written recipe. With no means of independence, she is fated to continue living with her husband. She said, "I don't know how to manage with myself, so what will be with the children?"

FIRST IMPRESSIONS

The most prominent feature of Sara's story is its low level of organization. Many sentences are incomplete, ideas are fragmented, and the style is often repetitive. She seldom used personal names, so that when she introduces a new person into the story, it is unclear about whom she is speaking. Many parts of the story are bizarre. The way in which she describes her muteness and the operation on her armpit arouse suspicion and even ridicule. When she is unable to give her children's ages, she sounds pathetic. When she describes her daughter's strangeness and the way she and her husband maltreat her, she seems shut-off and provokes anger. Sara's view of the world and her perception of self are to a large extent chaotic, disconnected, and disintegrated. When I asked her to talk about her life and childhood, she said, "I was born and that's it" as if she has no story, no interconnection between the events and her role in the way the events unfold. When she described the operation she underwent as a child, it seems as if her perception of her body is completely distorted, and it is clear that no one ever explained to her what she underwent. Even if Sara is describing a real operation, the way it is described points to complete ignorance and an inability to communicate details of her congenital defect in a way that the listener can relate to seriously.

Sara's story hardly rouses feelings of respect or admiration for its protagonist; rather pity for a somewhat negligible or worthless object. Sara is, it seems, a clear example of the victim whose "suffering may be pitiful and heartrending . . . but it cannot be tragic" (Krook, 1969, p. 12). Nevertheless, I would argue that Sara, despite these first impressions of her story and despite her own unawareness of being anything but a helpless victim, exhibits in her behavior and in her narrative features that qualify her as a tragic protagonist. The class, gender, and family conditions of her life constitute the arena of her unremitting struggle against those very conditions, despite her inability to withstand or overcome them. The tragic paradigm of agency only apparently free but in reality fated offers a way of relating to Sara's trials and struggles as to those of an agent however unsuccessful she in reality is. I will clarify and expand on these features drawing on the work of two literary critics, Krook (1969) and Nevo (1972), who have analyzed tragic form and structure.

THE BIRTH AND THE HOSPITALIZATION:
THE SHAMEFUL DEFECT

Since Aristotle's treatise on tragedy (1970), the Harmatia, the fatal flaw or error, has been recognized as one of the elements motivating the tragic plot. The term, however, has been variously translated and interpreted. Krook interpreted it as "the act of shame or horror" but noted that "in modern drama it may refer to a situation or condition" (p. 8), whereas Nevo preferred the Aristotelian concept of fatal error, which places the emphasis on that action of the protagonist that inevitably involves him or her in his or her fate.

Krook's situation of shame aptly describes the beginning of Sara's story and her parents' reaction to it: "I was born in Tsrifin, that's what I know that they told me that I was small, and I was, about a year in hospital, because I didn't know how to speak, so my father would always say: I would visit you, visit you from the window. They wouldn't let him come in. Only after . . . about a month or two . . . they decided to do this operation on my armpit here, and after a month, I recovered, more or less they heard my voice. My father would always tell me that [when] they were going to visit me [they said]: She'll die, she'll die, all the time. And the nurses said: No, she'll be all right, it'll all be okay. 'Cause all the time they said that she is in a bad way . . . I even have, to this day, things that I can't say, that I hear, sometimes things that I don't catch onto."

The story of the birth is the exposition, the tragic predicament, in which the components of the sequence destined to develop afterward are found in embryo. From what Sara described, it is not clear exactly with what defect she was born. She was apparently born premature ("small") and with some impediment to her speech system. This defect, because of no fault of her own, accompanies her from birth and colors the course of her life. She attributed to it the shameful inadequacy that is her illiteracy: "When I was one year I had an operation 'cause I was dumb, I couldn't talk, then I recovered a bit . . . so for example . . . I couldn't understand things, even I was taken out of class in tests not to spoil the class grades." In Sara's life and narrative this shameful defect assumes the place of the fatal flaw in that it becomes the key to understanding her interpretative system. Throughout the interview, she connected all her distresses to her illiteracy: her marriage, her not getting divorced, her inability to cope with her daughter's problems. Thus her story is contained in embryonic form in the picture of the small baby being observed by the father full of foreboding and the soothing nurse through the window in the hospital.

The distress conveyed by the scene is clearly not only a result of the congenital defect but also of her father's attitude to it, as described in her story. The perception that the story of her birth already contains within it the potential for errors and distresses to be revealed in the future is expressed in a dramatic manner. Two voices argue like the prophetic chorus in a Greek tragedy: "She will die"; "She will live."

The statement, "I was born and that's it," expresses her perception that her story begins and ends with birth, with the father's fear that she is going to die, and his underlying fear of the possibility that the defective baby is actually going to live. This ambivalence finds no real repair or resolution during her life.

THE TERRIBLE SECRET

The two main themes in Sara's story are illiteracy and loneliness. Her illiteracy is an organizing theme through which she explained her feeling of helplessness and despair, of having no possibility of living life differently or in changing anything in her life. She agreed to marry her husband because of her father's pressure and because no one else would have taken an illiterate like herself. She remained married to him because she has no means of independent existence: She is illiterate. "Even if we get divorced, even if he gives me support, I don't know what to do with the money, where will I go? I can't go to the grocery, I can't pay the electricity, and what will I do with the house? Where will I live?" She provided specific evidence of the illiteracy: an inability to deal with the bank accounts or to use the automatic bank teller, to check her grocery bill or to bake a cake from a recipe.

It is interesting to consider why Sara takes her illiteracy to be the keystone of her difficulties. The choice attests, in my opinion, to a powerful awareness of difference. She lives in a world where people know how to read and write. Her manner of detailing her difficulties and connecting them to reading and writing leads us to reassess the way in which literacy is perceived in our daily lives; it is so automatic that we are not even aware of it. Sara's awareness thus emphasizes her difference and her loneliness. The illiteracy signifies not only a concrete obstacle but an emotional state, expanding from a feeling of inferiority to a sense of extreme marginality and to an abysmal aloneness. Her removal from the classroom during the examination is equated with a shameful removal from legitimate society. The school hides her away. Sara internalizes this attitude and continues to hide the illiteracy throughout her life, as if she fears that the rejection will return and, once again, she will be put outside the circle. The illiteracy becomes a signifier of her defectiveness and of the attitude of her father's home and of society to this defect. The conjunction results in the existential loneliness that she feels, her inability to make contact, to feel worthy. This is related to the experience of life as imprisonment and isolation, which Sara described in various contexts: "All the time I was closed in, even when I wasn't married I wouldn't go anywhere"; "I was a working girl, from work to home, I wouldn't go anywhere, because I didn't know how to read and write"; "It's difficult that everything is at home ... to be like an idiot between four walls"; "I wouldn't go on trips with the school, they wouldn't take me ... I was always at home." And about Yachdav, the group therapy that helped her, Sara said, "I didn't give up, I always came, because I said that this is a place that I have, you understand? I kind of join up with something" and she accompanied her words with a hugging movement.

Sara's relation to her illiteracy resembles that of the classic tragic hero to the decree of fate: This is the shameful defect that fate determined for her at birth. In Sophocles's *Oedipus Rex*, two attempts are made to alter fate. The first by Oedipus's parents who wish to kill him to prevent the oracle's fulfillment and the second by Oedipus himself, who flees to avoid killing those whom he wrongly believes are his real parents. Of course, all the efforts to evade his fate fail, and through a complicated turn of events, Oedipus arrives, as it were by chance, to the city of his birth, eventually carrying out the dictates of his fate.

Sara perceived her illiteracy as irremediable; as her fatal flaw—an irreversible destiny, a blot that cannot be erased. It is not only the lack of a specific ability but the inferiority, difference, and loneliness that form the central core of her personal experience. By marrying, she hoped to alter her fate, to repair the impairment and the marginality. She said, "At 20 we got married, a normal age, not early and not late," as if she is saying that marriage would enable her to become normal, to be like everyone else. Up until her marriage, there was insufficient normality in her development, and it seems to her that her marriage at a normal age would be the beginning of a new chapter in her life. Her dream of marriage extricating her from her plight is very characteristic of girls in her situation, and is rooted in our culture in the image of "the knight on a white horse" as one of the legitimate ways for girls to think of emancipation, of personal redemption, and of a better life (Krumer-Nevo, 2003b). Sara's dream itself is an expression of strength, of a refusal to bow to her oppressive life situation. The trouble is that Sara's knight himself comes from a marginalized family, drinks, is abusive, and lives in the shadow of mentally ill siblings.

That the hopes of a better life will be realized, Sara, with tragic irony, hid her illiteracy from her husband, as she was hidden during the school examination. Secrecy, Sara naively hoped, would protect her new life from the pain and the deprivation that were her lot until the marriage. However, not only is the secret inexpedient (for it will obviously be discovered), but it is also revealed in the context of her husband's devastating secret. The illiteracy, which stands between her and normality, is dwarfed by the complete inversion of normality—the madness in the husband's family and his parents' home in which the young couple live. It is not surprising that Sara described their home as a "madhouse" and the time they lived there as a period in which her mental state felt seriously undermined.

Ruth Nevo (1972) drew attention to the "cruel reversal of expectation, characteristic of tragedy, and the more poignant by virtue of whatever guilt, of whatever degree and kind, has been incurred by the protagonist, paradoxical victim–agent of his doom" (p. 29). Sara hoped that her marriage would constitute a joining and a belonging, but it brought disintegration and breakdown. "I want them (the children) to have a good life, get married and have a good mother-in-law because I didn't have a good mother-in-law. . . . When I got married I fell apart."

An additional irony is that the madness in the husband's family is actually related to intellectual superiority and Sara connected the two when saying: "My brother-in-law was also a top Torah student, and where is he now? In a mental hospital." The connection between educational powers, the opposite of illiteracy, and madness continues into the next generation. Sara's eldest daughter who, through her diligence and superior grades, could have compensated for Sara's defect, in fact embodies the conjunction between secrets and the two fateful forces in the family. She is an excellent pupil but behaves strangely. Sara is both proud and afraid of her.

Sara, initially defeated by illiteracy, is defeated again, this time by madness, drink, and violence. Sara's daughter has conquered illiteracy but it is not clear if she has the strength to emerge victorious in the battle for sanity. The way Sara and her husband react to their daughter only causes destruction and harm. The father beats her, Sara throws her school bag and old notebooks into the trash can and threatens not to buy her what she needs for school "until you stop moving your hands around." "If you don't want to change I won't buy you anything. Her father nearly had an attack because of her, 'cause he suffered enough with the problems with his brothers. . . . [I tell her] you're a hard worker, show people that you work hard, show them that you are better than them, you don't have to fall, do you know how hard it can break you?"

Sara's behavior at this point constitutes an equivalent to the tragic reversal in the classic tragic plot: The turn around from a high point of potential good fortune to downfall. A repetition of the tragic reversal of her marriage. She harms her daughter and causes her to fail precisely through a desire to protect her and precisely at the point where she herself feels most vulnerable. This is the point at which all the motifs converge—the secret illiteracy, the madness, the isolation, and fate. Fate indeed takes on the character of a repetition compulsion, which annuls any attempt at repair or restitution.

THE IMPOSSIBLE CHOICE

Schafer (1976) maintained that the perception of time among people who operate in the tragic mode is linear, as opposed to circular. Life is seen as progressing toward death without any possibility for rebirth. Time marches on and is irreversible, decisions and choices are irrevocable, the subsequent opportunity cannot undo mistakes.

To the issue of the irreversibility of tragic choices, Nevo (1972) added the claim that tragedy characteristically issues from what she calls the impossible choice. The tragic heroine finds herself at a crossroads where each of the alternative courses of action before her presents a life-threatening danger. The choice is impossible because "whichever . . . alternatives he chooses will seem to him deeply wrong, to involve him in great guilt, to constitute the greatest conceivable danger to . . . his life, to require him to place in jeopardy the goals and values to which he most passionately aspires" (p. 23).

The choice is impossible, therefore, because, in a sense, it is no choice at all but a trap or a double bind. This view is critical in understanding the tragic heroine, because without seeing the situation of choice through the eyes of the heroine as impossible, we as reader–therapists cannot empathetically understand her point of view or the complexity within which she operates. The concept of the impossible choice reflects the meaning that the tragic heroine gives to her situation, a situation in which she is compelled to act and to choose but that does not allow a real or beneficent choice to be made. This, of course, does not mean that we as therapists have to agree with the perception of the circumstances as offering only an impossible choice. We have only to recognize its existence to the protagonist and to understand its influence on her.

Let us examine how we can understand Sara's world and her experience of it with the aid of this concept. Toward the middle of the interview, it became clear that the problem that most disturbs her, to which she devotes all of the latter part of her narrative, is that of her eldest daughter. It is important to see that although Sara does not understand her daughter or help her with her difficulties, she repeatedly stated, "I try to talk with her, [it] doesn't help, I say: I want life to be good for you, I ask her so much . . . my parents didn't ask me like that, I try to say what haven't you got, I'll give it to you, what's your problem, tell me what's hurting you, she doesn't tell me anything, she's . . . so closed, she is breaking us, the whole family she is breaking up . . . I say, maybe God will help me a bit . . . maybe give me someone who can tell me what to do . . . a stranger . . . not from here . . . Maybe she needs help, this is what I thought to myself . . . maybe she's lacking something . . . I told him [her husband] don't hit her, explain to her." Sara does not give up easily; she attempted to talk with her daughter and to mobilize her husband, but without success.

This daughter, who could help Sara to defeat her past, fails dismally. Sara told her, "You are bright, show people that you are bright, show them that you are better than them, that you don't need to fall." Sara's difficulty begins to emerge with the knowledge that the neighbors know that her daughter is "not okay": "How I cried that day, I went into my room and cried . . . I don't want her studies, don't want anything, only that she will change, that other people won't laugh at us, only that."

The alternatives confronting Sara in dealing with her daughter and her special needs are these: to move emotionally closer to her daughter's strangeness, which she seemingly does in those moments in which she expresses the daughter's difficulties and her desire to help. But this forces her to confront her own helplessness and even worse, to feel exposed, vulnerable, and above all, ashamed—because the fragile internal balance of her self-esteem is only maintained by keeping the shameful secrets hidden. The other alternative is brute force or punishment, to withdraw her empathy toward her daughter, to hide her strangeness from everyone, including herself, to destroy the very symbols and tools of education. This of course leads to violent attempts to compel the girl to alter her behavior, and, in fact, to aggressively counterproductive abusive behavior toward her daughter.

Choosing between the two alternatives is impossible because for Sara each entails hurt, pain, and humiliation. Sara chooses not to choose. Throughout the interview, she vacillated between moments in which she described her pain connected to her daughter and her tremendous need to protect her and moments in which she described her inability to tolerate the feeling of shame the daughter arouses, and her fear of the danger that the daughter, by her behavior, will "expose" her and her secrets.

In fact, whenever there is open conflict in the family between the daughter and her parents, and Sara has to choose how to act, she feels that her internal balance is endangered. If she supports her daughter, she feels herself exposed and vulnerable. If she participates in the attacks against her daughter, she suffers from feelings of guilt. She identifies with the daughter as a victim and she has the maternal need to defend her. "I beg her so much (to stop her behavior). . . . my parents didn't ask me in this way."

Sara's way of dealing with the impossible choice is analogous to Oedipus's attempted escape from the knowledge of what he has unwittingly done to his biological parents. He blinds himself. Sara described the way she deals with the situation of conflict: After her drunk husband broke dishes in front of the children, "I ran to the room, shut myself in . . . by myself, I was scared that he would break other things that I would *see,* at least let him break things and I *didn't see* . . . sometimes I say to myself, God help me so that at least I *don't see,* the torture I'm going through." At another point, after she described her daughter's strange behavior, she said, "I say God come and take me, not *to see* these things or *not to know,* or that things will be good for me . . . I don't want *to see* . . . I *don't want to see* what's going on."

Sara thus deals with the situation by "not seeing." What is interesting is that she described the not seeing as a conscious choice. In this way she attests to herself as "seeing"; she feels the horror of the situation both for herself and for her daughter. If she did not see, she would not have to choose not to see. Both are a kind of death.

Undoubtedly, this kind of coping is unsuccessful. On the other hand, it shows that Sara is far from unaware. If she really could "not see," she would not be a tragic protagonist. Her being such is inherent in the fact that in spite of her minimal ability to influence events, she continues to see. Because she does see and does know—she begs not to see. This is the nature of the impossible choice and her kinship to the classic tragic hero. As Krook put it, "The tragic hero receives the full impact of [the world's] painful, terrible, humiliating unintelligibility, [and] by the extremity of his conscious suffering, renders it intelligible" (Krook, 1969, p. 44).

It is interesting to note the continuity between the wish to be blind and the experience of illiteracy—Sara's tragic plight. Both, in effect, are acts of self-sabotage, intimately interconnected. The illiteracy and the blindness seemingly allow her to remove certain elements that are intolerable from consciousness or to nullify action. Together they constitute a vicious circle and a fate.

THE HEROINE AND FATE

The genre of tragedy is the outstanding literary expression of an encounter with fate. Tragedy presents a paradoxical situation, a tension between what is determined by fate and what is determined by human beings, in which both exist simultaneously. Although the tragic hero is far from being victorious, he or she is also far from being a victim, because of his or her human stature and above all self-knowledge. The hero is neither passive, nor weak, nor lacking in value. He or she is considered a hero by virtue of his or her coping with the suffering, danger and harm in which he or she is in, and for which he or she is in part responsible, in spite of his or her inability to overcome them.

Despite the fact that fate determines the course of events, the tragic hero is such because he or she takes responsibility for his or her actions and decisions and is punished for them. The tragic hero existentially exercises free will and, therefore, bears both responsibility as well as its consequences.

Are we not doing an injustice to women when we interpret their tendency to speak of fate in terms of "an external locus of control" as pointing to their relinquishing personal responsibility? Do we not tend to ignore the fatalistic, inexorable elements in their lives? Can we deny the struggle that a baby born with a defect into a family that is unable to cope with defects—a family itself on the margins of society—will have for her whole life? If we adopt the notion that the most difficult environmental conditions, arising from poverty and its consequences, are really a kind of fate that affect all areas of life, and condition all choices, we can come closer to understanding how people who live in poverty experience themselves, their difficulties, and their prospects. Tragedy, with its tension between the power of fate and the power of the heroic will, which perceives both as powerful forces that command our respect, can help us to understand the complex relationship between these women and the often implacable reality that they inhabit and against which they fruitlessly struggle.

CONCLUSION

This chapter presents the story of only one woman. But the tragic components it exemplifies can be found in many other life stories of women living in severe economic and social deprivation (Krumer-Nevo, in press). The reading that I propose of Sara's life story is interpretative. It does not profess to constitute an impeccably objective report. Nor does it profess to describe the unmediated subjective truth of Sara, the protagonist of the story. The strength of interpretation of this kind lies in the possibility of telling a story in a way that presents a new look as the main character and the dilemma in which she is placed. Whether this new look is useful will be assessed in terms of how fruitful it is for therapists who encounter poor women and who look for ways to empathetically understand their difficulties, ways that the other models focusing on pathology do not allow.

The potential value for therapy of the tragic meta-narrative is that it offers a paradigm of women who live in a world so constrained as to preclude the chances of success yet who possess agency and choice. It enables therapists to take in the full force of the restrictions of social reality without reducing the women to the status of a one-dimensional victim. Change can only come about through such a nonreductive shift in the viewpoint both of the women with regard to themselves and their "fate" and of society with regard to poor individuals and its policy toward them. Recognizing the manifold expressions of "fate" within the story that professionals tell themselves about poor women, while seeing the women's efforts to escape this fate, however unsuccessful these may be, provides an opening for the empathetic understanding of their lives. This kind of approach is a first step toward an ability to work with and for these women toward change.

REFERENCES

Aristotle. (1970). *Poetics* (Trans. G. F. Else). Ann Arbor, MI: Arbor.

Corradi, C. (1991). Text, context and individual meaning: Rethinking life stories in a hermeneutical frame. *Discourse and Society, 2*(1), 105–118.

Crenshaw, K. (1994). Demarginalizing the intersection of race and sex: A Black feminist critique of anti discrimination doctrine, feminist theory, and antiracist politic. In A. M. Jaggar (Ed.), *Living with contradictions: Controversies in feminist social ethics* (pp. 39–51). Boulder, CO: Westview Press.

Etter-Lewis, G. (1991). Black women's life stories: Reclaiming self in narrative texts. In G. S. Berger & D. Patai (Eds.), *Women's words: The feminist practice of oral history* (pp. 43–58). New York: Routledge.

Fine, M. (1994). Working the hyphens: Reinventing self and other in qualitative research. In N. K. Denzin & Y. S. Lincoln (Eds.), *Handbook of qualitative research* (pp. 70–82). Thousand Oaks, CA: Sage.

Frye, N. (1957). *Anatomy of criticism.* Princeton, NJ: Princeton University Press.

Glenn, E. N. (1985). Racial ethnic women's labor: The intersection of race, gender and class oppression. *Review of Radical Political Economics, 17*(3), 86–108.

Hamilton, G. (1940). *Theory and practice of social casework.* New York: Columbia University Press.

Krook, D. (1969). *Elements of tragedy.* New Haven, CT: Yale University Press.

Krumer-Nevo, M. (2003a). *"I got married to get free of home": Why young women marry. The case of women living in poverty in Israel.* Manuscript under review.

Krumer-Nevo, M. (2003b). *Poverty industry: Research models and products.* Manuscript under review.

Krumer-Nevo, M. (in press). *From "noise" to "voice." Women, poverty, gender.* Tel-Aviv: Hakibutz Hameuchad.

Nevo, R. (1972). *Tragic form in Shakespeare*. Princeton, NJ: Princeton University Press.

Novick, R., & Krumer-Nevo, M. (1993). *Yachdav: From multi-generational poverty to nurturing and independent parenting. Research and evaluation report*. Jerusalem: Bayit Lekhol Yeled—Ministry of Labor and Social Affairs, Hebrew University.

Omer, H. (1994). *Critical interventions in psychotherapy: From impasse to turning point*. New York: W. W. Norton.

Polatnick, M. R. (1996). Diversity in women's liberation ideology: How a black and a white group of the 1960s viewed motherhood. *Signs, 21*(3), 679–706.

Rosenfeld, J. M., Schon, D. A., & Sykes, I. J. (1995). *Out from under: Lessons from projects for inaptly served children and families*. Jerusalem: JDC–Brookdale.

Rosenthal, G. (1993). Reconstruction of life stories: Principles of selection in generating stories for narrative biographical interviews. In R. Josselson & A. Lieblich (Eds.), *The narrative study of lives* (Vol. 1, 59–91). Newberry Park, CA: Sage.

Schafer, R. (1976). *A new language for psychoanalysis*. New Haven, CT: Yale University Press.

4

BETWEEN ABSTRACT INDIVIDUALISM AND GENDERED LIVES: NEGOTIATING ABUSED WOMEN'S AGENCY AND IDENTITY IN THERAPY

SUVI KESKINEN

Narrative identity consists of stories that we tell about ourselves and others, as well as stories others tell about us. The construction of narrative identity is a collective act that includes the presentation of the self (or some parts of it) to the world and the world's recognition of the self. Recognition by others and the ability to tell stories that are socially and culturally embedded are therefore an important component in constructing narrative identities (Whitebrook, 2001). In therapy, the client and the therapist engage in a dialogue of constructing narratives and narrative identities. In the therapeutic encounter, some narratives and narrative identities receive recognition and are supported, whereas others are discouraged by the therapist. The negotiation of which narratives and narrative identities

I wish to thank Suvi Ronkainen, Jeff Hearn, Tarja Pösö, Harriet Silius, Marjo Kuronen, and Minna Nikunen for their valuable comments regarding the chapter. The research has been conducted as part of the research project The Violence of Sex. Meanings, Emotions, Practices, and Policies of Sexualized Violence, which is funded by the Academy of Finland (2000–2003).

receive recognition in therapy is also negotiation over a possible and preferable agency. Narratives suggest visions for the future and of different forms of agency (Ochberg, 1994).

This chapter discusses the construction of narrative identity of women who have experienced violence from their partners. The analysis focuses on how agency and narrative identity are negotiated within the therapeutic process. These negotiations are set in a sociocultural context of abstract individualism, which includes expectations of agentic behavior performed by a rational, independent, and autonomous individual. However, the rhetoric of abstract individualism is not always easily reconciled with abused women's gendered lives and the gendered expectations they meet. The chapter looks at how the therapist and client negotiate the discrepancy between the implicit agentic expectations of abstract individualism and the gendered, embodied lives of abused women during the therapeutic encounter. The ethnographic study, conducted at three family counseling centers in Finland, concentrated on how the therapists worked with intimate violence and on the rhetorical spaces opening up for abused women in the encounters.

EQUALITY DISCOURSE AND GENDER
IN THE NORDIC WELFARE STATE

The Nordic welfare state has broken down some of the traditional gender differences, but at the same time other gendered patterns have remained untouched and some new ones have been introduced (Gordon et al., 2000). For example, women's participation in the labor market is extensive. The welfare state gives access to economic independence also for women who are not employed. Even single mothers are able to support themselves with the combination of wages and social security benefits (Nousiainen & Niemi-Kiesiläinen, 2001). This allows Finnish women enough economic independence to divorce violent husbands.

However, the emphasis on gender neutrality and the widely used rhetoric of gender equality make it difficult to address gendered inequalities, such as violence against women. These issues receive little attention and tend to be discussed in gender-neutral terms (Gordon et al., 2000; Ronkainen, 2001). When violence in intimate relationships was taken up in Finnish public debate at the end of the 1970s, it was treated as "family violence." According to this view, all the family members were seen as responsible for violence within the family. Violence was not regarded as an issue related to gender and power but as a form of argument–conflict occurring between two equal partners. This rhetoric was institutionalized in the practices of shelters and other social and health care organizations. Working with both partners to solve their common problem was the preferred way of dealing with family violence. In the 1990s, issues of gender and power started to be associated with the understanding of intimate violence, and the phrase "violence against women" was introduced (Ronkainen, 2001). Despite these recent changes, ideas of gender neutrality and of violence occurring between two equally situated partners are still widely shared.

THE NOTION OF ABSTRACT INDIVIDUALISM
AND EXPECTATIONS OF STRONG AGENCY

Gender-neutral rhetoric and the discourse of equality are based on what Joan Scott (1995) called abstract individualism. According to Scott, this way of conceptualizing the individual relates to the development of the modern notion of citizenship. With the formation of the modern nation state, individuals are conceptualized abstracted from their social location. Citizenship is exclusive of gender, "race," and social class. An abstract individual is seen as disembodied and without particularities. Furthermore, all individuals are considered to be equal holders of rights and duties (Gordon et al., 2000; Scott, 1995). However, the construct of the abstract individual has been shown by feminist analyses to be either an explicitly masculine subject or linked with attributes that are historically associated with men, such as rationality, autonomy, and independence (Ronkainen, 2001; Scott, 1995).

Abstract individualism is also normative. A woman who has been subjected to violence in an intimate relationship is expected to react as an abstract individual, thus she faces expectations of rational and autonomous agentic behavior. An autonomous individual can choose whether to leave or to stay with a violent partner. If an abused woman does not make the rational choice to leave, her behavior is seen as irrational and thus may be considered the cause of the problem. This point of view does not take into account emotions such as shame, hope, and love. In addition, the effects of violence and victimization are discounted. (Ronkainen, 2001.) Research on the attitudes of Finnish social and health care workers toward intimate violence shows that these professionals often regard a woman's depression and passivity as explanations for the violence perpetrated against her (Perttu, 1999). Even when professionals know a woman is a victim of violence, they regard her as an autonomous actor who is responsible for the continuation of the violence. In addition, expectations of rational and autonomous behavior are evident in court practices. For example, in cases where abused women who have killed their husbands try to present proof of previous violence, if the women have not contacted the police or seen a doctor, or left the batterer, it can be regarded as evidence that there was no violence or that it was not as frequent as claimed (Ruuskanen, 2001).

CONFLICTING PERSPECTIVES

During my research at the family counseling centers, it became clear that much of the therapists' work revolved around the issue of the abused women's agency. For the therapists, it was critical for their clients to learn to survive the effects of violence and gain their strength. The capability of an abused woman to take action and maintain her rights was seen as part of this. Autonomy and independence in a relationship with a violent man were clearly regarded as desirable by the therapists.

To a large extent, the family counseling centers work with these women at a point when they consider leaving the abusive men or have already divorced them. The discussions at the family counseling centers often deal with questions of agency in relation to the violent (ex-)husband and the various institutions with which the women are involved when they leave him—for example, the police, the courts, or the social or health care systems. The matters concerned include, for instance, arranging child custody and contact, reporting the man to the police, or applying for a restraining order. In their interactions both with these institutions and with violent men, abused women are expected to act as individuals who claim their rights. It is assumed that they will be able to stand up against threatening men and negotiate with them as equal partners—and do this free from emotional ties. This places normative expectations of agency on abused women at a time when they may find such actions especially challenging. Abused women are treated from the perspective of abstract individualism, excluding any admission of emotion. Yet emotional bonds are an essential part of the problem of intimate violence. Love and hope for improvement have often tied women to abusive relationships. Besides physical violence, abusive men use power through emotional means. This web of emotional violence is built on fear, adjustment, and responsibility (Kirkwood, 1993).

In the lives of women who have experienced intimate violence, gender-neutral rationalizing expectations are confronted with gendered expectations, especially those connected to heterosexual and family relations. Maintaining family relations, emotional closeness, and taking care of others are highly gendered expectations: Women in particular are linked to this emotional work and are culturally regarded as responsible for it (Jackson, 1999). Even in a society espousing a rhetoric of equality, these gendered expectations are widespread and influential. How do abused women respond to this conflict? How do they combine these contradictory elements when they narrate their lives? How do therapists take part in the constructing of narratives?

MATERIAL AND METHOD

This ethnographic study was conducted at three family counseling centers in Finland. Data were collected over a period from 3 to 18 months, depending on the center. As a context for narrating lives, family counseling centers are both similar to and different from individual therapy settings. Family counseling centers offer therapy for the woman client who has experienced violence. Meetings are also arranged with other family members, most often with the children. Counseling in the form of giving advice and information about social and legal services is part of the work. Family counseling therapists are considered to possess professional knowledge on child development and family questions. In my study I attended meetings between therapists and clients at the centers and made field notes. The ethnographic method mainly relies on field notes, but to be able to analyze the discussions in detail, I also taperecorded the encounters. Thirty-three meetings were taped and transcribed. The therapists were also interviewed about their perspectives on working with intimate violence. In addition, the analysis material included newspaper articles and project reports. The consent of the clients and therapists for my presence and the recordings was obtained before the meetings.

The therapists in the centers are specialists in domestic abuse. They are well-versed in the processes of victimization and regard the supporting of abused women an essential part of this work. The centers willing to participate in this research are probably more reflective about their work practices and most likely regard intimate violence as a more important issue than most Finnish family counseling centers. The theme of abused women's agency and the obstacles to it was constantly discussed in the therapy sessions. It was also frequently raised as an issue in my interviews with the therapists. The therapists regarded supporting a strong agency important to secure a future without violence for their women clients. In this work they are, however, compelled to rely on the discourses available in society. The rhetoric and narratives based on abstract individualism form an influential yet contradictory resource that is drawn on in these discussions. In the following analysis, I will highlight the discussion of abused women's agency and the role of abstract individualism in this. I also trace the process of negotiation between this discourse and women's gendered lives. I approach the theme by presenting two encounters in which these issues have a central role and the patterns can be seen in detail. These patterns can, however, be discerned in other therapeutic encounters as well. The analysis is based on taperecorded and transcribed material.

I have analyzed the encounters with reference to how agency and narrative identities are constructed in them. When doing this I made a closer analysis of the passages where the description related to these questions is extensive. I have been influenced by the idea of key rhetoric (Komulainen, 1999), according to which the analysis focuses on the rhetorical means used by people when describing their lives and the changes in them. The course of events is not as essential to analysis as are the ways in which the events and characters are constructed and the meanings attached to them.

The first encounter presents a dialogue between Julia and her therapist Helena; the second that between Anna and her therapist Paula. Narrative identities are not necessarily stable but may be shifting, fluid, or multiple (Whitebrook, 2001). In the encounter between Julia and Helena, Julia's narrative identity is constructed as fairly coherent. The construction of Anna's narrative identity, on the other hand, involves more shifts and negotiation of possible identities.

AN ADVOCATE OF HER CHILDREN

The encounter between Julia and Helena took place when Julia was facing the threat that her two children could be kidnapped and taken out of the country by their violent father. During the discussion, Julia recounted in detail how she had contacted several officials and how she had been treated by them. She presented herself as an active and competent agent who managed to overcome difficulties and to find the right persons to contact. Helena supported and reinforced this construction of Julia as agentic and capable.

In the beginning of the discussion, Julia told Helena that she had been busy lately. She had organized all the papers necessary for applying for a restraining order. This was needed to prevent her former husband from carrying out his threats of taking the children with him to his home country. Julia also reported on a meeting with a lawyer who was helping her. With a slight laugh, she made the following comment to Helena[1]:

> And well . . . I have such a lot again and I don't know how much time we have to spend. That I at least, for my own part, have accomplished a lot.

---

[1] The parts italicized in the excerpts were stressed in speech. The symbol [. . .] indicates that part of the discussion has been omitted. The symbol . . . indicates that the speaker's thought was not completed or she paused.

Julia stressed that she at least has accomplished a lot. She then told about her meeting with the lawyer and said (again with a short laugh) that the lawyer seemed to appreciate her way of handling the process with the restraining order. She continued her story about encounters with different officials.

Julia: I wrote out this application myself for [H: Umm.] a restraining order for the court in that office and now Anita K. has agreed to be my lawyer and I only need this one appendix for it.

Helena: Umm. Yes. So that would be one of the things?

Julia: That would be one of the things. And another thing is what I was explaining . . . this chief of the border control . . . a man called Hannu Laukkala. I phoned him myself. And gave him all the personal particulars about Linda, Alex, and their father. I explained my errand to him. He was able to give me very practical advice and guidance on what to do and then I sent it all to him in writing. So now they know all about this.

In this excerpt, Julia told how she managed to find her way in the legal and bureaucratic settings. Helena helped Julia to structure what has happened. She also suggested a categorization of the events: This is one thing and that is another. Julia then told Helena about other precautions she has taken in the situation.

Helena: So you've done everything you could?

Julia: Yes.

Helena: Is that so?

Julia: Yes. I also gave the child custody office all personal details and told them I have sole custody of the children. I mean how do I know which papers he'll use . . . if he tries to take the children away. (sighs) This is . . . these are these secur . . . certainty . . . trying to stop him.

Helena: You're making plans for your safety. Is this what it is?

Julia: Yes. But this has been a very long process . . . it took the whole of Monday and Tuesday (laughs). For instance I called the central criminal police, but they couldn't advise me. And then on Monday I phoned the local police, they connected me with the duty room. I explained [what I needed] . . . the man who took the call did have time to listen to me, but then he said "Well, what do you mean, are we to go to this man and tell him not to travel with the children?" [H: Umm.] But he couldn't give me any advice about what I should do. [H: Umm.] I said of course not. I was also laughing like he was. So I mean, there's a lot of ignorance there also.

[*H:* Umm.] I mean you'd assume that an authority . . . that they would at least tell you where to ask.

Helena: Sure. And you've gone through a lot of trouble and then apparently found exactly the right. . . .

Julia: Yes, exactly the right . . . exactly the right person. (laughs)

In the two last excerpts, Julia described the obstacles she has faced and the fact that she has found the right ways of acting in this difficult situation. She is the clever and active main character of the story. There are even traits of heroism in her struggle with the ignorant and unhelpful officials. During the discussion, Helena supported this way of narration. She emphasized that Julia has gone through a great deal of trouble and used much energy to solve the problem. Helena also noted that Julia has been skillful enough to find the right person to talk to and has not let herself be put down by the difficulties. Helena strengthened Julia's construction of herself as a competent actor who deserves admiration for everything she has done.

Helena: What I meant to ask you . . . this sounds like you knew exactly how you wanted things to be and if they weren't, what you'd do then and you have also made sure of some things beforehand . . . with this Hannu Laukkala and . . . taken care of this restraining order and made a sort of safety plan. So can you *remember*, Julia, having been in a situation like this earlier . . . that your plans and thoughts of how to act would have been so clear? And of how to take care of things?

Julia: Well, I've had this thing—for instance, that the children have not been returned, so I've called social services. But they have *not taken care of* the matter. [*H:* Umm.] So when the father . . . the father breaks the contact arrangements, the social services office kind of looks at it . . . umm through their fingers.

Helena: Does this mean that you're not going to let this happen again?

Julia: No, I won't!

Helena: Okay.

Julia: I won't!

Helena: (laughs) Judging by your voice you won't, either. (both laugh)

Helena continued to give credit to Julia for knowing how to act even when things do not go according to plan. She suggested that this is connected with a change in Julia's agency: Her thoughts and plans have become clearer. Helena did this in a very sophisticated way. She emphasized the present positive situation and asked Julia if she remembered having been in a similar situation earlier. Formulating herself as Julia's ally, she concentrated on the idea of positive development and indirectly raised the delicate issue of problems in the past. Here, Helena tried to construct a narrative of development that is based on constructions of a previous and a present Julia. Julia, however, does not take up Helena's suggestion of change in her agency and identity but regards it as a question of continuity. She sees herself as having been active and capable of handling difficult situations even before, but her actions have been limited by officials who have not taken the situation seriously. Helena turned this latent disagreement into a reinforcement of Julia's identity as a strong actor who does not accept ignorant and indifferent treatment. The alliance is restored and strengthened by a short dialogue during which Julia showed that she is determined not to accept such treatment any more.

In her analysis of women's educational life stories, Katri Komulainen (1999) described women's "independence narratives." She argued that independence narratives construct a discontinuity in the presentation of self: a division between a previous and present self. In Komulainen's analysis, the previous self is construed as dependent and adjusting to external expectations, whereas the present self "stands on her own feet," is independent and able to defend herself. The demarcation between the previous and present self in the independence narrative is dichotomous: The two selves are presented as contrasts to each other. The previous, dependent self is gendered. It is "the subordinated Woman" (see de Lauretis, 1984)[2] who has to be projected onto the past to facilitate an independent and autonomous present self. Within the masculine-based construction of the abstract individual, all bonds and care-taking become defined as expressions of dependency and subordination. According to Komulainen, in the independence narrative the discrepancies between the abstract individual and the gendered, embodied aspects excluded from it are resolved in a dichotomous way. Thus, the "new," present self is independent and completely different from the "old" self, conceptualized as dependent and subordinate.

It is this independence narrative that lies behind Helena's suggestions to Julia. Helena suggested that Julia has recently become agentic and clear in her thoughts and implies that she has had another kind of identity in the past. What is interesting, however, is that Julia did not join in this narrative. She held on to a construction of continuity. She resisted the

---

[2] Komulainen's way of using "the subordinated Woman" can be compared to the distinction made by Theresa de Lauretis (1984, pp. 5–6). de Lauretis distinguished between "women" as historical subjects and "woman" as the representation (the other-from-man) constructed by theoretical discourses and expressive practices (such as language, cinema, narrative, imaging). The relationship between these two is not a one-to-one correspondence but is mediated by language and is thus culturally set up. At times the notion of "woman" is written in the form "Woman" to mark the difference to "women" as historical beings.

narrative that would require her to construct herself as dependent and passive in the past. However, in testimony to the strength of the independence narrative and its conceptualization of identity, Helena returned to it after a while, as discussed next.

> Helena: Another thing I would like to ask you is that when you think of just yourself . . . you (J laughs), a grown-up woman, Julia, the mother of your children . . . when you think about yourself, about your own resources and how you . . . have started to stick up for yourself and kind of find out about things and . . . kind of act in a way that shows your will. [J: Umm.] I mean what you want as a mother. [J: Umm.] And you have gone about this really great and if we were to make a kind of picture . . . like this is where you started and this is your goal. That when you've got here you can say that things are pretty good for you now. That nobody's going to walk all over you and you stick up for yourself and won't agree to just anything. So how far on the line are you now? You?

> Julia: Just on the home stretch. [. . .] Or maybe I'm even further, because I think . . . I mean I know now, like the children's father and I, we brought these children to the world as parents . . . so I have thought that I may actually be one step ahead of the officials who also deal with these things. Who I have to work with.

> Helena: Yes. So in that sense . . . dealing with yourself . . . you have come a long way? [J: Umm.] And you are [J: Umm.] quite close and may even already be in a situation where no one is going to walk all over you and you know [J: Umm.] what . . . how to act and can make safety plans [J: Umm.] and have your own way [J: Umm.] and kind of set your own conditions. You don't have to give in and adjust yourself [J: Umm.] and do what others want you to do [J: Umm.]. Congratulations! (J laughs) It's great. And I also think that it's the most important thing for the children. That you as a mother have become stronger in the sense that . . . well . . . you will not be kind of . . . be manipulated or . . . how would I say . . . umm you won't adapt and adjust yourself any longer and do things. . . .

> Julia: I can't be made to do things, or if someone does, you'd really have to ask *who* that could be.

Helena assessed the situation and once again introduced the idea of a dichotomous change in Julia's identity. Helena mostly talked of the present, positively defined Julia. Julia agreed with the construction of this present identity and added that she was even ahead of the officials with whom she has to work to secure her children's well-being and safety. The independence narrative is present, but hidden, because Julia did not join in the construction of a narrative that would require projecting "the subordinated woman" onto the past (e.g., Komulainen, 1999). This makes it problematic for Helena to follow the narrative. When comparing the present and the previous Julia, Helena began to falter. She described the subordinated and passive previous Julia, but with some lack of confidence. The culturally influential independence narrative would give a strong backing for Julia's present identity and agency. However, it is precisely the dichotomous construction of self and the need to describe the past and her own identity in such negative terms that made Julia resist the independence narrative. Instead, she responded by giving her own version of the situation. At this point, Julia and Helena find they can agree about the present identity of Julia as a competent actor.

> Julia: I mean that all through this . . . process [. . .] I could have had an advocate with me [H: Umm.]. That that I . . . I am my own advocate now . . . a representative of myself and my children. [H: Umm.] Because all through this process [. . .] I've felt that parents don't necessarily understand what they are expected to do. That the authorities should bring this up much more . . . discuss, speak about it. [. . .] I have felt myself . . . that I would have had . . . should have had . . . or I've felt at times [H: Umm.] that . . . an *advocate* who knows these things [H: Umm.]. But I've felt after all this (laughs) that I've managed quite well.

> Helena: I'll say (laughs).

The narrative identity that Julia and Helena constructed together during the session is crystallized by Julia. She again constructed a continuity between her past and present identity and named this as being the advocate of her children. She has been skillfully defending herself and her children, although it has not always been easy to deal with unhelpful officials and a threatening ex-husband. But she found the strength and agency that made it possible for her to stand up against these external forces. The way in which she achieved this is based on her motherhood. She has been the advocate and the representative of her children. Her strength and agency are *not* based on abstract individualism, which would exclude relational and emotional ties. Instead, Julia's narrative identity has been built on relational and gendered characteristics, thus avoiding the conflict for women inherent in abstract individualism.

Motherhood and being an advocate of children or other persons in need of care have provided acceptable ways for women to join in public activities and public discourse. With the development of modern society and the modern state, women's citizenship was linked to motherhood. Being a mother became women's social status: Women were expected to give their contribution to the nation by giving birth and raising children, taking responsibility for the home and the family. Even the public positions gained by women within politics or later in the institutions of the growing welfare state in Western societies were to a large extent connected to children, families, and care (Anttonen, 1997). In feminist analyses of women's citizenship this historical background has been analyzed with concepts such as social motherhood (Anttonen, 1997) in the Nordic countries or as maternalism (Elsthain, 1992; Prokhovnik, 1998) mainly in the United States, Britain, and France. Feminists have directed much criticism to the narrowing effects of defining women's citizenship primarily in relation to motherhood and the family. However, motherhood and family-related advocacy have also served as a basis for women's initiatives and enabled women to hold positions of authority. Thus there is a powerful discursive and social potential in motherhood—one that can form an alternative to abstract individualism.

A YOUNG GIRL IN NEED OF GUIDANCE

The encounter between Anna and her therapist Paula occurred in a situation in which Anna had recently been attacked by her former husband. In this encounter the conflict between emotion and rationality plays an important part.

> *Paula:* It's been about . . . over a month since we met last . . . at the end of March?
>
> *Anna:* Yes. And a lot has happened since then. [P: Yes?] Around the 15th . . . of April . . . something very bad happened. I'd been to a party with my coworkers in the evening and one of them gave me a lift home, left me at the parking lot and drove off. And I walked towards the door of the block of flats where I live and as I came to the corner of the house I noticed that Joel was hiding behind the corner and started to run, heading towards me. I turned on my heel and just as we have gone through here, I did as I'd been told here. In other words, I ran in the opposite direction and also started to shout, but he caught me almost at once. And knocked me down on the ground and beat and kicked and hit me. Then some neighbors happened to come out of the building and that was what stopped it in the end. . . .

When Anna told about her actions during the assault, she referred to previous discussions with her therapist. She followed Paula's instructions about what to do in a situation of this kind. When Anna said that she had done as she was told, she placed Paula in a relationship of authority to her. Compared to Anna's earlier meetings with Paula, the element of obeying instructions is stronger in this encounter. I interpret this to be connected to the violent attack and aspects of victimhood. Anna told about being a victim, of being weak and in need of help. During the assault her agency was gravely restricted and she was not able to end the violence by herself but needed the help of her neighbors. In a similar way she needed Paula's advice and was trying to follow the guidelines given to her previously.

Anna then told about what followed the assault. She went to see a doctor to have her injuries treated. She also said that Joel phoned her later and apologized.

Paula: What did he . . . you said that he apologized?

Anna: He only said "please forgive me, I didn't mean to, it was a complete misunderstanding."

Paula: A misunderstanding that he hit and kicked you?

Anna: Yes, that's what I said to him myself. (laughs) [P: Umm.] I told him on the phone that it wasn't because . . . that even if it had been, it can't be justified.

Paula: Well of course not. Well well.

Anna: That even if in a way maybe *I* could think it's possible that if it had been a man who left me there [P: Yes.] . . . I could have imagined that I was provoking him . . . [P: Umm.] in some ways. [P: Umm.] Although it wouldn't be that anyway [P: Umm umm.], but knowing myself I probably would have thought like that.

Paula: You would have felt that it was your fault . . .

Anna: Yes, in a way. Yes.

Paula: Nothing stops you . . . you are a free person. . . .

Anna: Yes I am. Yes. It's true. But I mean, your own patterns of thought, are not like . . . they are like stuck in there [P: Oh yes. But I mean . . .] But I do understand that myself. I can easily imagine that I would have thought so.

Anna took up two different ways of responding to the assault and to assuming responsibility for the violence. On the one hand, she told Joel on the telephone that he had no right to attack her, not even if she had been brought home by another man. This line of reasoning is supported by Paula. Yet on the other hand, Anna also wanted to talk about her thoughts concerning her emotions and her responsibility for the situation. If she had been brought home by another man she would have felt responsible for the attack, she assumed. She was divided between these two ways of thinking. She held on to the rational arguments presenting her as a free, independent person who can do what she chooses. But she also had to come to terms with the emotions and lines of reasoning that placed her in relation to her former husband. The cultural ideas about marriage include expectations of monogamous behavior and respect for both partners' feelings. Even though Anna no longer lives with her ex-husband, the ties that bind her to their relationship have not totally been severed. Anna thus presented herself as having a divided identity where one part is rational and willing to act as an abstract individual and the other part is the emotionally involved and gendered identity that she carries from the past. Paula reacted to this division by trying to convince Anna that she is a free, autonomous person who can do what she wants. She did not join in the discussion of this division or the possibilities of bringing these two parts together. After a while Anna returned to the telephone call and her response to it.

> Anna: I told him that it's not ... I mean that I have no obligation to account to you for this. [P: Umm umm.] That I only ... I said only that *even if it had been a man* [P: Umm.], you *wouldn't have had the right.* [P: Umm.] I mean he didn't get the ... the message. He just repeated over and over again, tell me if it was a man or a woman. [P: Hmm.] I mean I think it's obvious if you listen to me [P: Umm.], that even if it had been a man [P: Umm umm umm.] ... I didn't feel at that point any more that there was any kind of need to put him right about whether it was a man or a woman who happened to give me a lift.

> Paula: Umm umm yes. In a situation like that of course always ... always when you take a taxi or a friend gives you a lift [A: Yes.], it's probably important that this person *stays* a while and sees to it that you get home safely.

> Anna: Yes, I learnt that too now.

By declaring that she is a free person who can do what she wants, Anna strengthens the rational and autonomous part of her identity. By this process she attached herself to the values and arguments put forward by Paula in the earlier excerpt. Paula quietly agreed with her, but turned the discussion to more pragmatic matters. She gave advice to Anna about the safety precautions that she should take in the future, thus showing recognition of Anna's position as a possible victim and her need for help from others.

Anna continued by describing her actions after the violent event. She went to the police and reported the assault. However, she did not do this immediately but waited for a week after the event. During that week, she said, she simply rested and collected her strength. She felt very tired and had to almost force herself to go to the police. She knew that this was the proper way to act in a situation such as this, but her emotional contradictions made her feel ambivalent.

Paula: So what do you think made it so difficult to talk to the authorities, to the police?

Anna: I'm so tired by now, I don't have the strength.

Paula: Umm. Are you scared about what will happen then?

Anna: N–, it's some kind of strange . . . well like, it's not fear. It was . . . some kind of like . . . *pity*. [P: Umm.] I mean I thought wait a minute, he doesn't . . . he can't help his emotions. [P starts to say something] I mean they are so totally out of his control. He's completely helpless in the face of them [P: Umm.]. And how mean I'd be if I now reported it to the police [. . .] If it ends up with imprisonment, what will it do to him? That that's not what he needs. [P: Umm.] He needs another kind of help. [P: Ummh.] So these thoughts started to go round in my head and . . . I really had to try hard to realize . . . or come to think that it hasn't . . . it hadn't helped earlier either. [P: Umm umm.] It hadn't helped earlier one bit. And it does not lead to anything either. That I'll start now . . . I just have to go ahead and . . . take this matter . . . to the police.

Paula: Where did you get this idea that . . . that Joel can't help his emotions?

Anna: Umm, it's the general impression and the fact that I know him [. . .] I mean he couldn't explain earlier *why* either. He just felt angry. [. . .]

Paula: But even in this situation, when he was hitting and kicking, he noticed that your neighbors were coming. [A: Yes.] So he stopped it. I mean . . . I was just thinking that . . . (sighs) has *he* kind of managed to get this thought into your head that "I just can't help myself and that's why I lash out"?

Anna: It could be.

Paula: It looks like it was *your* thought. Very many men say things like "I blacked out," [A: Umm.] "I was so drunk I didn't know what I was doing," but yet they know exactly whether they [. . .] hit a spot that's visible or hit a spot that's covered by clothes. And it's conscious then, it is a conscious choice. [A: Yes.] I mean most of the time it's not only that he'd be overcome by emotion or something. [. . .]

Anna: Yes. I've never thought about it that way. [. . .] Am I naïve.

In this excerpt, Anna discussed her pity for her former husband, a feeling person whom she knows well. She felt responsible for what happens to him. Based in relationship and emotion, this part of her identity includes the elements that are excluded from the rational, autonomous part. At the same time it is the identity construction that connects her to a relationship where she was subjected to violence and threats. Aware of this, Anna struggled to cut the ties that have bound her to her former husband and to take the position of the abstract, rational, autonomous individual. She managed to act on the agentic expectations that she has recently been taught: to go to the police and report the assault to them. She left the emotional contradictions behind her and started to act as she is expected to.

Paula's handling of Anna's emotion talk aims to further rationalize the event and the violence. Paula asked Anna why she thought Joel cannot control his emotions and Anna referred to their common history. Anna returned to the emotionally involved and relational identity construction. Paula questioned all of Anna's arguments and descriptions at this point. She used her professional knowledge to point out that many violent men are actually highly aware of the means and effects of violence. In doing this, Paula simultaneously rejected Anna's identity construction. She presented Anna almost as a puppet, with her former husband pulling the strings. Paula suggested that Joel has planted the idea in Anna's head. Anna solved the situation by defining herself as naïve. She placed herself and was placed by Paula's reasoning in the position of a young, uninformed girl who needs to be taught and guided.

> *Paula:* It's still important . . . an important observation, this that pity never helped you before either.
>
> *Anna:* Never did. It was just so weird when these thoughts start going around in your head and I mean they're really anxious thoughts.
>
> *Paula:* Umm, well for goodness sake, he is the father of your children.
>
> *Anna:* Yes.
>
> *Paula:* So to report him to the police [A: Yes.]. I mean obviously . . . there are . . . obviously it would be a lot easier to report some *completely* unknown person.
>
> *Anna:* It would be a lot easier. . . .
>
> *Paula:* Who you've never had any feelings for.
>
> *Anna:* Yes, it would be a lot easier.
>
> *Paula:* And none of these ties either, which are there because of the children. [A: Yes.] Of course it . . . these kind of things also have an impact there.
>
> *Anna:* Yes they do.
>
> *Paula:* But I think it's extremely important that you do report him. Because for years the pattern has been that he's asked you to

forgive him [A: Umm.], in other words he *asked* and you went and *forgave* him. [A: Umm.] And these things were kind of repeated and repeated and repeated [A: Yes, umm.] over and over again. I mean if you [reported him] you would communicate to him that it's *over* now [A: Umm.]. That you won't be treated this way. [A: Yes.] That you *won't* downplay it any more.

Anna: Yes, like I told him then . . . nobody will . . . *nobody* will kick or hit me any more.

After Anna defined herself as naïve, some space opened up in the discussion for an understanding and recognition of the emotionally involved and relational identity that Anna was trying to build earlier. Paula noted the ties of parenthood between Anna and Joel and their former relationship. She agreed that these former and present relations make it more difficult to report Joel to the police. But she still wanted to underline that there is a need to reject these emotions and take action to make this a legal issue. Paula reminded Anna about the history of their relationship and about the connection between violence and forgiving. Emotional and relational involvement becomes defined in negative terms and as dependency. Anna's answer shows that she was determined to stop this negative and dependent pattern. In the end, Paula and Anna found some common ground after many partially conflicting interpretations and identity constructions. The discussion has provided Anna with arguments that place the responsibility on the violent man, and this has given her justification for defending herself against additional violence. At the same time, however, this rationalizing talk rejected Anna's attempts to discuss emotional involvement and the meaning of the relationship with her ex-husband.

In the interchange between Anna and Paula, we again see, as we did with Julia and Helena, a dichotomous division between the rational, autonomous, and independent ideal and the gendered, emotional, and relational parts that are excluded from this category. In this encounter, too, the discrepancy between the category and the parts excluded by it is resolved by the use of the independence narrative. The relational and emotional parts of life need to be projected to the past as traits of the subordinated and dependent Woman. To be able to take the position of an autonomous and rational individual, Anna must define emotional and relational aspects as negative and exclude them from the present. They become defined as irrational and "incorrect" ways of feeling and thinking. At times, the subordinated and dependent woman returns from the past to haunt the new individual, but is then rationalized back to its place. Although Anna was trying to introduce a discussion of herself as a woman in the present and negotiate the meanings that could be attached to this, Paula was holding on to the independence narrative and the abstract individual as its ideal outcome.

When Anna brought elements of the subordinated woman to the present, it shows that she had not yet reached the ideal of the abstract individual. She had not become independent enough but needed guidance and careful teaching to reach that phase. Anna was thus left with an evolving identity construction, as someone who needed the advice and knowledge of others.

> Paula: I mean ... no matter how *terrible* it is, falling victim to an assault like this [A: Umm.], so ... it mostly results in fines. [A: Yes.] I mean that aggravated assault is a bit different. That you can get a suspended sentence for that. [A: Yes.] What kind of sentence it will be depends on what actually happened.
>
> Anna: But I don't think about that. I mean ... what's happened has happened ... I have taken it up the way you are supposed to and it's the experts who will decide about that then. [P: Umm.] I mean they will give their reasons then.

When discussing the possible legal effects of the violent attack, Anna said that she would leave the decisions to the professionals. She did not have expectations or make claims on the consequences for the assault. She described herself as someone who has done what she should in a proper way and leaves the rest to the experts. They have their rules to follow and their reasons for making decisions. She is acting in a competent way within structures determined by others. Anna found the means to an agency and the arguments to legitimate her actions. The rationalizing arguments and identity construction strongly supported by Paula have given Anna guidelines for agency and protection. Yet, she has also had to exclude large parts of her life and relegate them to the past as the dependent and subordinated woman. She needs a teacher who can guide her on the path to becoming an autonomous individual and an independent subject. Anna's situation resembles that of young students at school. They have been characterized as "adults-to-be who are in need to be raised and educated to be proper 'citizens' able to exercise their rights, duties and responsibilities in acceptable ways" (Gordon et al., 2000). Anna is constructed as still in a process of becoming independent and thus is still in need of guidance.

CONCLUSION

Dealing with the consequences of intimate violence and finding ways to survive its effects are the focus of therapy for the abused women in this study. Although the combination of power, emotions, and relations is essentially linked to intimate violence, in these encounters it seems to be difficult for the therapists to engage in a discussion about this. When therapists seek to support women's survival and agency they rely on culturally strong rhetoric and narratives based on abstract individualism. Abused women are encouraged to tell about their lives in ways that suit the patterns of the independence narrative. In this narrative, gendered, emotional, and relational aspects are defined in negative terms as subordination and dependency. The present identity as independent and strong is created in a dichotomous way.

In a society that, despite its attempt at gender-neutral public policy, continues to be characterized by gendered norms, women are constantly confronted with expectations of caring and taking responsibility for others. In the context of relationships, women are assumed to be flexible, forgiving, empathetic, and so forth. Women who have experienced violence are confronted with the question of how to combine conflicting expectations and norms in their lives and narratives. On one hand, they are expected to be agentic and independent, and on the other, emotional and relational.

The therapeutic encounters analyzed in this chapter suggest the independence narrative as an idealized way for the clients to conceptualize their stories. In both encounters, the women clients tried to introduce their versions of what had happened and how their identities could be constructed. They brought into the discussion the aspects excluded by the rhetorics and narratives based on abstract individualism. The abused women were not willing to totally exclude the relational aspects of their identity nor relegate them to the past as negative. At times, the therapists also recognized the importance of relationships and emotional bonds for their clients and included these aspects in the discussion. Although autonomous and independent agency was most often presented as the ideal in the encounters, the logic of abstract individualism was not overly convincing. The therapists and their clients engaged in negotiations of how to combine this rhetoric with women's gendered lives and experiences. In the end, the narrative identity that emerged from the therapist–client dialogue included gendered and relational aspects as well as an agentic autonomy.

This resolution was achieved in two ways: First, by building an identity on motherhood and second, by relying on appropriate authority. An identity built on motherhood expressed the agency required by institutional expectations while still allowing for gendered, relational elements. Being an advocate for children and other people in need of care has been a common way for women to enter the public sphere and public discourse. The normative expectations associated with motherhood can thus be called forth as an alternative to the expectations associated with abstract individualism. Motherhood can include both elements of agency, decisiveness, and assertiveness, as well as caring and emotionality.

Another way of finding an expression of appropriate agency was to rely on the guidance and advice of the authorities. In this example, a comparison with the abstract individual and the independence narrative showed that the abused woman had not reached these ideals. But if she were willing to follow the guidelines provided by the authorities, she might gradually come closer to this kind of identity construction. Her dependence on authority resulted in a relative individuality (cf. Yuval-Davis & Werbner, 1999), placing her in a situation resembling that of the adolescent.

The constraints of the independence narrative highlighted in this article raise a question: What other ways could there be of organizing experiences involving gender, violence, and survival? Opening up space to other kinds of narratives and rhetoric could make it possible to include emotional involvement and relational aspects as part of abused women's stories and positively defined identities. In their effort to support their clients from slipping back into victimizing patterns of control and violence, the therapists in this study discounted the importance of emotional ties and relationships. The therapists were caught in a discursive conflict, trying to combine support for abused women with the inherent contradictions of rhetoric based on abstract individualism and expressed in the independence narrative. This chapter analyzed these contradictions and their manifestations in institutional encounters to suggest that there may be alternative ways of narrating experiences of violence and abused women's agency. This does not have to result in losing the orientation to resist violence and control. Therapy sessions contain many other possibilities for constructing narrative identities—possibilities that can be used if the rigid rhetoric of abstract individualism is questioned.

REFERENCES

Anttonen, A. (1997). *Feminismi ja sosiaalipolitiikka* [Feminism and social policy]. Tampere, Finland: Tampere University Press.

de Lauretis, T. (1984). *Alice doesn't. Feminism, semiotics, cinema.* London: Macmillan.

Elshtain, J. B. (1992). The power and powerlessness of women. In G. Bock & S. James (Eds.), *Beyond equality and difference. Citizenship, feminist politics and female subjectivity* (pp. 110–145). London: Routledge.

Gordon, T., Holland, J., & Lahelma, E. (2000). *Making spaces. Citizenship and difference in schools.* London: Macmillan.

Jackson, S. (1999). *Heterosexuality in question.* London: Sage.

Kirkwood, C. (1993). *Leaving abusive partners.* London: Sage.

Komulainen, K. (1999). A course of one's own: The rhetorical self in educational life stories by women. *NORA, 7*(2–3), 124–137.

Nousiainen, K., & Niemi-Kiesiläinen, J. (2001). Introductory remarks on Nordic law and gender identities. In K. Nousiainen, Å. Gunnarsson, K. Lundström,

& J. Niemi-Kiesiläinen (Eds.), *Responsible selves. Women in Nordic legal culture* (pp. 1–22). Aldershot, UK: Ashgate.

Ochberg, R. L. (1994). Life stories and storied lives. In R. Josselson & A. Lieblich (Eds.), *Exploring identity and gender. Narrative study of lives* (Vol. 2, pp. 113–144). Thousand Oaks, CA: Sage.

Perttu, S. (1999). *Domestic violence in social welfare and health care. A survey of professional workers and the areas for development in their work 1998.* Helsinki: Federation of Mother and Child Homes and Shelters.

Prokhovnik, R. (1998). Public and private citizenship. From gender invisibility to feminist inclusiveness. *Feminist Review, 60,* 84–104.

Ronkainen, S. (2001). Gendered violence and genderless gender. *Kvinder, Kön & Forskning, 10*(2), 45–57.

Ruuskanen, M. (2001). The "good battered woman": A silenced defendant. In K. Nousiainen, Å. Gunnarsson, K. Lundström, & J. Niemi-Kiesiläinen (Eds.), *Responsible selves. Women in Nordic legal culture* (pp. 311–329). Aldershot, UK: Ashgate.

Scott, J. (1995). Universalism and the history of feminism. *Differences, 7*(1), 1–14.

Whitebrook, M. (2001). *Identity, narrative and politics.* London: Routledge.

Yuval-Davis, N., & Werbner, P. (1999). Introduction: Women and the new discourse on citizenship. In N. Yuval-Davis & P. Werbner (Eds.), *Women, citizenship and difference* (pp. 1–31). London: Zed Books.

5

ECHOES OF SILENCE: REMEMBERING AND REPEATING CHILDHOOD TRAUMA

LYNN SORSOLI

Since Sigmund Freud developed psychoanalysis in the late 19th century, the world has been largely convinced that talking can cure psychic ailments. The trauma, sexual abuse, and psychoanalytical literatures still tend to stress the importance of reviving memories of traumatic events and expressing those memories verbally with appropriate affect (Davies, 1997), just as empirical studies continue to link the development of narratives with recovery (e.g., Amir, Stafford, Freshman, & Foa, 1998; Pennebaker & Seagal, 1999). In fact, the research literature on disclosure repeatedly connects it to positive changes in physical health, as well as to beneficial cognitive and emotional effects. As Pennebaker (1995) noted, the increasingly clear relationship between disclosure and health exists on multiple levels of analysis and across the cognitive, emotional, and social dimensions of experience. The picture painted by these literatures is that the development and delivery of a personal narrative is unidirectionally linked to psychological health.

However, perhaps the relationship between disclosure and health is less straightforward than it would seem, particularly at the level of the individual, where understanding this phenomenon may require a consideration of life history. My in-depth narrative study of the experiences of a small group of women survivors of childhood sexual abuse revealed a great deal of conflict around disclosure, highlighting the ways words can simultaneously reveal and conceal their experiences and the tensions existing between a desire to tell their stories and a desire to hide or forget them. For these women, words have often evoked overwhelming emotions, including feelings of fear, anger, and sadness, as well as distressing bodily sensations, and seem to offer little by way of relief or security, whether they are revealing their abuse histories or simply what they feel and need in a relationship. In my mind, the depth of their struggles with "telling" raises questions about the nature of disclosure and complicates the assumption that constructing a complete narrative will heal or even that the verbal translation of lived traumatic experiences will automatically move survivors down the path toward psychological health (Grand, 1997; Wigren, 1994). In this chapter, I suggest that certain aspects of disclosure may be closely related to childhood desires for rescue in the face of traumatic experiences and that problematic patterns of speaking and not speaking in relationships may be repetitions of those early traumatic experiences in ways that could be compromising its healing capacities. Although clinicians have often discussed the ways relationships can be complicated for trauma survivors (Chu, 1998; Davies & Frawley, 1994; Miller & Stiver, 1997), for these women it may not only be relationships in general but the process of disclosure specifically that has become untrustworthy and fraught, leading to additional challenges for therapists who work with this population.

METHOD

Victims of Violence (VOV) is an adult outpatient clinic at Cambridge Hospital in Massachusetts that provides a range of clinical services to victims of violence in the community. In an effort to understand the differing paths to recovery, the program conducts in-depth interviews with trauma survivors taking part in their clinical treatment program. The small study described in this chapter was associated with the larger VOV study but recruited a community sample through flyers describing a study about the ways survivors of sexual abuse used personal and community resources to deal with their experiences. When participants were screened, they were asked about past experiences with therapy and research studies and informed that the first interview would involve talking about their life histories, including their experiences of trauma, whereas the second interview would focus on the ways they were or were not able to disclose those difficult stories in relationships throughout their lives.

The four women interviewed for this study were between 22 and 35 years old, currently involved in supportive nonclinical relationships, and living apart from their families of origin. Although they differed greatly in terms of their backgrounds and abuse histories, all of these women had been sexually abused before they were teenagers and none of them had extensive experiences with psychotherapy: Although one had seen a therapist for about four years, another had seen a therapist for only six months, the third had attended workshops, and the fourth had never seen a therapist at all. For three of the women, the abuse had lasted over a period of several years between the ages of 4 and 13 (their memories about their exact ages were not clear), whereas the other had experienced two separate incidents: one with her father at the age of 11 or 12 and an earlier incident with a stranger.

Joining a growing body of research combining an interest in narrative methods with an interest in the effects of trauma (Harvey, Mishler, Koenen, & Harney, 1998; Rogers, 1999), my own interest was not only in the kinds of stories these survivors could tell but in how they would share these stories and understand their experiences. Because traumatic events are difficult, if not impossible, to relate even under ideal circumstances (Caruth, 1995; Laub, 1995), and because I was interviewing a population for whom silence and secrecy about the past may have become habitual, it seemed critical to acknowledge that there would be limits to what could be said in an interview and to use a method of analysis that both assumed and explicitly examined this phenomenon. Adopting a layered method of reading personal narratives (see Rogers, Casey, Ekert, & Holland, 1999),[1] I conducted a detailed exploration of these stories that are marginalized in society and possibly even within these storytellers.

In this chapter, I am only able to present a sliver of this complex and intensive analysis, relaying findings arising mainly from a content analysis designed to explore the experience of disclosure in addition to the experience and impact of trauma as revealed by these women's narratives. This layer of analysis revealed recurrent themes across interviews but also recurrent experiences within interviews in ways that systematically connected the past with the present. In particular, by differentiating trauma stories into separate narrative threads, I was able to closely examine the behavioral impact of trauma, its emotional impact, and these women's reflective understandings of their experiences and to observe the nuances among these differing threads of experience. Although it was clear that these women

---

[1] This method (called interpretive poetics) is modeled on a voice-centered method of analysis (Brown et al., 1988; Brown & Gilligan, 1992) and formed from multiple interpretive readings involving four complementary dimensions: (a) re-storying narratives; (b) tracing shifts in relational dynamics within the interviews; (c) identifying and interpreting languages of the unsayable (Rogers et al., 1999); and (d) listening for figurative thought in language contrasts.

engaged in behavioral repetitions of early experiences, their words, silences, and emotions in attempts to reveal their stories to others can also be seen as essential elements of the traumatic experiences that persistently repeat in their lives. Considering the nature and power of these repetitions and their potential effects on experiences in relationships offers a way to understand why, for these women, disclosure was not always experienced as healing or even comforting.

REMEMBERING AND REENACTING

Elizabeth Loftus, a leader in the research against the reality of repression, is also a survivor of childhood sexual abuse at the hands of a babysitter. She wrote, "I kept the secret to myself. But I have never forgotten this memory, nor did I repress it. And even though it affected me deeply, I choose to leave it in my past. I think that's where it belongs" (Loftus & Ketcham, 1994, p. 226). I believe that many survivors would make the same choice, if they could. The problem is that for so many, the past does not stay relegated to the past. It tends to return, again and again, permeating the present and often their visions of the future as well—whether or not they consciously remember these experiences.

The repetition of trauma is conspicuous in life history narratives: The links between adult behaviors and painful childhood experiences are often so clear that very little interpretation is required. In behavioral reenactments, the survivor typically plays the role either of the victim or the victimizer, although the stories being told may involve a range of behaviors, including harm to others (such as physical or sexual violence and criminality), harm to self (such as self-mutilation, drug dependency, and eating disorders), or revictimization (such as repeated rape or domestic violence; van der Kolk, 1989). For example, Lauren,[2] 33, is White, and had been raised in Western Europe. She had never seen a therapist at the time of these interviews and had spoken to only two people, neither one a family member, about her history of abuse. Although she is not certain how old she was when it began, one of her brothers had repeatedly sexually abused her when she was a child. Recalling one of her early sexual experiences with her older brother, she narrated her helplessness in that situation. After long pauses that seem to perfectly illustrate her self-acknowledged tendency to lose words, she drifted off while saying "I was, you know, the little sister and . . . and . . ." In an effort to bring her back into the interview, I offered, "You just sort of complied." "Yeah," she said, and looking away, asked a question into

---

[2] All names, places, dates, and certain other identifying details have been altered throughout this chapter to protect the confidentiality of the study participants.

space, phrased poignantly in the present as if she had been taken back in time, "What can I do?"

Later in this first interview, when we spoke about her life as an adult, Lauren reported a long history of undesired sexual encounters, including "horrible experiences" with intimacy and many "one-night stands" and "short stories," in which she was not interested in having sex but "just went along." She spoke about these encounters in ways that reflected her early sexual experiences with her brother. Reviving a familiar air of helpless compliance, she explained:

> In all of these encounters, most, I would more often than not, uh, I didn't really want anything. But *I just, you know . . . complied to . . . obliged—I wouldn't say obliged, but I just went along.* "Well, if he wants that, let's just, you know, do it." And, and um, I think also . . . I had this idea that everyone was doing that so that, you know, there was just nothing wrong with that and I just had to get used to it. So, you know, if anyone was to be pushy on me, *I just would never . . . refuse or . . . push them down or . . . or, you know, state my limit.*

The reenactment pattern Lauren described is clear: In sexual relationships with adult men, she literally repeated her early experiences with her brother, continually fulfilling sexual desires that were not her own. Other behavioral reenactments are not quite as clear. Elena, for example, is 32 and originally from South America. She had not remembered her early experiences until after her son was born, six years before the interviews, but she had since told a therapist, an ex-boyfriend, and her mother. At her babysitters' house as a child, Elena was sexually abused and often witnessed other physically violent behaviors, although she denied being hit herself. In stories of these childhood experiences, she revealed fears about telling her mother what was happening to her, putting herself in the position of protecting her mother's job and telling herself that if she did not say anything, then "*everything is going to be fine.*"

For Elena, a behavioral reenactment took the form of physical abuse at the hands of a boyfriend. When she was revictimized in this way, Elena also repeated her earlier method of coping, again putting herself in the position of "protecting" another person, "making excuses" for him, she said, while silencing her own sense of reality. Although never acknowledging a link between her experiences, she once more described silent attempts to understand her situation, repeatedly telling herself that "he needs to," "he's having a bad time," and "he's tired." Like Lauren's inability to "state her limit," Elena's silence in this situation is telling. In addition to the more obvious behavioral reenactments taking place, silence can be observed as an aspect of their experiences that echoes intriguingly across their narratives, marking a possible return to childhood coping mechanisms and setting the stage for the "return of the repressed" (Ainsworth, 1967; Freud, 1961/1975; Frieze, 1983; van der Kolk, 1996a).

The uncanny accumulation of traumatic experiences across a lifespan can be understood as repetitive reenactments of "real events from the past" (van der Kolk & McFarlane, 1996, p. 11), although the tendency for trauma to return may seem paradoxical to both researchers and survivors alike. In fact, the feeling that they could not control what did and did not happen in their relationships and at the same time did not understand why certain things would repeatedly happen the way they did was incredibly frustrating for the women I interviewed. Hearing their stories gave me the sense that they were routinely ambushed by their pasts in ways that tended to leave them completely baffled. Shauna, for example, holds a master's degree and, at 32, was in the beginning stage of opening her own business. After telling me numerous stories about the depths of her struggles in relationships, she sighed, shifted her body toward me, and said, "It's like, okay, here I have *another* friend who doesn't have time for her friends! *How come I keep making friends with people who are unavailable?*" Although she knew that her father molested her on one occasion when she was 11 or 12 years old, she also had vague memories of an earlier incident with a man who had been invited into her house by her mother. Shauna had disclosed these experiences to many people, including her mother and sister, beginning in late adolescence; and had confronted her father, who begged for her forgiveness but insisted he did not remember his actions and must have done it "in his sleep."

At times, like Shauna, each of these women related a struggle to understand why certain patterns repeated in their lives, and yet each remained confused, apparently never clearly connecting past experiences with struggles in the present. Amy, at 22, was the youngest of the women interviewed. She had been raised in the Midwest and, after attending and graduating from college, was completing a fellowship. "The man," as she called the husband of her babysitter, sexually abused her over the course of 3 years, from the age of 4 or 5. She told her mother about the experience when she was 12, but had told few people since then. Amy's abuse had occurred on the frequent occasions when her mother was late to pick her up from her babysitter's house. Her father had died when she was an adolescent, and her first memory is one of being alone and lost. However, although I hear a clear thematic connection between her stories of isolation and abandonment, she tended not to make this connection and did not understand her "really terrible fear of people going away" or her tendency "to push them away . . . before they [got] a chance to go."

Freud associated the tendency to repeat with unresolved neurotic conflicts that arise in the absence of conscious memory. Thus, the compulsion to repeat is a way of putting childhood attitudes and expectations into present-day relationships, a different "way of remembering" (Freud,

1914/1963).[3] These pieces of a dis-membered past float into present relationships and come back together, re-membered in myriad new ways. Because of the inevitable transference of emotions and desires from one relationship into another, this way of remembering can be understood as a relational process, through which trauma continues to reside in relationships even when conscious links to the past are lost. However, although certain reenactments may be more readily recognizable than others, such as behavioral reenactments with clear and obvious ties to the original traumatic events, many different layers of repeating themes can be heard in narratives of trauma survivors. Among the most powerful in this set of narratives were repetitions of the silence surrounding their childhood experiences, punctuated by the deep emotions of that time, recognizable now in the tendency to long for friends who are never "unavailable," "horrible" experiences with intimacy, and "terrible" fears of abandonment.

REPEATING EMOTIONS, SILENCES, AND
THE SEARCH FOR CONNECTION

Comparing narratives of their earliest experiences and relationships with those of later experiences through my analyses, the presence of these echoes of early experience clarifies the ways the present can be haunted by the past. As these women told stories about their childhoods, their voices often sounded wistful or sad and they tended to drift off into long silences. They made repeated references to not having adult attention, and in fact to not having any close relationships with either adults or children in the early portions of their lives. In addition, they tended to describe their pasts using figurative terms and phrases that served as audible indicators of a history filled with feelings of alienation and isolation. For example, they described being or feeling "lost," "left behind," "left out," "never at ease," and "far away" from other children as well as adults. Meanwhile, they remembered words they said to themselves but never said aloud and spoke of ways "silence translate[d] into not caring." In narratives of adult life, they revealed significant difficulties in sustaining relationships coupled with an intense desire for particularly deep emotional connections.

The experiencing of intense but failed relationships is common in survivors of childhood sexual abuse (van der Kolk, 1996a). My analyses suggest that these relational difficulties, and in particular their difficulties around disclosure, may be strongly related to words they needed to say or hear at the time of their painful experiences. Thus, rather than characterizing

---

[3]Such repetitions are seen as an unconscious method of gaining active mastery over passively endured experience (Freud, 1961/1975).

them as pathological disturbances, these difficulties could also be seen as yet another traumatic pattern persistently repeating in their lives.[4] In a way that seemed powerfully connected to their pasts, this second repeating pattern involved distinct fears of betrayal and abandonment coupled with rigid ideas about what could not be said or asked for in relationships, what seemed to be difficult or impossible for them to hear or remember, and the desire for others to know what they felt and needed in spite of their inability to directly relay that information.

What Cannot Be Said: "I Really Need You Right Now"

All of the women I interviewed, at one point or another, alluded to the fact that they had great difficulty both with disclosing their emotions and asking for what they needed in relationships. Lauren, for example, told me "I can *talk* about all kinds of things. I mean, *except my emotions*." Elena said she finds it difficult "to ask what I really really need . . . so, to say, 'Look what I really need is this, this and this.'" She added that it can also be hard for her to share her feelings, particularly sadness, explaining, "*Because I wonder in my head if people are gonna take advantage . . . of what makes me sad.* And every time they need something . . . from me, they, you know, what I mean? They gonna . . . press that button. Yeah. *So I don't I don't really want to . . . be vulnerable.*"

Considering Elena's feelings of vulnerability in light of her experiences as a child reveals a possible connection. She mentioned that as a child she did not have close relationships with anyone, including her family, and did not have anyone in her life she felt she could trust, particularly with her story of abuse. Although an aunt tried to get closer to her when she was an adolescent, she still decided not share her story. When she told me what she remembered about this experience, I heard her perception of the risks involved in telling her story and the ways those risks are intertwined with her relationships:

> Well, at first I remember that I didn't really trust her. You know, I thought that everything that I that I I would tell her, she would tell my mother. . . . *But I didn't want anybody to know . . . how I I was.* I I

---

[4] The emotional pattern seemed to operate separately and somewhat independently from the behavioral pattern. For example, although behavioral reenactments seemed to occur in relationships with men, the pattern related to disclosure seemed to occur more often with women—although obviously I am not able to generalize beyond this very small sample. In addition, because repetitions did not occur in all of these women's relationships, I came to see repetition as a phenomenon catalyzed within particular relationships, as opposed to a pathological symptom carried into relationships by a particular person.

always had that that that fantasy, in my head. So I say, if I started, like, sort of, you know, *if I start telling her . . . something—or she start to knowing me—then she's going to go and tell my mother and then everybody's going to know . . . how I am.* You know, some something like that.

I asked her what she thought would happen if they started to know her and she said, "I don't know. *I I always thought that my mother would get mad with me for some reason.*" In these words, I again notice the terrible danger these women feel with regard to speaking about their experiences and the sense that safety, for one reason or another, can be found in silence. Rather than understanding speaking as a means to make connections or deeper relationships, they seem to see words only as a way to destroy them. If she spoke or let herself be known, Elena suggests, she would risk someone getting "mad" or "taking advantage" of her. Being known, then, is dangerous, and silence continues to offer an alluring sense of safety, just as it did during her childhood.

Also dangerous, it seems, is asking for what one needs. When I asked Amy how she went about getting emotional support when she needed it, she mimicked her way of asking for support, a process that revealed a number of betrayals. She ended the series of examples by saying, *"Really, I really need you right now. But I can't ask you for that."* After pausing, she added, "I would never say that. 'I really need you right now.'" She told me she did not "want to be a burden . . . ever." It is as if stating what she wants and needs means risking the relationship, a risk she cannot bear to take. Thus, even when a friend says explicitly that Amy can call if she needs her and promises to be there in that event, Amy is not able to call and say those words and she is left with an unbearable feeling that "everyone" has let her down, a feeling that leads far back into her past.

As with Elena, I see Amy's inability to say the words "I really need you" as a repetition of earlier experiences. As a child, Amy would fight with her mother, yelling out angry clues about her abuse and screaming, "You don't know what it means to be attacked!" When she finally told her mother about her experiences, she pretended not to need anything. She said, "And I said 'This is what happened . . . um . . . I was . . . abused by . . . him. *It's not a big deal. I just want you to know. That's the end. I don't want you to tell Dad.'* So that's what my mom did. *She didn't tell my father. She didn't do anything.*" Even though at the time she actually did not want her mother to do or say anything, she as an adult has realized that she "wasn't in a place to be able to make that decision." Unfortunately though, Amy still feels too vulnerable to make her needs clear, and the silence of others still "translates into not caring." "*When people are silent to me,*" she said, "*I feel like they don't care.*"

What Cannot Be Heard: "It's Not That You're Not Important"

Not only did these women have difficulty expressing their emotions and needs in relationships, they also were plagued by a story about abandonment they seemed to hear everywhere they went. The tendency to feel "let down" interacted with an occasional inability to let in words of support and care when they were offered, leading to a great amount of pain in their lives. Shauna, for example, told me a great deal about her struggles with women friends. In our first interview, she explained her practice of trying to get clarity between what has really happened and her interpretation of those events. When revisiting this practice later, I asked if she ever felt as if she struggled between those two things. She laughed and said,

> Oh all the time! 'Cause we are just meaning making machines. We just add interpretation to everything. For example, my friend Abigail, she was going to school and teaching *and* trying to get other things happening in her life and, you know, she had no time. And I interpreted that as, "she's abandoned me for the semester," you know. You know, and that's not what happened, what happened is we . . . got together at the beginning of the semester and at the end. So . . . I might not be satisfied with that, but *it's not like she abandoned me*.

Although Shauna concluded that "it's not like she abandoned me," this particular interpretation is fragile and tends to slip back into a very real feeling of abandonment, as if she does not hear herself making this shift and as if she cannot take in what friends are trying to tell her. I heard this slippage a few moments later in the interview as I asked if, when people say they do not have time in their schedules to see her, she interpreted that as them *not wanting* to see her. She said,

> Like it's not important enough for them to . . . make the time. I mean, we *decide* what we're going to spend our time on. You know, and if you decide, you know, if her priority is more . . . her husband and her son, then *that's* her priority. *And* if she told me, "You're one of my priorities in life" and then the other ones, you know, take over . . . then *I'm no longer, I'm not a* . . . like I was *on* the list of, you know, things to actually handle or do or something, to be with, and then *I got . . . taken off the list*.

I noted the subtle shift in interpretation: This new story was about the experience of being abandoned, or as she put it, getting "*taken off the list*." Sensing her distress, I asked if she could share her thoughts with her friend to get some support. She paused for a long while, then asked me what they could do that would be supportive. Caught a little off guard, I stuttered, " 'It's not that I don't *want* to see you? It's not that you're not important? It's just that I have a lot of things going on?' " She responded,

"Yeah, see that wouldn't, that wouldn't do it . . . for me. That wouldn't be supportive. I would go, 'Well, that's what you've been telling me is . . . you know, the other things going on in your life are more important . . . you know . . . than I am. That's what you've been saying!" Struggling both to reassure and understand her at the same time, I said, "But that's *not* what I just said though. What I just said was that it's *not* that you're not important." She responded,

> Like it's subtle, *it's like what's behind, what's behind them saying* "It's not that you're not important, I just have other things in my life." It's that "The other things in my life are *more important* than you. That's why I'm doing it. I'm choosing to do them instead of being with you!" And for what other reason could it be?

In this painful story, Shauna showed me how she listens behind the words that are said, hearing words that were not said instead. Because the words that were unsaid cover over the words that were actually said, she does not hear that her friend is still present. Not only is she not able to tell her friend how she feels, being "taken off the list" feels like desertion, permanent abandonment. Looking back into her life, I found that she never told her mother about being molested by her father when she was a child. She first revealed this fact as an adult, during a telephone call. About that experience, she said, "I think she seemed like she didn't even believe me or something. It was very strange . . . how things happened. And then um . . . it was either that she didn't believe me or she said something like it was a very stressful time in his life or something."

Three hours later, however, her mother called her back crying. Shauna said, "She told me that she remembered us talking about it, and that she had had a conversation with my dad and had made sure that it wouldn't happen again. But this makes no sense at all." Confused as well, I asked, "But how—if you didn't say anything to him and you didn't say anything to her, then how could they have talked together?" Her story got quite confusing as she considered how her mother might have known in spite of the fact that she never told, but in conclusion she said, "So it—I'm not really clear, what happened, who talked, who said what to whom. They didn't—my mom certainly did *not* come back to me and say, *'Oh Shauna, I talked to your dad yesterday and I made sure* that you would be safe,' you know, *'Don't worry about it.' There was none of that.*" What is striking in this story is that the words she emphasizes never hearing from her mother as a child, "Don't worry. I made sure that you would be safe," are now the very words she seeks in present relationships, the words she hopes to discover lying "behind" whatever else is being said, as if the emotions of her past have drifted into her present.

The Good Relationship: "You Don't Have to Tell the Whole Story"

In spite of their struggles with communication and complicated fears about being seen or heard too clearly (or not well enough), these women consistently expressed a desire to be known, to feel connected, and as though they "mattered." However, for women who as children found safety in disconnection and silence, developing and maintaining relationships that rely on words for making contact is a difficult business. In addition to my analytical process, during the interviews I sought the meanings these women had made from their experiences by asking direct questions about the qualities of good or authentic relationships. In response, although they often mentioned both listening and speaking one's mind, what they emphasized were relationships in which words were *not* required. Elena, for example, indicated that it is actually *not* needing to speak that defines a good relationship:

> I know that he has his mess and I have my mess, but we'll get together and we, you know. But the the the simple fact that you are with a person and *you don't have to tell the that other person the whole story* . . . *for the other person to realize what's going on with you*, that's a that's a really important thing, because sometimes, you know . . . you don't, you don't feel like . . . you know, telling them the *whole* story. But uh, *to be good friends, you know, it's like, realizing that the other one is cold before he say something*, you know, because *it's that connection*.

The role of speaking itself was often de-emphasized, as in this excerpt, and instead, specific kinds of "connection" and consciousness were described as fundamental elements of authentic relationships. Amy, for example, talked to me about her disappointment that when people ask how she is, they do not seem to be aware that the abuse is still present in her life. She told me that her experience of being abused is not something that ever goes away for her. Her friends, however, tend to forget that if she looks sad and says that she is not doing well, it might not be because she has failed a test. She wished that people could be conscious of her abuse in the same way she was and said, "I think it's impossible to ask that of people, but at the same time . . . when I think about a relationship and relating, *that's* what it means." Later, she added,

> There's um there's this passage in the Talmud that talks about um . . . how when when your brother reaches out his his hand, brother in the kind of generic word of it, that you should always pull him up. You should always help him. And my sense is that . . . that when people are in a really dark place . . . maybe they don't have the strength to reach out their hand, *maybe they need people to reach to them and just*

know . . . sometimes I I think that I would want people just to know and they don't and I I know that's an unrealistic expectation, but . . .

Although on both occasions Amy chastised herself for wanting to ask the "impossible" and having "unrealistic" expectations, she is very aware of the reality of these desires in her relationships. Listening to the wavering of her voice during this portion of the interview, I too understood that her longing for someone who will reach out and "just *know*" was very deep. Because each of these women voiced confusion about whether a parent or sibling had known about her experience of sexual abuse and had never said or done anything, I have come to believe that the intensity of this present need to be known without or beyond the presence of words links back to a long and painful history. Rogers (1999), in her study of sexually abused girls, mentioned a similar distrust for words, a similar capacity to read the unspoken, and a similar search for connections going beyond words.

Shauna shared the desire for someone who "knows," but said she believed that words could not create the kind of knowing she needed. Our shared understanding about this develops unexpectedly from a point in the first interview when she told me that the memory of her abuse experience was "totally silent." She said, "There's no sound in that memory . . . all I have is this image." Intrigued by the silence in her memory and the way it might relate to the unsayable, I revisited this idea toward the end of the interview. Unfortunately, my attempt to explore this link caused a rupture in our relationship when, in my urgent exploration of my own interests, I did not hear what she was trying to say. Feeling like I was missing something and wondering how the silence in her memory might be linked to the silences in her life, I asked, "Why can't I put those two pieces together? Why does that seem so important to me?" She answered,

> It seemed very important to me when I remembered that it was . . . that it was silent . . . but I really don't think that there's anything that I'm aware of that I didn't s—haven't told at least *one* person . . . you know, sometime in my life. It's like the memory itself is silent, but there's, you know, *I have words for all of the emotions that I felt that I remember feeling*, and the things that happened, and even the thoughts that I had at the time, I can remember thinking them.

As I continued to muse aloud about whether words can ever capture something that is silent in memory, her tone shifted and she began to sound irritated. She said, "Well, I can describe a painting." Not recognizing her irritation at the time, I pushed my point, saying, "That's true, but are you really capturing the painting? Don't you just have to see it?" Audibly frustrated, she said, "*Well, nobody* can really understand what it was like for me, you know, through words. So they wouldn't get the memory of what I what I actually experienced, what I actually experienced, whether I remember sounds in it or not!" Finally, I heard and understood her exasperation. What I was wondering about did not matter to her because either way she would feel alone with this memory. I told her about a television show I had seen recently, an episode of "Voyager," a show she said she watched too. The episode was about a monument in a society where a terrible injustice had occurred. Rather than simply marking the site with a display of words for people to read, the monument sent out the actual experience straight into the minds of passersby. I said that perhaps my story was irrelevant, but it seemed like that was the only thing that would allow someone else to really "get" it. She told me that I am right, that it is not irrelevant at all and added, "It's insightful." I sensed a reconnection at this point and believe I finally" got" it.[5]

Notably, these conversations about relationships revealed a belief in what seems to feel like an inevitable rift between the outside world and the experience held inside, a chasm that words cannot bridge, resulting in a desire for another to simply read one's mind. Shauna's silent memory involves moments in which she most desires to be joined, and in this segment of the interview, I sensed that I betrayed her by not listening closely enough to what she was trying to say. A desire for mind reading is not exclusive to trauma survivors; it has been observed in certain types of intimate relationships as well, such as romantic relationships (Fitzpatrick & Sollie, 1999). However, because the lives of these women would have been so profoundly affected if someone *had* read their minds when they were children and acted on what they found, it is understandable that this desire may take on a unique sense of urgency or power in their relationships.

Telling: "You Need Somebody to Walk You Back There and Walk With You"

The fact that they have constructed a good or authentic relationship as one that does not require telling "the whole story" is particularly interesting given the deep desire for others to know and hold their stories of abuse. However, telling is an inherently relational practice, and these particular stories, even more so than everyday emotions and desires, are extremely difficult to tell. This difficulty holds across many different types of traumatic experiences (Erikson, 1976; Langer, 1991; Shay, 1994) and has not only to do with the ways traumatic memories are encoded or internal psychological and physical responses but also with the responses of the audience. Unfortu-

---

[5] This interaction highlights the ways disclosure patterns were repeating even within these research relationships and deserves discussion that is beyond the scope of this particular chapter.

nately, as Langer (1991) wrote, "The more painful, dramatic, and over-whelming the narrative, the more tense, wary, and self-protective is the audience, the quicker the instinct to withdraw" (p. 20). For survivors primed to *sense* withdrawal, this ground may be particularly treacherous. Amy, for example, has clear perceptions of the words other people can and cannot "handle." As we discussed the ways words could possibly come to feel safe, she said,

> I think some of it has to do with how people react. Um. People can handle . . . um . . . people can usually handle "I'm a survivor of . . . childhood sexual abuse." They can handle . . . "Something bad happened to me." Um. "I was a victim." I don't like to use the word victim. They can't handle . . . I can't even handle . . . what I was going to say. *And I think that that's where the real healing . . . will happen for me is if I can . . . can be pushed pushed into that zone.*

I asked her whether, when she told her story to people, there was ever more she wanted to say but felt she held back. She said, "Sure, I mean, I'd love to talk to someone about it for a long time, but . . ." When she paused, I asked her what she would say. She responded, "I don't even know what I would say. Maybe they would ask me some questions. Um . . . *maybe they would walk with me in some of that . . . space that doesn't feel so safe.* Talk about what everything meant." In addition to simply saying the words, for Amy, it is about not feeling alone with them. Safety, she said, is "them . . . instead of saying, you know, 'Why do you get so upset?' Just being willing to sit there while I *am* upset."

For these women, telling involves an inherent vulnerability, both in terms of internal physical and psychological reactions and in terms of the possible reactions of listeners. When I asked her how she had come to understand safety and wounding in her life, Amy told me about a process of "trial and errors." She gave an example about a person who once asked her about "all of [her] cuts." Although she was originally hesitant to talk with him about her experiences with self-mutilation, she "finally [told him] that I do it all to myself and he *freaked* out, like so much. And um . . . and it was it was so painful, it was like my nightmare becoming a reality, telling somebody the truth and them thinking I'm so ugly that they couldn't deal with me." Shauna, on the other hand, told me that she had never had a bad experience telling her story. Even so, she echoed Amy when she said, "*I have to work really hard at expressing myself to people.* Um. Like what's really true for me. Um . . . especially people that I'm in an intimate relation-ship with. *Like I need a certain kind, I need a certain kind of response to make me feel safe.*"

The response these women seek is less about spoken words of support and, again, more about someone being with them in the space where they feel the most alone. It is about a companion who will "just know" what they need, who is willing and able to act as a guide, and who will "push" for words when they are wordless, making it safe to speak. Although I was always careful to clarify the difference between research and therapy, the interview process often seemed to illustrate the importance of someone "just sitting there" as well as paying continual attention to "reconnecting" after the many potential relational ruptures that can occur during the process of revealing traumatic experiences. In our discussions about the experience of the interviews, these women told me, in addition to what they "sensed" about me, who I was "as a person," and the fact that this was a relationship that held no risks because I was a "stranger" and what they said could not "leak out," it was the *way* I listened that actually allowed them to speak so openly and to continue to speak, even when it was very difficult for them. As Amy mentioned, "You know, people are are so good about listening that they forget to help you to get to a space that's . . . uncomfortable and . . . um . . . you know, *when you're running away from something . . . it's like, you need somebody to walk you back there and walk with you.*"

Given all of the emphasis on their needs for particular kinds of reactions from people to feel safe, and their vigilance in that arena, I was surprised to notice that where I heard the most stumbling and uncertainty was not in the stories of their childhood abuse but in the stories about telling other people about those experiences. When it came to questions about what they had actually said or how people had reacted when they told their stories, they simply could not remember—even when their initial responses suggested familiarity with those experiences. For example, Amy first suggested that she had clear memories of telling her friends she had been abused; however, when I asked her to say more about what she remembered, she said, "*I remember telling all three of my girlfriends who were there. And I don't remember them. I don't remember how they reacted or anything. But I do remember telling them.*" Although it could be that these adolescent experiences have faded over time, it was as the women told their stories about "telling" that uncertainty suddenly seemed to creep into their narratives for the first time.

Shauna's responses to my questions about disclosure were similar to Amy's. In contrast to the certainty with which she told me about her experiences with her father, during this portion of the interview, Shauna began to say things like "I think" and "I guess." She said, "*I think* [the first person I told] was Gabby, my senior year. Yeah, and *I guess* it was just that she was really . . . supportive and open and . . . like everybody, like nobody has ever even seemed uncomfortable about me bringing this stuff up." I asked if she remembered how she brought it up and if she could tell me the story of how she told her friend. She said, "*I don't know.* I I remember being at her house. And like talking about everything, talking about the whole mess with David . . . um . . . *I don't know*." Later, after struggling, but still not being able to give me a clear example of a time she has told this story in a relationship, she told me that "it just comes up." She added, thoughtfully, "It seems like this would be very useful to the kind of research *if I could remember this*, you know, the research you're doing." She knew she had told her story many times, and had the sense that people had been supportive, and yet she was not able to tell me a single detailed story of the way she told her story to these people and what exactly had happened when she did.

Listener involvement has been found to have an important effect on the development of narratives and the construction of a personal past (Bavelas, Coates, & Johnson, 2000; Pasupathi, 2001). However, because hearing these difficult stories may cause the audience to withdraw (Langer, 1991; Pennebaker, 1997), in spite of the desire for a companion who will "ask questions" and push them to reveal uncomfortable details, these storytellers might repeatedly find themselves alone in the attempt to construct a story, possibly complicating identity development and memory. Attempts to tell may also be marked by certain psychological defenses, such as denial, that may actively shape these life stories (McAdams, 1998; Sorsoli, 2000). Meanwhile, the apparent tendency of the storytellers themselves to dissociate from the telling experience, coupled with the expressed desire for a companion who would just know their stories, further illustrate the tensions, possibly arising as repetitions of earlier traumatic experiences, existing in the disclosure process for these women.

CONCLUSION

When survivors of trauma become fixated on the past, as Janet (1911) wrote, it is as if their personalities "cannot enlarge any more by the addition or assimilation of new elements" (cited in van der Kolk, 1989, p. 53), conclusions that paralleled those of Freud on the same issue (Freud, 1961/1975). Van der Kolk (van der Kolk, 1996b; van der Kolk, Burbridge, & Suzuki, 1997), however, explained that high levels of emotional arousal (which occur frequently for survivors of childhood trauma) can actually interfere with the integration of certain experiences, which means that a traumatic past may contribute to the likelihood of repetition by preventing new experiences from being registered, integrated, and remembered, particularly when those experiences are emotionally charged. Interference with the integration of new experiences is one way of understanding why, even when these women disclosed their experiences in adult relationships, the devastation that no one heard their stories or cries for help as children may continue to repeat itself. For example, although Shauna had told her story many times, she concluded that telling her story did not actually help her to heal because speaking the words did not keep her from feeling depressed. She said, "Well, okay, so telling my story . . . was fine. It was okay. Was it healing? I don't think so." In spite of her insistence that "everyone" had been supportive and that "no one" had ever seemed uncomfortable about her "bringing this stuff up," Shauna was not able to recall the details of any of these experiences of disclosure. Meanwhile, she continues to feel unseen, unheard, and abandoned in many of her relationships, indicating that, for Shauna, healing may require something more than simply telling her story.

Davies and Frawley (1994) have provided a second way of understanding why, for some, disclosure may not always be experienced as healing. They stressed the importance of the analyst as "an adult who will contain, listen, and believe in the child's inexpressible nightmare" and suggested that without such containment, "the reemergence of the traumatic material will represent only a dissociated reenactment within the transference and not the necessary type of integrative work" (p. 59). Thus, a lack of effective containment may result in a situation in which reenactment occurs during disclosure, rather than integration, which also may help to explain why these women have such difficulty remembering their disclosure experiences. Effective containment within a relationship, however, may allow the integration necessary to interrupt the repetition of behaviors and emotions that torment these women's lives. Although such a relationship does not necessarily have to be clinical, given the propensity for transference and reenactment on the part of survivors coupled with the tendency of listeners to withdraw, professional training could be of significant benefit. Unfortunately, as has often been noted (e.g., Chu, 1998; Davies & Frawley, 1994; Herman, 1992), traditional talk therapies can be incredibly challenging, particularly for clients who distrust relationships. The results of this analysis expose additional challenges arising from the fact that, for certain clients, repetitions of trauma may complicate not only the ability to develop and tolerate intimate relationships but even the process of personal disclosure, a process that might otherwise be experienced as healing.

In addition, although it is clear that within these women's lives a great deal of what could be said was purposefully kept inside, there were also elements of their experiences that could not be presented in a coherent, logical narrative and thus would require a new understanding of what it means to tell or what telling might sound like. Often, the array of traumatic symptoms in their bodies, repetitive patterns in relationships, and strange or outwardly incomprehensible behaviors and beliefs signaled the significance of their experiences more clearly than the actual words they were sharing. However, it was also clear that the ways the words these women were not able to say or need to hear, as well as the ways they defined authentic relationships, were strongly tied to the original experience of trauma.

Because words and silences permeate relationships and have the power to create as well as disrupt connections, focusing on the therapeutic relationship more broadly may cause us to overlook particular struggles around telling that exist both because of fears that words can compromise or even destroy relationships and because of a deeply held belief that if people cared, they could and would "just know." The struggle of telling, which seems to range beyond the disclosure of traumatic experiences to include everyday emotions and relational needs, occurs at the intersection of these conflicting fears and desires and is complicated both by the effects of traumatic experience on mind and body and by the incessant repetition of those experiences in relationships. Based on these women's narratives, it seems that healing disclosures may require continual attention to safety and the presence of a caring witness who, although constantly holding what can be known of their experiences, will "push" them for words, tolerate whatever words can be spoken, recognize and honor the struggle, and invariably offer the opportunity to reconnect—an approach that is also supported theoretically (e.g., Herman, 1992). In addition, for these women, because the struggle for relationships has, in some senses, moved beyond words, it would seem that a good therapeutic practice must also involve a way of listening to what remains unsaid, even in the midst of whatever else is being said and worked through, and a way of inviting the unsaid back out into an authentic relationship.

REFERENCES

Ainsworth, M. D. S. (1967). *Infancy in Uganda: Infant care and the growth of attachment.* Baltimore: Johns Hopkins University Press.

Amir, N., Stafford, J., Freshman, M. S., & Foa, E. B. (1998). Relationship between trauma narratives and trauma pathology. *Journal of Traumatic Stress, 11*(2), 385–392.

Bavelas, J. B., Coates, L., & Johnson, T. (2000). Listeners as co-narrators. *Journal of Personality and Social Psychology, 79*(6), 941–952.

Brown, L., Argyris, D., Attanucci, J., Bardige, B., Gilligan, C., Johnston, K., et al. (1988). *A guide to reading narratives of conflict and choice for self and moral voice.* Cambridge, MA: Harvard Graduate School of Education, Center for the Study of Gender, Education, and Human Development.

Brown, L. M., & Gilligan, C. (1992). *Meeting at the crossroads: Women's psychology and girls' development.* Cambridge, MA: Harvard University Press.

Caruth, C. (1995). *Trauma: Explorations in memory*. Baltimore: John Hopkins University Press.

Chu, J. A. (1998). *Rebuilding shattered lives: The responsible treatment of complex posttraumatic and dissociative disorders*. New York: John Wiley.

Davies, J. M. (1997). Dissociation, repression, and reality testing in the countertransference. In R. B. Gartner (Ed.), *Memories of sexual betrayal: Truth, fantasy, repression, and dissociation* (pp. 45–75). Northvale, NJ: Jason Aronson.

Davies, J. M., & Frawley, M. G. (1994). *Treating the adult survivor of childhood sexual abuse: A psychoanalytic perspective*. New York: Basic Books.

Erikson, K. (1976). *Everything in its path: Destruction of community in the Buffalo Creek flood*. New York: Simon & Schuster.

Fitzpatrick, J., & Sollie, D. L. (1999). Unrealistic gendered and relationship specific beliefs: Contributions to investments and commitment in dating relationships. *Journal of Social and Personal Relationships, 16*(6), 852–867.

Freud, S. (1963). *Therapy and technique*. New York: Collier Books. (Original published 1914)

Freud, S. (1975). *Beyond the pleasure principle* (Ed. and trans., S. Rickman). New York: Norton. (Original published 1961)

Frieze, I. (1983). Investigating the causes and consequences of marital rape. *Journal of Women in Culture and Society, 8,* 532–553.

Grand, S. (1997). The persistence of nonlinguistic testimony. In R. B. Gartner (Ed.), *Memories of sexual betrayal: Truth, fantasy, and dissociation* (pp. 209–219). Northvale, NJ: Jason Aronson.

Harvey, M. A., Mishler, E. G., Koenen, K., & Harney, P. A. (1998). *In the aftermath of sexual abuse: Making and remaking meaning in narratives of trauma and recovery*. Unpublished manuscript. Cambridge, MA.

Herman, J. (1992). *Trauma and recovery: The aftermath of violence—From domestic abuse to political terror*. New York: Basic Books.

Langer, L. L. (1991). *Holocaust testimonies: The ruins of memory*. New Haven, CT: Yale University Press.

Laub, D. (1995). Truth and testimony: The process and the struggle. In C. Caruth (Ed.), *Trauma: Explorations in memory*. Baltimore: Johns Hopkins University Press.

Loftus, E., & Ketcham, K. (1994). *The myth of repressed memory: False memories and allegations of sexual abuse*. New York: St. Martin's Press.

McAdams, D. P. (1998). The role of defense in the life story. *Journal of Personality, 66*(6), 1125–1146.

Miller, J. B., & Stiver, I. P. (1997). *The healing connection: How women form relationships in therapy and in life*. Boston: Beacon Press.

Pasupathi, M. (2001). The social construction of the personal past and its implications for adult development. *Psychological Bulletin, 127*(5), 651–672.

Pennebaker, J. W. (1995). Emotion, disclosure, and health: An overview. In J. Pennebaker (Ed.), *Emotion, disclosure, and health* (pp. 3–10). Washington, DC: American Psychological Association.

Pennebaker, J. W. (1997). *Opening up: The healing power of expressing emotions.* New York: Guilford Press.

Pennebaker, J. W., & Seagal, J. D. (1999). Forming a story: The health benefits of narrative. *Journal of Clinical Psychology, 55*(10), 1243–1254.

Rogers, A. G. (1999). *Two related layers of psychological trauma in the life-narratives of sexually abused girls.* Unpublished manuscript, Cambridge, MA.

Rogers, A. G., Casey, M. E., Ekert, J., & Holland, J. (1999). Unpublished working papers of the Telling All One's Heart project. Cambridge, MA.

Rogers, A. G., Casey, M. E., Ekert, J., Holland, J., Nakkula, V., & Sheinberg, N. (1999). An interpretive poetics of the languages of the unsayable. In R. Josselson & A. Lieblich (Eds.), *Narrative study of lives, Vol. 6: Making meaning of narratives* (pp. 77–106). Thousand Oaks, CA: Sage.

Seidman, I. E. (1991). *Interviewing as qualitative research: A guide for researchers in education and the social sciences.* New York: Teachers College Press.

Shay, J. (1994). *Achilles in Vietnam: Combat trauma and the undoing of character.* New York: Simon & Schuster.

Sorsoli, L. (2000). *Paper tigers: Remembering, repressing, repeating and relating stories of childhood sexual abuse.* Unpublished manuscript, Cambridge, MA.

van der Kolk, B. A. (1989). The compulsion to repeat the trauma: Re-enactment, revictimization, and masochism. *Psychiatric Clinics of North America, 12*(2), 389–411.

van der Kolk, B. A. (1996a). The complexity of adaptation to trauma self-regulation, stimulus discrimination, and characterological development. In B. A. van der Kolk, A. C. McFarlane, & L. Weisaeth (Eds.), *Traumatic stress: The effects of overwhelming experience on mind, body, and society* (pp. 182–213). New York: Guilford Press.

van der Kolk, B. A. (1996b). *An integrative view on the neurobiology of developmental trauma.* Unpublished manuscript, Brookline, MA.

van der Kolk, B. A., Burbridge, J. A., & Suzuki, J. (1997). The psychobiology of traumatic memories: Clinical implications of neuroimaging studies. In R. Yehuda & A. C. McFarlane (Eds.), *Annals of the New York Academy of Sciences, Vol. 821: Psychobiology of posttraumatic stress disorder.* New York: New York Academy of Sciences.

van der Kolk, B. A., & McFarlane, A. C. (1996). The black hole of trauma. In B. A. van der Kolk, A. C. McFarlane, & L. Weisaeth (Eds.), *Traumatic stress: The effects of overwhelming experience on mind, body, and society* (pp. 3–23). New York: Guilford Press.

Wigren, J. (1994). Narrative completion in the treatment of trauma. *Psychotherapy, 31,* 415–423.

6

ON BECOMING THE NARRATOR
OF ONE'S OWN LIFE

RUTHELLEN JOSSELSON

"Whether I shall turn out to be the hero of my own life, or whether that station will be held by anybody else, these pages must show." So begins *David Copperfield* (Dickens, 1962, p. 13). Charles Dickens engages us with the question of what it might mean for someone else to be the hero of one's own life. But we are clear from the outset that David Copperfield will be the narrator of his history, beginning from his birth. What might it mean, though, not to be the narrator of one's life—for someone else to fill that station?

I began to pay attention to the incapacity to create a narrative of one's life and the delegation of that role to someone else during a session with one of my most challenging patients. This young woman, Heidi, whom I began seeing for psychotherapy when she was 19 and stopped seeing after her graduation from Columbia at the age of 21, was strikingly brilliant and beautiful and, on the surface, quite well-adjusted. She had been sent to therapy by her mother, who believed she was an alcoholic. Heidi was engaging, lively, and full of the social graces of the upper class. The difficulty of working with her was that her hours were filled with events and description but never connected stories.

The session that first caught my attention in regard to how she narrated her life occurred after her academic advisor pointed out that she had enough credits to graduate a semester early and she agreed to do so. I asked her what had gone into her decision and she replied, "I don't know. He said I could and seemed to think I should, so I said okay." But she added brightly and ingenuously, "I will be home this weekend and I'll listen to my mother tell it as a story. She weaves it into a plot with logic and a goal." Heidi reacted to my surprise at this with her own surprise, and then declared that all her life her mother had been making her life into a story. Even as an older child, she would eavesdrop as her mother talked about her while on the phone with her friends and then she would know *why* she was doing what she was doing. For example, in the current circumstance, Heidi said her mother might say, "Heidi has decided to work and gain experience for medical school" or perhaps "Heidi has been working so hard in college that she decided to take a break from studying and relax a bit before medical school." As we explored this further, I came to understand that listening to her mother make a story of her experiences had always been a soothing experience for Heidi. She felt as if her mother took "ragged fragments" and made them into a whole so that Heidi could know that her choices made sense. In Heidi's case, the issue was not so much that she depended on her mother to tell her what to do as that her mother had, at some point, taken over the function of telling her *why* she was doing what she *was* doing.

Charlotte Linde (1993), a linguist who studies life stories, made the crucial distinction between the narrator and the protagonist, the difference being that the narrator does the reflecting. The act of narration creates a space for reflection in which the narrator can observe, correct, and comment on the self that is being created. The narrator possesses superior knowledge of why the protagonist acted in a certain way or of how the protagonist should act. In Heidi's case, she was the protagonist of a story her mother was narrating, a phenomenon that resonated for me with Dickens's evocative question about being the hero(ine) of one's life.

Heidi had initially consulted me because her mother declared that Heidi was an alcoholic—even though Heidi asserted that she had never drunk to excess and, in fact, had rarely drunk alcohol at all. In response to Heidi's protests, her mother told her that she was "in denial"—just like her father. The story, as best I could gather from Heidi, was that on New Year's Eve of Heidi's sophomore year of college, she had been at a party, had a few drinks, and decided that rather than stay at the house of the hostess as planned, she preferred to drive herself home. On the way, she was stopped by police, failed a Breathalyzer test, was given a DWI, and a court date was subsequently set. Heidi told me, in response to my question, that she had not had a drink for at least a month before this and that she drank rarely, only at parties, to be social. She maintained that her drinking was "normal."

She said she had not drunk that much on New Year's Eve, did not feel impaired, and was surprised that her blood alcohol level was so high. Still, Heidi was not exactly outraged by her mother's declaration that she was an alcoholic. How does one know, she asked me pointedly, if something is not so or if one is in denial? This I found a most intriguing question—but I had no ready answer.

Over the course of 2½ years of therapy, my initial impression of Heidi did not change. She did exceedingly well in her demanding college courses, maintained friendships, had a boyfriend, and had no "problems" to speak of. She could feel joy, sadness, anxiety, and guilt as well as a range of other feelings that she often articulated in colorful ways. She worried about her exams and described in detail her efforts to study for them; she attracted needy and troubled friends whom she struggled to help. She was certainly not psychotic or borderline; she was not alcoholic; and she was not deeply disturbed. There was no evidence of dissociation either. She perhaps most resembled what Bollas (1987) described as the normotic patient—that is, a person with an abnormal compulsion to be normal.[1] But the diagnostic question interests me less than the matter of the authorship of a life narrative. Although I early on harbored a suspicion that she was in therapy to impress the judge who would hear her case, I came to recognize that she was in therapy to try to find a self, even though her stated reason for being in therapy was because her mother had "put it on my schedule." (Indeed, she had been referred to me by her mother's therapist in another city.)

Heidi was well able to relate the facts of her life. The youngest of five children (ranging in age from 20 years older than herself to 3 years older), her parents divorced when she was 13. Her father, a physician, had been distant and demanding, critical and controlling, engendering the rage of his ex-wife and children. Heidi's mother said that he was an alcoholic in denial and Heidi had never questioned this. Her mother had had bouts of depression throughout Heidi's life, and more recently, several episodes of cancer, one quite serious. Several years before, Heidi's mother had found a new "religion" in Alcoholics Anonymous-Alanon and used this philosophy as a way of understanding the world. Heidi described her mother as both "super-competent and hysterical" and explained that this was typical for daughters–wives of alcoholics. All of her siblings were superachievers, all graduates of Yale, her father's alma mater, and all had become, or were becoming, physicians. Only Heidi had gone to a different school and that only because she had been accepted to Yale off the waiting list too late to

---

[1] Mcdougall (1985) similarly discussed what she would term "normopaths," people who seemed to have achieved in early childhood "a robotlike adaptation to the demands of external reality" (p. 156). In analysis, such people tend to recount endless chains of external events that appeared to have little emotional significance for them.

easily change her plans—at least her mother told her that it was not worth it to do so.

Heidi's therapy sessions were filled with details of events in her life and her efforts to succeed in everything. She spoke of her course assignments and the challenges they presented for her, the arguments with her parents about money, her worries about the court case, the efforts she made to calm herself when she felt "stressed out"—usually with exercise or reading. Sometimes she berated herself for making mistakes while playing the flute in the university orchestra, especially when the conductor noticed, but then would double her resolve to practice more.

When her roommate left town for the summer, Heidi was surprised at how lonely she felt, and she discussed this over many weeks, especially because it seemed to her that she "shouldn't" feel lonely or miss her roommate. But no matter what the event of the week Heidi was reporting, there seemed to be no meanings attached or linkages made or efforts to think of herself as a person with a history that has influenced her becoming. Although there was no question of her intellectual capacity and development, she seemed to lack a necessary ingredient for what cognitive psychologists call "autobiographical reasoning," which involves "a process of self-reflective thinking or talking about the personal past that involves forming links between elements of one's life and the self in an attempt to relate one's personal past and present" (Bluck & Habermas, 2001, p. 136). What Heidi was missing were not the cognitive components but the imagination necessary to make her story go beyond logical, causal coherence to a story rooted in subjectivity.

Heidi, for example, remembered that she "hated" her father between the ages of 8 and 12, and when I asked her what she recalled about this time, she told me about the conflicts between her parents and how she always took her mother's side. I invited her to try to reconstruct this time from her own point of view, but she was only able to remember through her mother's experience. She remembered her mother's anger at her father for being so controlling about money, for not paying enough attention to the kids, and for being moody and often withdrawn. "I think my feelings will always be linked to my mother," she told me. "At least," she added, "that's what my mother says."

I thought that the history of Heidi's romantic interests might be one place where I might find a self-reflective story. I struggled to get a picture of her relationship with her boyfriend, Phil. She mentioned him, but acknowledged no feelings about him except that he was her boyfriend, "nice," a "good friend," and they "went out." Phil helped her with things she needed help with, like moving from one apartment to another. Once she told me that she thought she liked being with him in a group more than being alone with him and that they usually did things together with other friends. She denied that the relationship was sexual, but I have no idea what was taking place in this regard. Although the relationship lasted nearly three years, they broke up after he graduated (one year before her), and she said only that she ended the relationship because it seemed like the right thing to do—after all, Phil was graduating and moving away. Heidi hesitated to tell her mother that she had broken up with Phil, however. Her mother always heartily approved of Phil because Heidi's connection to him proved that Heidi "had broken the cycle of choosing an alcoholic partner." (Heidi's mother was the daughter as well as the ex-wife of an alcoholic, as had been her own mother.) She worried that her mother would be distressed at the breakup; she herself did not seem to be. As I realized later, despite her anxiety about telling her mother, her mother came through with a storied response in the guise of support. She told Heidi that she could understand her doing this because Phil was not the right one for her. Subsequently, Heidi felt relieved to be able to explain to others that she had broken up with Phil because he was not the right one.

I, too, was busy creating a story around this, making up a Phil to go with Heidi. I imagined Phil as someone with a low need for intimacy who was probably impressed to have such a beautiful girlfriend and did not demand much from her either sexually or emotionally. Only well after the breakup did I understand that Phil served the purpose of keeping other men away from her so she did not have to deal with them or make choices and decisions.

And what about her relationship to me? Heidi related to me politely but at what I experienced as an emotional distance, absorbing anything I might say rather than reacting to it. If she were late to an appointment, she apologized profusely and detailed a welter of external reasons to explain her lateness—the traffic, the bus not coming, and so forth. She seemed to want me to like her—and I did. She found my questions of her "interesting" and she said that it was "good to have someone to talk to." We did not have a usual kind of therapeutic contract because there was no particular problem that Heidi brought to solve, but I felt that any effort on my part to question her being in therapy would seem to her to be critical of how she had been behaving as a patient. I believed that simply making a space for self-reflection was probably good for her. And, because her mother was paying for the "treatment," at least I did not have to try to narrate what was happening in the insurance company language of symptoms and short-term goals.

As I try to reconstruct the 2½ years I spent with Heidi, I realize that anything I might write about her would be my story rather than hers because in most important ways, she did not have a personal story. Largely, she took herself for granted, without much autonomous interest in self-reflection. She had always taken as a given that she would become a doctor, like her father and siblings, and oriented herself to realizing this goal. In place of stories of her becoming were the stories her mother created for her, primarily the story of, "You poor thing. You've been through so much in your life." Although Heidi could describe the events she'd "been through," she had no sense of having experienced the "being through" or having attached meanings to it. And she did not *feel* like a "poor thing," although she acknowledged that she had been through some difficult experiences—or at least experiences that she recognized that others would mark as difficult. But she was not curious about her parent's divorce—the explanation that her father was an alcoholic sufficed for her; she did not wonder about her mother's bouts with depression because there were always others to take care of her when her mother was hospitalized. She had not worried that her mother would die of her cancer because people assured her that it was treatable. (All of these denials of significance were in response to my questions.) When her mother was having surgery, Heidi was not frightened because her father told her it would turn out fine, which it did.

The shocking discovery, at age 11, that two of her siblings were adopted and therefore not her "real" brother and sister must only have added to Heidi's sense that the real narratives of life were outside her control. Her task was to learn what they were rather than to create them. This discovery was particularly painful to Heidi because it was her older (adopted) brother to whom she felt closest in the family; he seemed to pay most attention to her. After the revelation, however, she felt distant from him; today he behaves like an outsider and does not play by the family rules. Her mother says he used to beat Heidi up when she was little, but she does not remember this, adding again to the confusion about which narrative is the right one.

Sometimes Heidi talked of people she admired—her mother and her siblings. What she always admired was their academic or professional success or their capacities to manage people or be funny and get attention. It was clear to me that the therapeutic task was to help Heidi locate a sense of self, to find a way to recognize her own emotional complexity, which involved, in many ways, learning to construct her own story of her life. But it is not my purpose to explore the process of the therapy. Rather, I wish to try to conceptualize the meaning of her incapacity to story her life.

As we began to explore the origin of the stories others told about her and her reliance on her mother to story her life, Heidi explained to me that her own experience of life is in pieces—"I'm not sure how they fit together." When she hears others' stories of their own lives, they sound certain, purposeful, and goal-directed. It is reassuring to hear other people tell her story because then it sounds the same way. For example, the story Heidi imagined her mother would tell about her early graduation was, "Heidi is so brilliant that she can graduate early. Since she's about to go to medical school, she's going to do research at Sloan-Kettering for a few months first to gain experience." I asked Heidi what her own true story would be and now, nearly 2 years into therapy, she could reply to this. "My story is I don't know what to do. I feel empty, not sure." But this was not a story she intended to live. Even when Heidi got her college diploma, she did not quite believe it. She felt they might take it away from her somehow—until her mother incorporated its arrival into her narrative of Heidi's experiences.

The challenge of telling Heidi's story parallels the therapeutic challenge in that any story I might create of Heidi's fragmented experiences would simply re-enact what her mother has always done. Indeed, I could weave a developmental story around the pieces I heard from Heidi—but the point is that it would not be *her* story, because she had not created one. Her life was built around trying to achieve perfection in whatever goals others set for her and worrying about how well she was doing. Her therapy hours were filled with recitations of events and plans for future events—largely academic, sometimes interpersonal. She rarely left room for me to take part in her monologue. It was hard to keep notes on her sessions; once they were over, they did not stay in my mind because I was at pains to find something coherent around which to organize my own narrative of the session. I gleaned only tiny fragments about her inner experience. Once she said fervently, in response to a question from me about what she thought of as the central theme of her life, "I just want to get to the end of the race without tripping." Later, she told me, "I want to be finished—to have arrived."

What I learned of Heidi's inner world from this was that her wish not to trip during the race overshadowed any consideration of who set the terms of the race or of her own experience running in it. The race was there— she simply wanted to show well in it. And she had little patience for or interest in process or for the conflicts and struggles along the way. The point was to arrive at a finish line she imagined as being like "the aura of being at the pearly gates—special, accepted, a good person." So, as with the material she generally brought to her sessions, either she was running along just fine or worried about some danger of tripping up. Bollas (1987) described this process in making the distinction between the drive to *be* and the drive to master being, the latter involving a kind of objectification of the self in which the inner world and the psychic tensions that it contains is obliterated.

THE THERAPEUTIC MASTER NARRATIVE

Therapy exposed Heidi to *my* master narrative that values inner experience and felt connection to others. I refrained from interpretation, recognizing that this ran the risk of offering her linkages that she could not make on her own—which would thereby repeat her mother's behavior. Instead, I asked her lots of questions about her inner experience, her feelings, her wishes. Mostly, this perplexed her, but she tried, in her persistently compliant fashion, to produce something to please me. She wanted to succeed in the therapy arena as well, although it was never clear to me if success had any definition for her beyond my seeming pleased with her enough so that she could tell her mother, in response to her questions, that therapy was "going well."

Given her high intelligence, she asked challenging questions of my master narrative. When I would ask her to try to distinguish between thoughts or ideas that came from her mother and those that felt like her own, she asked me, "How do you know if something is yours or if you've gotten it from someone else?" After all, she pointed out, her hair and her smile are her mother's—as were many of her beliefs. How could one say what belonged to whom? In some sense, one might regard Heidi as the ultimate social constructionist. Still, these questions served to illuminate the gap between my (therapeutic) narrative in which one is always the hero of one's own life and her sense of life in which one lives competently the plots constructed by others.

In time, though, Heidi came to describe the difference between the "gilding" she presented outside and her fears that what was inside was "flawed." Her dream of her life had always been to have a successful career and live in a perfect little white house. I told her I did not think there was any *perfect* little white house, but she could not quite cross the border to look at what might be flawed inside. At the same time, Heidi grew panicky in the weeks preceding her appointment with a medical school admissions counselor. She felt she could not tell him her usual story of single-minded drive toward a medical career because she was not so sure any more that that was really her story. But such a thought left her not knowing what her story was—or what she wanted, or what she has done throughout her life. She felt called to give an account of herself, as though she were a character in a movie called *Defending Your Life*, and she recognized that this is a feeling she had had to some extent throughout her life. She remembered that in her adolescence, she lived in fear that her actions would be misunderstood and woven into a story that framed her actions in a blameworthy light—which is, of course, exactly what happened in the DWI incident.

Shortly before termination, which occurred when Heidi moved to Colorado to attend medical school, Heidi related her first self-created narrative—and this was in regard to her father, not her mother. At her formal graduation, which occurred a semester after her official graduation, she was aware of her father saying and enacting a narrative of, "See, I got my last child through college and she's going to be so successful."

Spontaneously, Heidi told me, "But my story is, 'No thanks to you. I did pre-med at Columbia to *escape* your pre-formed story about me.'" This was the first time Heidi ever related an episode that included her own motivations or wishes as linkages between events. She saw herself as having acted to escape the tyranny of another's narrative form for her life.

EPIC FORM AND NOVELISTIC FORM

There are individual differences in how life events are narrated, how pieces and fragments of experience are joined, how individuals conceive themselves and the genre of their life story. Literary theorists use the term *genre* to describe a mode of representing the world. In what Bakhtin (1981) termed the high-distanced genres, such as the epic, individuals were represented so that there is not "the slightest gap between his authentic essence and its external manifestations. All his potential, all his possibilities are realized utterly in his external social position. . . . He has already become everything he could become and he could become only that which he has already become. . . . his internal world and all his external characteristics, his appearance and his actions all lie on a single plane. His view of himself coincides completely with others views of him" (p. 34). Similarly, MacIntyre's (1984) analysis of heroic poetry depicts a world in which epic narrative enacts heroic social structure. In these Homeric epics, the self is a character only through its social role and has no means of reflecting on itself outside of the conceptions that inform the existing world view.

This is largely how Heidi viewed herself—as living a predesigned narrative created by her mother, and she felt shamed by the moments of recognition that her inner world and her outer presentation were not precisely identical. But she largely ignored and suppressed these moments. Her reliance on her mother to form her story was the certainty that her mother could make the elements, such as Heidi's decision to graduate early from college, fit the unfolding chronicle. The epic character, which, in Bakhtinian terms, Heidi was trying to be, "sees and knows in himself only the things that others see and know in him" (p. 35). In addition, Heidi's narrative form required that she regard her life from the vantage point of its ending, turning away from the open-endedness or indecision that might make the present a re-evaluating juncture with an uncertain future. She largely took herself for granted, which in Schutz's (1967) terms means that she did not regard her experience as being in need of further analysis; she felt she simply was what she appeared to be and that her stated goals contained all there was to say about her.

According to Bakhtin's analysis of the history of literature, the novel brought a radical new view of the individual in which "a dynamic authenticity was introduced into the image of man, dynamics of inconsistency and tension between various factors of this image; man ceased to coincide with himself, and consequently men ceased to be exhausted entirely by the plots that contain them" (Bakhtin, 1981, p. 35). In the contemporary novel, the protagonist is regarded as a being in the process of evolving and developing. It was precisely this discourse that was missing from Heidi's therapy. She could recount events, but she could not view her own evolution. Indeed, she was quite intolerant of any suggestion on my part that there could be aspects of herself in dialogue on the way to growing a different sort of self.

Therapeutic narrative is implicitly and inherently novelistic in that it is based on the premise of an evolving self with a history that includes meaningful linkages among life events and inner meanings, meanings linked to a self that grows in self-understanding. When Heidi entered therapy, such a narrative was foreign to her. Linkages among events were absorbed through her mother's narration, and this narrative thread generally related to success.

Contradiction between what inner experience she could allow into awareness and her mother's narration created confusion in Heidi, but she had few resources to battle for the supremacy of her own experience. When her mother declared her an alcoholic and laid out a convincing story of how daughters of alcoholics frequently become and marry alcoholics themselves, regarding the denial of alcoholism as part of the disease, this "made sense" to Heidi. The fact that she did not drink was not for her an adequate refutation of this narrative; thus, she did not resist her mother's demand that she be in therapy to treat her "denial." I remained troubled that Heidi was so unconcerned with resolving the question of whether she was or was not an alcoholic. I was outraged by her mother labeling her in this way; Heidi was not. She simply accepted that this is how her mother thought of her and, although she abstained from drinking, lived with the possibility that she nevertheless *could* be an alcoholic—or maybe even *was*. Once the court case was past, the issue simply no longer concerned her and seemed peripheral to the epic form of the trajectory of her life.

A related episode occurred when one of her professors suggested that she might have plagiarized some ideas in a paper she turned in. Although Heidi said that these ideas had been her own, she was left feeling that she must nevertheless have unwittingly taken these ideas from somewhere else because her professor thought she did. (As it turned out, her genuine puzzlement about this as well as her ability to discuss the ideas fully persuaded her professor that there was no plagiarism involved. Heidi, however, told me that she remained unable to believe that she could know more about this topic—of all things, medieval literature—than her professor.) Heidi, however, had little conviction that she could have "thought" these ideas on her own and instead tried to figure out the difference between ingesting ideas and plagiarizing them.

EPIC AND NOVELISTIC MASTER NARRATIVES IN PSYCHOLOGY

The tension between the unidimensional and the dialogic narratives of self also exists in psychology, enacted between those who would like to regard human life as goal-directed, all motivation and action subservient to an individual's sense of purpose in life, and those whose sensibilities require the recognition that for every purpose there is a counter-purpose as the individual struggles through life against his or her own dividedness.

But such tension may reflect differences in people—differences psychologists have not yet adequately reflected on; differences between people who are living chronicles and those who are living novels. Phillip Roth wrote of using his memories of the past for "an intricate explanation to myself of my world" (1988, p. 4). By contrast, others seem more to store experience untransformed by the imagination necessary to elevate it to narrative.

We understand now that trauma is often unstoried (Bar-On, 1999; Greenspan, 1998; Herman, 1992; Rogers et al., 1999). But perhaps more of life is unstoried than we have suspected. What we consider the "good patient" in psychotherapy or the "good informant" in narrative research is the same: a person who novelizes his or her experience into a multivocal, evolving text. As therapists, one of the first things we try to inculcate in our patients is curiosity about their own life histories, which involves suggesting that there is more to the initial narrative than has yet been presented or understood. The epic character takes this inquiry as mystifying or even confrontational.

Heidi, for example, when I inquired about the effects on her of her parents' divorce, said that it was painful in destroying the image of perfection she had felt herself living out. She could remember the events—her parents fighting, their announcement of their decision to live separately, the calendar of visits to her father. But her emotional reaction, to the extent she could reconstruct it, was distress that the narrative of perfection was disturbed— "it meant my family wasn't a perfect family."

It was in this and related contexts that I offered to Heidi my narrative stance of the difference between external appearance and internal reality— how things happened or looked versus how she felt or experienced (there being no point in talking about fantasy in this context). In effect, I was, as most therapists do, offering another narrative template for her to fit her experiences into, my story mold perhaps as ready-made as Heidi's mother's. To my mind, the therapy really took off only after Heidi spoke of the contrast between her "gilded" and "flawed" selves—that is, when she joined my dialogic way of thinking about the self. It is, of course, our assumption that joining this narrative form represents health and growth, much as Bakhtin presented the novel as "progress" over earlier genres.

PSYCHIC REALITY

What psychoanalytical thinking adds to literary theory is the idea that the multivocality and dialogism that Bakhtin highlighted in the contemporary novel are rooted in often chaotic and irrational aspects of unconscious and preconsious psychic reality. The essence of the dominant therapeutic narrative is that truly dialogic life narratives are centered in psychic reality. Knowing, to Bion (1962), always involves an integration of multiple psychic realities with material reality. Early in life, the baby may fall into relying exclusively on the sensory apparatus and, in naively realistic fashion, conclude that what is sensorily apprehended is reality itself. When psychic reality loses its psychic features, thoughts are reified and turned into concrete entities, which foreclose the possibilities for psychic linkages. Rather than experiencing the inner world as inner, the individual feels it to be identical with and determined by what is external; thus, the "psychic" aspects of internal life disappear. What we conceive to be making sense in a life narrative is always psychic sense—the integration of emotion, wishes, thoughts, and fantasy with external events and niches for the self to express itself. This is what, in Bakhtin's terms, is always multivocal. Development is hampered by overconcern with the external facts of life, because the concrete replaces psychic elaboration and may be logically, but not psychologically and emotionally, linked. This was Heidi's situation: She had all the facts, but needed her mother to narrate the missing affective and agentic pieces to connect them. The process of creating and telling a life narrative is the transformation of facts into psychic reality. This is what both good novels and good psychotherapies do. All good stories are, in their essence, psychological stories in that it is the complex interpretive interplay of desire, fantasy, feeling, and action churned through the imaginative processes of the living person that imbue events with meaning.

The facts of a life only assume narrative meaning when they are embedded in the emotional coherence of a life story. All children are initially reliant on their mothers to interpret and cope with their emotional experiences (McDougall, 1985; Target & Fonagy, 1996), but with adequate containment (Bion, 1957) eventually take over this function for themselves. In Heidi's case, it appears that what occurred developmentally is that her mother narrated her emotional experience without being able to contain it in and of itself. That is, Heidi's mother told her that she (Heidi) was angry or sad but could not experience and bear Heidi's actual anger or sadness.[2] Disavowing the experiential core of Heidi's inner world, her mother substituted a narrative structure in its place. Thus, Heidi came to experience herself as though in the third person, not the owner of the anger or sadness but the protagonist of it.[3] She could not experience as real any feelings that did not correspond to external reality or her mother's version of her inner states (Target & Fonagy, 1996). Because she regarded herself in objective, rather than subjective, terms she was quite ready to allow others to create the formal structure of a story about her life.

To achieve the knowing of one's own life history, one must be able to tolerate the ambiguity and uncertainty of process, process rooted in shifting subjectivity. Heidi's wish to be finished, to be at the end of the race, represents the opposite pole. Because of her need to already have a coherent, structured—and socially valued—life story, she was unable to engage in the process of creating one, and thus used her mother's willingness to fashion one for her as a way of defending against this anxiety. Heidi tended to the overuse of what Kleinians call manic defenses, a turn to external reality to deny the depressive anxiety that is inherent in emotional development and forms the core of inner reality (Winnicott, 1975). It was no surprise to me when, able to pull away the manic defensive mask for a moment, Heidi found herself empty, deadened, and at a loss about what she wanted from life.

The turn away from inner reality pervaded Heidi's life, including her relationship to her literature courses (she was majoring in Spanish while doing premed). She tended to do well looking at language structure and analyzing how a work of literature hung together. She was less interested in plot or emotional content. If she were reading a novel, she nearly always read it through to the end so that she could know in one sitting how it turned out. Most interesting to me, she enjoyed poems because she could say them—not their meanings but her ability to recite them (this latter, we later discovered, related to an early memory of her father's joy in her ability to memorize poems—even poems far too complicated for the child she was to understand, and his requests for her to recite in front of his guests was one of the few times she remembered him paying attention to

---

[2] For a discussion of how deviant affect-mirroring can result in the failure of ownership of one's own experiences, see Gergely and Watson (1996).

[3] Bollas (1987), discussing a case of a young man who was living out his mother's mythic projection, refers to his patient's weekly visits to his mother as a "narrative feeding." In another paper, Bollas also discussed the parents of the normotic person as being insufficiently alive to their child's inner reality and thereby not facilitating the creative expression of the inner core of the self. "Instead of being mirrored by the parent, the child is deflected. This is accomplished by diverting the child from the inner and the psychic towards the outer and the material" (1987, p. 151). Bollas's idea of deflecting and diverting extends similar observations made by Klein, Winnicott, and Bion about the processes of parental unresponsiveness to the child's imaginative inner life.

her as a child). Heidi enjoyed poems as puzzles of language structure, but was mystified by my asking her if a particular poem had personal meaning to her. Opening herself to the meanings of poems seemed to invite too much internal chaos, and her effort was to shore up and understand their scaffolding, a process very much a metaphor for what was taking place in the therapy.

Bion (1962) quoted Poincare: "If a new result is to have any value, it must unite elements long since known, but till then scattered and seemingly foreign to each other, and suddenly introduce order where the appearance of disorder reigned. Then it enables us to see at a glance each of the elements in the place it occupies in the whole. Not only is the new fact valuable on its own account, but it alone gives a value to the old facts it unites" (p. 72). The facts Bion has in mind are emotional experiences, the emotional experience of a sense of coherence that he views as epistemological rather than logical.

Facts of a life, although logically ordered, do not make for a coherent life story. A person's story may evince the characteristics of a coherent narrative—continuity of self through time, relation of self to others, and a moral evaluation of the self (Linde, 1993)—but still not, in a fundamental way, emotionally belong to the person whose story it is. Winnicott (1975), in discussing the manic defense, contrasted adventure stories that overlook internal reality with those that portray, tolerate, and bind depressive anxiety and doubt. Like Heidi's mother, we therapists may be able to link aspects of our patients' life experience into a kind of epic form (which leads to the simplistic formulations some people seem to take from their therapists), but this does not offer them the emotional coherence necessary for a life story. Life narrative is always open-ended, always revised and expanded, and it is important that, as therapists, we recognize the relativism inherent in life narratives we hear and cocreate. Spence (1982) wrote of lending form and coherence to the fragments of memory, fantasy, and association that the patient has produced, and I think that *lend* is an apt term. Our interpretations should only be lent, as provisional transitional tools. All life stories can be told many ways. It was this that I think the therapy offered Heidi—my continuing to raise questions in the absence of answers, my not expecting conclusions but insisting (to Heidi's dismay) on the exploration of the multiple layers of experience through self-reflection.

My own temptation to link the elements of Heidi's memories into a story that I thought was coherent and psychological was nearly overwhelming at times. And it taught me how easy it is, in the therapist's chair, to become like Heidi's mother and weave the narrative structures and linkages for the patient. Heidi once told me that when she related an event to her mother, her mother would often say, "I know how you feel." Together, we came to understand the double meaning of this phrase. On the one hand, her mother was trying to express a form of sympathy and care, but on the other, she was taking over the knowing function from Heidi. I think that therapists too easily "know" prematurely how their patients feel. The rush to coherence in patients, therapists, and the field of narrative psychology itself is often a defense against the anxiety of sitting with undigested elements of experience until they take meaningful shape, however transitory or provisional this shape may be. Spence warned us about how the "effort after coherence" may lead patients and analysts to "collude in an attempt to prematurely streamline a chaotic life" (p. 23). Heidi's example offers a caveat from the other side—the way in which the demand for coherence may lead us to prematurely narrate an impoverished one.

Of course, to some extent, everyone borrows narratives from others. Familiar to every parent is the moment when his or her young toddler falls down unexpectedly, seems confused, and looks at them searchingly to see if this should be cause for wailing or just for picking oneself up and going on. The parent who responds, "You poor baby—you fell down" will likely elicit wailing, because the baby frames the confusing experience as a painful one. The parent who responds cheerfully, "Oh, a little bump. You're okay and didn't hurt yourself," narrates for the toddler a story that will likely lead to continued exploration or play, without tears. As adults, we similarly take confusing or upsetting moments in our lives to talk over with friends and confidants. We are likely to come away saying that this discussion helped us put our experience in perspective and it is that perspective that forms the narration we are likely to carry with us about that experience. Like the toddler, and like Heidi, we seldom look too closely at whose perspective it is or how that perspective was created. Heidi's is thus an extreme case that illustrates more universal phenomena.

CONCLUSION

The two questions Heidi asked me in our first month together proved to be central to the therapy: How do you know if something is not so or if you are in denial? And how do you know if something is yours or if you got it from someone else? The course of therapy for her was a project of discovering answers to these profound questions—of unearthing and feeling her way into some of her own unprocessed experiences. Once she could catch some glimmers of this inner reality,[4] she could begin to story her own life, or at least to do so more on her own. My input was still

---

[4] A number of writers have emphasized the role of playfulness in being able to access psychic reality (e.g., Khan, 1973; Ogden, 1985; Winnicott, 1971).

very much present, but I like to think that I was less intrusive than her mother had been.

Heidi's first effort at a self-authored life story chapter—"I went to Columbia to escape . . ."—may or may not reflect what she, at any level, actually experienced then. But it seemed to her, on her graduation, to be emotionally true—as she prepared herself to encounter life as a more independent person, trying to forge her own path. The fact of going to Columbia instead of Yale is autobiographically identical, yet now she uses this piece of her past as a basis for transformation (Roth, 1988, p. 4) of herself in the present. This for her seemed to be a suitable "I am born" beginning, and thus contained an emotional truth of her past and a direction for her future. Perhaps down life's road, she will completely forget that she would have gone to Yale if she had been admitted earlier, because that is an element that will not fit her emerging life story. And if Heidi is truly the heroine of her own life, will that matter?

REFERENCES

Bakhtin, M. M. (1981). *The dialogic imagination*. Austin: Univeristy of Texas Press.

Bar-On, D. (1999). *The indescribable and the undiscussable: Reconstructing human discourse after trauma*. Budapest: Central European University Press.

Bion, W. R. (1957). Differentiation of the psychotic from the non-psychotic personalities. In W. R. Bion (Ed.), *Second thoughts* (pp. 43–64). New York: Jason Aronson.

Bion, W. R. (1962). *Learning from experience*. London: William Heinemann.

Bluck, S., & Habermas, T. (2001). Extending the study of autobiographical memory: Thinking back about life across the life span. *Review of General Psychology*, 5(2), 135–147.

Bollas, C. (1987). *The shadow of the object*. New York: Columbia University Press.

Dickens, C. (1962). *David Copperfield*. New York: New American Library.

Gergely, G., & Watson, J. S. (1996). The social biofeedback theory of parental affect-mirroring. *International Journal of Psychoanalysis, 77*, 1181–1212.

Greenspan, H. (1998). *On listening to Holocaust survivors: Recounting and life history*. Westport, CT: Praeger.

Herman, J. (1992). *Trauma and recovery*. New York: Basic Books.

Khan, M. (1973). The role of illusion in the analytic space and process. *Annals of Psychoanalysis, 1*, 231–246.

Linde, C. (1993). *Life stories*. New York: Oxford.

MacIntyre, A. (1984). *After virtue*. Notre Dame, IN: University of Notre Dame Press.

McDougall, J. (1985) *Theaters of the mind*. New York: Basic Books.

Ogden, T. (1985). On potential space. *International Journal of Psychoanalysis, 66,* 129–141.

Rogers, A., Holland, J., Casey, M. E., Nakkula, V., Ekert, J., & Sheinberg, N. (1999). An interpreive poetics of languages of the unsayable. *Making meaning of narratives. The narrative study of lives* (Vol. 4, pp. 77–106). Thousand Oaks, CA: Sage.

Roth, P. (1988). *The facts.* New York: Farrar, Straus, Giroux.

Schutz, A. (1967). *The phenomenology of the social world* (G. Walsh & F. Lehnert, trans). Evanston, IL: Northwestern University Press.

Spence, D. (1982). *Narrative truth and historical truth.* New York: Norton.

Target, M., & Fonagy, P. (1996). Playing with reality: II. The development of psychic reality from a theoretical perspective. *International Journal of Psychoanalysis, 77,* 459–479.

Winnicott, D. W. (1971). *Playing and reality.* New York: Basic Books.

Winnicott, D. W. (1975). *Through paediatrics to psycho-analysis.* London: Hogarth Press.

7

LIVING TO TELL THE TALE: REDEMPTION NARRATIVES, SHAME MANAGEMENT, AND OFFENDER REHABILITATION

SHADD MARUNA AND DEREK RAMSDEN

"My name is Bill, and I am an alcoholic." Those simple words may be the beginning of one of the best known and most influential narratives in 20th-century American life. The preamble to the Alcoholics Anonymous (AA) public speeches has been repeated so often in church basements, school gymnasiums, and (increasingly) Internet chat rooms over the past 60 years that it is easy to overlook just how powerful the phrase is. Far from peripheral to the method of recovery in Alcoholics Anonymous, the sharing and reconstruction of one's own life history *is itself the core* of the Alcoholics Anonymous method (Cain, 1991; Rappaport, 1993). According to O'Reilly, in *Sobering Tales: Narratives of Alcoholism and Recovery* (1997):

> Telling the story—it may be said that, in a sense, there is only one story in AA—enables the speaker to reconstrue a chaotic, absurd, or

---

To preserve the spirit of authenticity, the words of the speakers have been reproduced in their original form. In a few cases, this entails some profanity.

violent past as a meaningful, indeed a necessary, prelude to the structured, purposeful, and comparatively serene present. (p. 24)

Indeed, the edited volume *Alcoholics Anonymous* (1939), the primary text (or "Big Book") that has introduced millions of people to the 12-step philosophy, is itself a collection of 29 life stories of the original members of the organization. Alcoholics Anonymous Founder Bill Wilson has said, "The 400 pages of Alcoholics Anonymous contain no theory; they narrate experience. . . . Being laymen, we have naught but a story to tell" (O'Reilly, 1997, p. 129). Recovery stories continue to be told at Alcoholics Anonymous or related 12-step fellowships around the world. "Rarely is any point made in Alcoholics Anonymous meetings or publications without at least a few fragments of some individual's life history being presented to support it" (Thune, 1977, p. 79). And it is through this sharing of stories that Alcoholics Anonymous members hold on to their recovery.

This narrative reconstruction can be understood as a prototypical form of "shame management"—helping outcast groups overcome their stigmatization and realign themselves with mainstream society (Braithwaite & Braithwaite, 2001). The significance of this process transcends the problem of alcohol or drugs (evidenced by the fact that many of the spin-off 12-step groups have nothing to do with the use of substances), and can be understood as a general principal of self-change and reintegration. As such, the recovering people who founded and have continually fueled the 12-step social movements seemed to intuitively understand what academics have only recently started to explore: *The management of shame involves a social process of autobiographical reconstruction.*

In recent years, the self-narrative has become a central concept in the social sciences in general. In fact, Sarbin (1986) has argued that the narrative should be seen as the root metaphor for the entire field of psychology. Driving this new interest is the idea that narratives are the way that humans make sense out of an otherwise chaotic existence. According to Dan McAdams's theory of the life story identity (1993), the construction and reconstruction of one's autobiography—or personal myth—integrating one's perceived past, present, and anticipated future, is itself the process of identity development in adulthood. McAdams has argued that modern adults cultivate these life stories to provide our lives with unity, purpose, and meaning, and, hence, keep a creeping sense of meaninglessness or existential void at bay.

This may be particularly important during traumatic periods in one's life. For instance, considerable research suggests that when individuals experience life-threatening illnesses or other serious traumas, they frequently seek to find some silver lining in the experience or otherwise convince themselves that some benefits have emerged out of their adversity (Tedeschi & Calhoun, 1995). Persons who are able to construct these positive illusions seem to suffer less psychological distress and are less prone to depression than are other survivors of similar ordeals (Taylor, 1989).

Personal myths may also be the primary mechanism through which individuals are able to maintain a sense of self-worth in the face of moral, social, and personal failings. In particular, self-narratives may be crucial in the management and resolution of the shame that results from violating shared ethical codes. Wurmser (1994) characterized shame as a "betrayal of a global or gestalt image of the self because it is a threat to the whole framework of one's identity" (Harris, 2001, p. 185). According to Ahmed (2001), shame is thought to encompass feelings of inadequacy, inferiority, humiliation, dishonor, and a sense of despair and deep suffering. Ahmed chose the word *shame* rather than *guilt* specifically. Whereas guilt concerns discrete misdemeanors or transgressions, shame is "concerned with the overall tissue of self-identity" and the "exposure of hidden traits which compromise the narrative of self-identity" (Giddens, 1991, p. 67). Although guilt involves regretting one's behavior, shame is about the "whole self" (Lewis, 1971).

Not surprisingly, therefore, individuals have developed numerous sophisticated and unsophisticated defenses to deflect feelings of shame (Ahmed, 2001, p. 229). Individuals who commit socially disapproved acts seek some means of maintaining their own sense of pride and self-respect in the face of personal and public stigmatization. Externalizing one's feelings of anger or escaping shame through the escapism of drugs or materialist consumption (e.g., buying another new suit to hide one's shame) are among the options available for deflecting or avoiding shame according to Nathanson's (1992) "compass of shame" theory. Deviance, shame, and the deflection of shame, therefore, become a sort of unending cycle.

In this chapter, we argue that a social process of narrative reconstruction—similar to what takes place in 12-step meetings every day—provides a means of escape from this chimera of deviance and shame. We begin by critically reviewing the traditional understanding of narratives of deviance in criminology and related disciplines. Many of our examples will focus on addiction and recovery because this is where the narrative perspective has been best developed (e.g., Diamond, 2000; O'Reilly, 1997; Singer, 1997; White, 1996), yet our interest is in "deviance" more generally, with implications for disapproved behavior of other sorts. (Indeed, a case could be made that besides addiction research, the area in which the narrative model is most dominant is in research on sexual offending and pedophilia; e.g., Scully & Marolla, 1984; Ward, 2000). There are, of course, significant differences between addiction to substances like alcohol and the habitual commission of crimes such as burglary. We contend, however, that the two share enough similarities to be considered together under the generic label of "deviant" behavior.

Indeed, this view on the generality of deviance is largely shared in the applied world of offender treatment, where behaviors as diverse as stealing cars, using heroin, or cheating on taxes are often addressed under a single offending behavior rehabilitation program. In the next section of the chapter, we review the dominant paradigms in offender treatment and describe how the deconstruction of deviant narratives has become a central activity in the rehabilitative work with offenders. We argue that although the correctional system has become adept at breaking down deviant self-justifications, the system does less well at the more challenging task of helping clients develop new, positive life scripts for themselves. In support of this argument, we briefly present an analytical portrait of the subjective world of 30 persistent deviants—individuals in their 40s who have spent much of their adult lives going to jail. This section is provided as something of a context for readers with little experience of the types of issues faced by individuals in these circumstances.

Finally, in the remainder of the chapter, we outline what is known about the social process of narrative reconstruction (again drawing mainly from the addiction recovery literature). On some levels, this process is rather easily explained, as in White's (1996) elegant summary of the narrative premise: "By telling you who I am, I tell you my fate. To change my fate, I must redefine who I am; I must reconstruct my story" (p. 423). Yet research on how this process works and what self-narratives are the most supportive of reform is only in the earliest, most exploratory stages, even compared to the literature on the cognitive patterns associated with addiction and criminality.

FALSE PRIDE AND DEVIANCE: DEFLECTING SHAME

The stories that offenders tell to make sense of their behaviors has long been a side interest of criminologists. Donald Cressey (1963, p. 151), for instance, argued that "criminals and delinquents become dishonest because of the words available to them." According to Cressey, "Listening to people tell you why they did it does not give you explanations of why they did it. When you ask people why they commit crime, they make sounds. I call them verbalizations. These are data. You study them" (Laub, 1983, p. 139).

The most influential theory of these verbalizations is Sykes and Matza's (1957) techniques of neutralization theory. According to this view, "Much delinquency is based on what is essentially an unrecognized extension of defenses to crimes, in the forms of justifications for deviance" (p. 666).

These include denial of responsibility, denial of injury, denial of the victim, condemnation of the condemners, and appeal to higher loyalty. In this formulation, delinquents are thought to embrace conventional moral values, but allay the pangs of conscience involved in breaking these rules by internalizing a system of rationalizations for criminal behavior. Neutralization techniques, in other words, are a form of "shame deflection" (Harris, 2001)—they allow offenders to feel good about themselves despite violating a shared moral code.

Related research on the psychology of addiction suggests that addicts engage in a parallel process. Bateson (1971), for instance, described addiction as a disease of "epistemology" or, in the vernacular of Alcoholics Anonymous, a disease involving "stinking thinking." Habitual drinkers and drug users are thought to deny their addictions (and hence maintain their dignity) through an elaborate sort of "false pride" characterized by rampant individualism, materialism, and egotism.

Like neutralization techniques, the alcoholic's doomed narrative does not emerge from nowhere; it is drawn from prototypical narratives in the wider culture, and nurtured and celebrated in specific subcultures complete with their own mythology, rituals, symbols and language (White, 1996). Drug- and alcohol-based "tribes" are able to simultaneously celebrate the specialness of heavy drinking or drug use and also deny that members are deviant. In words that could just as easily describe delinquent gangs, White (1996, p. 36) wrote, "It's as if members have entered into an unspoken pact to mutually support the minimization, projection, intellectualization, rationalization, grandiosity, and aggression that allow them to sustain and deny their addiction." Equally, the "cultural script of addiction" (Singer, 1997) is thought to be reinforced by the rampant consumerism of the wider culture. Both the addict and the modern consumer are thought to be in a state of denial of sorts, masking their shame behind a materialistic veil.

NO MORE EXCUSES: UNMASKING THE DEVIANT

Although relatively neglected in criminology, narrative research (and in particular Sykes and Matza's theory) has had an enormous impact on the applied world of offender rehabilitation with the ascendancy of cognitive-based correctional treatment (e.g., Gibbs, Potter, & Goldstein, 1995). Cognitive-based programs—with titles like Reasoning and Rehabilitation (Ross & Fabiano, 1983) and Thinking for a Change (Bush, Glick, & Taymans, 1997)—have dominated practice developments in correctional programming in the United States and internationally. The primary aim of much of such cognitive programming is simple: Offenders need to "accept responsibility" for their actions and stop "making excuses" (or neutralizations) for their deviance. In *Changing Criminal Thinking: A Treatment Program*, Sharp (2000, p. 2) wrote, "Criminals do not think like law-abiding prosocial people. Criminal behavior is the result of erroneous thinking . . . which includes rationalizing, justifying, excuse-making, blaming, accusing, and being a victim."

The solution offered in Sharp's (2000, p. 3) treatment program and others like it is to convince convicts to internalize responsibility for their actions: "We believe that optimum opportunity for success in a treatment program requires that clients be held accountable for all their actions, past, present and future" (p. 3). These confrontation-based "technologies of the self" seek to "subjectify" or "responsibilize" convicts through the ritual of confession, forcing them to own up to their past sins and stop making excuses (Garland, 1997). The focus (best explained in a barrage of mixed metaphors) is to unmask offenders, tear down their well-developed defense mechanisms, and shine the mirror of reality at them, confronting them with the shame of their lives.

Unfortunately, these attempts at confrontation are only occasionally successful in practice (see especially Fox, 1999). Recent research suggests that direct identity confrontation is most likely to be effective when the confrontation is done "by those whom we respect very likely" (e.g., family members or peers; Braithwaite & Braithwaite, 2001, p. 32). The extreme subjugation of prison inmates and the moral distance between the captors and the detainees in the prison world makes this sort of emotional penetration unlikely (and is one reason for the popularity of therapeutic community models in the prison system). Building on Sherman's (1993) defiance theory, Braithwaite and Braithwaite (2001) argued that "disapproval perceived as communicated by people who are despised will increase predatory crime" (p. 44). That is, individuals with weak bonds to the moral community will deny their shame by rebelling against the sanctioning authority, which they perceive as illegitimate.

Braithwaite and Braithwaite (2001, p. 318) wrote, "Psychologically, we will be better off if we reject our rejectors. The shame will be resolved by rejecting their ethical view; we have nothing to be ashamed about and thus our self-esteem can be preserved." Observational research by Fox (1999) provides vivid evidence of the ways correctional clients can resist and subvert heavy-handed attempts to responsibilize and subjectify them. In the same way, "The solemn pronouncements of judges about the relative wrongness of this offense versus that will matter not a jot to the most critical audience for these censuring messages—criminal offenders" (Braithwaite & Braithwaite, 2001, p. 33).

Finally, little correctional counseling focuses on developing positive, redemption scripts for the future. As a result, after rationalizing identities are torn down, the correctional clients are left in a state of identity anxiety, not knowing who they are anymore. In such circumstances, it is often easiest to revert back to a self-justificatory narrative to preserve one's self-esteem and sense of identity. Sutherland and Cressey (1978) perceptively wrote,

> Once a man has gone through the impersonal procedures necessary to processing and labeling him as a criminal and a prisoner, about all he has left in the world is his "self." . . . If it should be taken away from him, even in the name of rehabilitation or treatment, he will have lost everything. (p. 558)

Removing the deviant's shield of false pride is only worthwhile if one can address the underlying shame being deflected. Feelings of shame, after all, are thought to be a principal cause of criminal behavior. For instance, arguing that deviance is primarily motivated by deep feelings of injustice, Katz (1988, p. 313) asked, "Is crime only the most visible peak of a mountain of shame suffered at the bottom of the social order?" Fashioning themselves "street elites," young offenders ward off "the increasingly humiliating social restrictions of childhood" by creating a world of mythology for themselves, according to Katz (1988, p. 313). "As one ex-punk explained to me, after years of adolescent anxiety about the ugliness of his complexion and the stupidity of his every word, he found a wonderful calm in making 'them' anxious about *his* perceptions and understandings" (p. 312).

RECIDIVIST PRISONERS: STARING INTO THE VOID

Like addicts who find themselves in hospital wards for treatment, prisoners facing long sentences behind bars are already "stripped of most of the defenses, positive and negative, that we use to protect ourselves from a confrontation with naked existence" (Singer, 1997, p. 35). Goffman (1961) described the process of institutionalization as a "mortification of the self," and the "loss of identity" is listed as a primary consequence of imprisonment in almost every study of the psychosocial effects of prison. Essentially, it becomes awfully difficult to maintain a sense of false pride—keeping up the fiction that one has everything under control—when one finds him- or herself locked in a prison cell. Lacking familiar defenses, therefore, it is not uncommon for individuals in prison to experience profound emotional emptiness, shame, and existential despair.

These themes emerged repeatedly in a recent study involving one-on-one interviews with 30 persistent prisoners in two different men's prisons in the United Kingdom. (For details of the sampling procedure and methodology, see Ramsden, 2002.) The 30 research participants had a combined total of 1,068 convictions and 291 custodial sentences between them. One of the questions each participant was asked was how he would characterize his life up to that point. The responses were remarkably consistent for such an abstract question:

> It's been a fucking waste! That's all, a waste. (46-year-old, seventh prison sentence)

> What a waste! There have been good points like me kids and women but most of it has been a waste. I would like to start again—but you can't. (40-year-old, 10th prison sentence)

> I mean, I'm not silly, in the sense of—this is a waste of life. We know that. I mean put all my sentences together and I've probably spent 9 years, probably 10 years, out of my life, a whole 10 years in through the prison service, through the system. (42-year-old, sixth prison sentence).

> Um, I wish it [my life] had never happened. (44-year-old, 10th prison sentence)

Braithwaite and Braithwaite (2001) discussed the need for offenders to undergo a process of shame management. From the quotations earlier, *waste management* might be the more appropriate (if misleading) term. What can one "make" of a life that is, on some level, "a fucking waste"? Personal reform, in such cases, is not as easy as simply changing course and forging a new start.

Indeed, not surprisingly, the vast majority of respondents were staunchly pessimistic about their chances for turning their lives around. When asked what it would take for them to avoid future criminal behavior, most of the respondents found the question almost absurd.

> Winning the lottery. If I had the money, Guv, to do what I wanted to do, then there'd be no need to go thieving or earning dollars the way I have to do. (47-year-old, 8th prison sentence)

> Um, death? Yeah, that's it. Because when I get out of here, fair enough I've got loads and loads of fucking good intentions, but it's like anything else, one little thing can smash it all to pieces. (41-year-old, 12th prison sentence)

> Impossible, impossible. . . . It's the system. The system won't let you out. (44-year-old, fifth prison sentence)

Dozens of valid justifications were offered for these pessimistic assessments, but the most common explanation focused on the inability to escape one's past. In particular, participants spoke passionately about their sense of being stigmatized and condemned to criminality by others:

> It's just a case of, "Fuck off, criminal, we don't want to know you," and that's it. And you'll find that nearly all the lads in this jail, or any other

jail, when they get out of prison, they go through the same shit, and it's bang out of order. (41-year-old, 12th prison sentence)

Well, a prime example is, you've got a criminal record and if you're stopped in the street (by the cops) . . . as far as they're concerned . . . you are a criminal from your past. . . . It's so frustrating because everybody gets this impression that because you're a criminal you'll always be so, it's hard to get away from it (41-year-old, 13th prison sentence)

Yes, and then they make you feel like a criminal when you get caught and it is all blown up larger than what it actually was without anyone looking into the meaning of why these things are done. They are not that interested. . . . They make you into criminals sometimes, don't they. (42-year-old, 11th prison sentence)

On an optimistic note, the research participants did seem, at the very least, to know what the challenge facing them entailed. Perfectly summarizing the shame management challenge, one prisoner answered the question, "What would it take for you to avoid criminal behavior in the future?" by saying,

Take away my past! I know you can't take away the past, but I need to learn how to cope with it. (41-year-old, eighth prison sentence)

Another interviewee, when asked to reflect on his life eloquently described the need to construct a new self-identity and the social nature of this process.

There was some exciting times, don't get me wrong, very invigorating and the adrenaline pumping and things like that. But I want to know who I really am. And when I know who I am, I want people to know who I am, where I come from. . . . That's basically it. (44-year-old, 10th prison sentence)

Finally, other participants drew on the language of religion or psychotherapy in the beginnings of an effort to write a redemption script for themselves.

I look back and I think I was misunderstood, you know what I mean. My intentions was good but methods was wrong, sort of thing. . . . I think now, as you get older, you get more religious and spiritual and I'm kind of like looking at it that way. I know I've done wrong. . . . And I tend to think I can make up for it. . . . I've always tried to pay for my crimes. . . . I've always tried to pay penance, that sort of thing. So I think there is still hope for me. (41-year-old, eighth prison sentence)

Still, making something positive out of this raw identity material in counseling, support groups, and other therapeutic efforts is anything but an easy task.

NARRATIVES AND RECOVERY: MAKING GOOD

According to McAdams's (1994) narrative identity theory, personality consists of three distinct levels or domains: dispositional traits, personal goals/strivings, and identity narratives. He referred to these levels, respectively, as the "having," "doing," and "making" of the self. Because they are constructions, identity narratives are not something that one has (like basic traits) or does (like goal pursuit), but rather are actively shaped or made to make sense out of one's life.

For this reason, Maruna (2001) referred to the social process of reconstructing one's self-narrative into a redemption script for the future as a process of "*making* good." The challenge faced by persistent offenders and addicts who want to change their lives is to make good out of a life that has been self-declared a waste. This process is explicitly narrative-based. The maintenance of long-term sobriety or desistance from crime in the face of the predictable setbacks, obstacles, and disappointments in the life of a recovering person seems to require the development of a generative story that can provide a new interpretation of such difficulties.

This narrative quality of the recovery experience (Morgan, 1995) has recently become a dominant paradigm for understanding how individuals are able to maintain abstinence from addictive substances (e.g., Cain, 1991; Rappaport, 1993) and is increasingly the reigning paradigm in counseling work more generally (Parry & Doan, 1994). Indeed, narrative reconstruction is thought to play an important role in recovery from many types of illnesses and accidents (Frank, 1995; Taylor, 1989). Advocates of narrative therapy have suggested that correctional clients be formally taught ways to reconstruct "more liberating life narratives" (Henry & Milovanovic, 1996, p. 224) in a process that Monk, Winslade, Crocket, and Epston (1996) called an "archaeology of hope." According to O'Reilly (1997), "Narrative is not a cure, but it is a method, a path toward redemption. Redemption lies in . . . a better understanding—an improved epistemology, . . . recognizing counterfeit, seeing through duplicity, and resisting snares and seductions" (p. 65).

The transformative power of stories and storytelling is well known to treatment practitioners and individuals in recovery. According to White (1996), "The most dynamic treatment milieus are filled with stories and storytellers. They are language laboratories through which addicts learn to change their future via the semantic reconstruction of past and present." A growing literature in addiction research is beginning to outline the inner workings of these language labs.

Traditionally, the identity transformation process has been understood as a whole cloth replacement of an old, failed self-identity for a new and improved one. Individuals seek out ways of "knifing off" their pasts, starting over anew and becoming "born again." Religious, therapeutic, and recovery narratives, such as those offered by mutual support groups, are thought to provide this opportunity for complete identity transformation. For instance, Antze (1987) described the Alcoholics Anonymous member's storytelling as a way of creating "a new understanding of himself (or herself) . . . in effect *a new identity*" (p. 149, emphasis added).

Drawing from a more sophisticated understanding of the role of narrative, O'Reilly (1997) argued that the term *identity* in such descriptions is used carelessly and without precision.

> Identity should not be construed as a commodity that may be exchanged, even pursuant to a state of crisis, for a "new" equivalent. That superadded newness breaches the integrity of the concept, stripping it of its essential differentia: coherence and continuity. The rhetorically devious term "new identity" is tendered to emphasize both the supposed cognitive susceptibility of (AA) affiliates and the voracity and relentless coerciveness of the (AA) program.

O'Reilly instead points to the "strong conserving trend" that is integral to narrative rehabilitation. "A recovering alcoholic is not a person with a 'new identity,' but someone who has reestablished those temporarily disrupted or disarranged thematic continuities that inform the significant plot lines of the life story" (p. 152). In other words, Alcoholics Anonymous and other forms of mutual aid or group therapy do not work through a cult-like process involving the wholesale replacement of one identity story with another, "approved" narrative. Instead, participants are offered opportunities for mining their own pasts for buried themes and alternative interpretations—means of maintaining continuity but altering course at the same time.

This narrative reconstruction is an imaginative process that blurs the distinction between fiction and nonfiction. For instance, on the theory that the greater the sin the greater the redemption, there may be a tendency by some former deviants to exaggerate the extent of their former badness (White, 1996). Yet this is not a process of explicit denial or identity propaganda. As Thune (1977) wrote, narrative reconstruction is "not so much a falsification of the past, any more than any other autobiographical creation is a falsification, as simply the application of a new model for conceptualizing it" (p. 84). In this framework, individuals are not coerced into accepting prepackaged realities, but rather are encouraged to develop their own stories in a more natural, gradual rearranging of their past lives.

Similarly, in his proposal for therapeutic rebiographing or rehabilitative storytelling, Rotenberg (1987) suggested that ex-offenders can learn to "correct" their pasts "for the sake of psychological continuity and cognitive congruity" (p. 49). By "selectively and creatively reinterpreting past events to suit future aspirations," the ex-offender is able to justify his or her past, while also rationalizing the decision to go straight (p. 50). Rotenberg called rebiographing a "legitimate historical rehabilitation method" through which the "failing parts in a person's history are contracted while the reinterpreted reconstructed parts are expanded to create a more congruent life story dialogue between the future-oriented present new 'I' and the past 'thou'" (p. 65).

In every version of narrative therapy, this reconstruction is thought to take place in a distinctly social process involving both shame acknowledgment and forgiveness and reacceptance into a moral–social community (Braithwaite & Braithwaite, 2001; Scheff, 1995). White (1996) argued that this is a staged process beginning with storytelling, moving toward a process of story sharing. In the early days of recovery, it is most important for the recovering person to find his or her own voice and work out a story that can make sense out of his or her past. Storytelling "explains and salvages one's past while generating esteem in the present," thus strengthening the person's hold on recovery in ways that should "never be underestimated" (p. 391). "The well-constructed story (at this stage) is like an incantation or chant that affords protection from evil" (p. 391). How long does one need to repeat this mantra? Carl Rogers's (1961) writings suggest that individuals basically need to tell the story until the story and its telling become more boring than healing.

As the person advances through the stages of recovery, listening to the stories of others may become more important for maintaining recovery than the telling of one's own story. The first time one is able to hear an "analog story" (or have the experience of hearing one's own story told by another speaker) is thought to be a critical moment in the recovery process (O'Reilly, 1997). Particularly for male addicts, who tend to lack listening skills, mastering the ability to empathize with, relate to, and learn from the stories of others might be more important to maintaining behavior change than telling one's own story (White & Chaney, 1993).

As such, this sharing often takes place in a setting made up of one's own reference group or persons thought to share a social identity (e.g., other alcoholics, convicts, or drug users). This can be achieved in a mutual aid format or through the use of "wounded healers" (Frank, 1995)—counselors and therapists who share many of the same experiences as the persons being counseled (Lofland, 1969, p. 268). In addition, the sharing of stories builds a strong sense of connection and fellowship, which itself is thought to counter the alienation and narrative incoherence connected to the addiction script of persistent offending (see Singer, 1997). One of O'Reilly's (1997, p. 123) research participants described the sharing of stories as "a terribly unifying, mentally unifying experience. It just gives me a sense of purpose a sense of, um, belonging to something, and a sense of direction."

Finally, narrative reconstruction tends to take place in settings in which individuals feel part of a community (sometimes referred to as a brotherhood or sisterhood) that transcends the present. In this process of historical connectedness, the individual is able "to seek strength from the experience of those who came before" and is challenged "to share strength with those who will follow" (White, 1996, p. 295). By linking one's own life to forces greater than one's self in this way, the individual is able to imbue his or her personal myth with greater significance and meaning, as well as coherence.

POSSIBLE COMPONENTS OF SUCCESSFUL REDEMPTION NARRATIVES

There is no single "redemption script" (Alcoholics Anonymous or otherwise) that is appropriate or beneficial to every individual seeking to make a change in his or her life. However, recent research has started to uncover both systematic differences (Hanninen & Koski-Jannes, 1999) and more universal similarities (Maruna, 1997, 2001) in the thematic content and style of the self-stories that seem to be associated with reform and rehabilitation.

Both patterns (differences and similarities) are important for those working in correctional treatment. For instance, research suggests that some of the metaphors that can be the most liberating for males in recovery from addiction can actually be detrimental to women undergoing the same process (White & Chaney, 1993). Continued research is necessary to uncover cultural and subcultural differences in the appeal of various metaphors, stories, and narrative themes. At the same time, it seems possible that some aspects of the redemption construct transcend constructions of race, gender, class, and even culture. For instance, Hannien and Koski-Jannes (1999) have identified four prototypical recovery narratives in addition to the Alcoholics Anonymous script that recovering alcoholics seem to rely on, which they label the growth story, the codependence story, the love story, and the mastery story. Although the authors highlighted the differences between the models in their typology, these master narratives seemed to share substantial similarities as well. At the heart of these commonalities might lie important clues to the essential phenomenology of recovery (or in other words, the most useful changes in self and identity for sustaining abstinence from alcohol abuse).

Extant theory and research suggests that the narratives that former deviants construct to help them create meaning out of their lives might possibly share the following five clearly interrelated themes:

- Themes of reparation and generativity;
- Themes of "tragic optimism" or providence;
- Themes of vulnerability and mutual dependency;
- Themes of social embeddedness; and
- Overall coherence and internal integration.

Each thematic element of this hypothetical redemption script—which White (1996) called the antiscript of the deviant's justificatory narrative—is discussed briefly. It should be noted, however, that although these hypotheses have been repeatedly generated in exploratory and descriptive research, they remain essentially untested because of the anecdotal nature of most of this research. Furthermore, although considerable research has analyzed the prototypical Alcoholics Anonymous narrative, "The accounts of (people in recovery) who do not belong to AA . . . have remained relatively unexplored" (Hanninen & Koski-Jannes, 1999, p. 1838). These hypothesized themes, therefore, may reflect a number of biases in the research literature that will only be corrected through the accumulation of more systematic narrative research.

THEMES OF REPARATION AND GENERATIVITY

Addicts and offenders are thought to be largely self-centered and suffer from an inability to empathize with others (Ross & Fabiano, 1983). In a sort of inversion of this egocentrism, redemption narratives tend to be characterized by recurrent themes of reciprocity, mutual obligation, restitution, making amends, and "carrying the message" to others. Maruna (1997, 2001) characterized this as a generativity script (see also McAdams, Hart, & Maruna, 1998), where generativity is defined as the concern for and commitment to promoting the next generation. By providing a "conversion from guilt to altruism through (a) process of repentance" (Peteet, 1993, p. 265), this element of the redemption script allows deviants to acknowledge and manage their overwhelming feelings of shame. In addition, shifting the focus of their identity narratives from narrow self-interest to a more generative concern for the next generations allows former deviants to shift from a backward-looking anger and guilt about the past to a forward-looking focus on the future.

Of course, the therapeutic value of becoming a wounded healer of others is well known by rehabilitation organizations. Alcoholics Anonymous members who have been sober for many years often remain with the organization, not so much because they need to *receive* any more counseling but because the act of counseling *others* can itself be empowering and therapeutic (Brickman et al., 1982). According to O'Reilly, "Next to avoiding intoxicants," the therapeutic power of *helping* is "the major premise upon which [AA] is built" (1997, p. 128).

TRAGIC OPTIMISM AND PROVIDENCE THEMES

Whereas the accounts of deviants often involve themes of luck (usually bad) and fate, individuals who overcome traumatic experiences such as addiction often reconstruct their lives as being planned, orchestrated, or "enfolded by care" (Morgan, 1995). Often this takes the form of "tragic optimism" (Frankl, 1984) or the idea that suffering can be redemptive (see also Taylor, 1989). Former deviants seek to find some reason or purpose for the long stretches of their lives for which they have "nothing to show." This rationalization usually takes the form of, "If it weren't for X (me going to jail; my life of crime; etc.), I never would have realized Y (that there are more important things in life than money; that I was good at helping others; etc.)." The good has emerged out of the bad, and indeed makes sense out of the bad.

As such, redemption stories tend to be forward looking, focusing on how the individual is going to take responsibility for righting past wrongs, rather than looking backward by endlessly blaming oneself for past mistakes (Braithwaite & Braithwaite, 2001). A common theme in redemption narratives is, "You're not responsible for being down, but you are responsible for getting back up" (Brickman et al., 1982; Maruna, 2001). For instance, a key element of the addiction recovery script is, "Addicts are not responsible for their addiction but, once educated, are responsible for their recoveries" (White, 1996, p. 438). The past, in the redemption script, becomes a useful preamble for a positive present and future.

VULNERABILITY AND MUTUAL DEPENDENCY

In marked contrast to the false pride of the deviant script, redemption narratives frequently recognize (and draw strength from) the fact that the individual is fundamentally imperfect and "other than omnipotent or absolutely autonomous" (Kurtz, 1979, p. 196). Whereas the addict or deviant's story is that they are "real men" and would never need to capitulate to something as weak and soft as attendance at a weepy support group, recovering persons are able to acknowledge their shared vulnerability and need for mutual aid.

One variant of the vulnerability theme is the well-known paradox of "empowerment through surrender" that is common to many recovery narratives. Central to many theories of recovery (e.g., Kurtz, 1979; Tiebout,

1949) is the paradoxical notion that to gain control over one's drinking or drug use, an individual needs to first admit his or her own powerlessness over the substance. Kurtz (1979) has eloquently labeled this theme as "not-God," as in, "The fundamental and first message of Alcoholics Anonymous to its members is that they are not infinite, not absolute, not God" (p. 3).

EMBEDDEDNESS

Relatedly, in what Bateson (1971) referred to as a sort of epistemological reintegration, redemption scripts are often characterized by themes of embeddedness (Singer, 1997) or deep connections to the social and natural world. Recovery, in Bateson's (1971) framework, involves the development of a complementarity of the self, characterized by feelings of unity, community belonging, cooperation, and inclusion. The anonymity in the Alcoholics Anonymous narrative, for instance, involves reminding addicts that they are no better or worse than any of their brothers or sisters. "And from this awareness of equality flows a liberating sense of true freedom" (Kurtz, 1979, p. 197). Indeed, recovery narratives are characterized by a sense of inner serenity and peace with one's self and the world (Tiebout, 1949).

COHERENCE AND INTERNAL INTEGRATION

Finally, whereas deviant narratives are thought to be fragmented, incoherent, conflicted, and ambivalent (Singer, 1997), recovery narratives are frequently said to be characterized by internal cohesion, personality integration (Emmons & King, 1988), and a sense of wholeness (May, 1988). McGovern (1999) wrote, "The addict's story is 'broken.' [Addicts experience] a feeling of incompleteness and a yearning for harmony. Through story, the recovering addict learns the boundaries that define him, restored to healing conversation with other human beings" (p. 10). Redemption scripts, on the other hand, are said to have the potential to forge "unity and coherence out of chaos and fragmentation" (p. 117) and "transform adverse circumstances into opportunities for personal growth, lasting happiness and quality of life even in the face of pain and suffering" (p. 139).

CONCLUSION

Although the self-narrative is an internalized construct, narratives are socially shaped and nurtured. Narratives are "in the air" in many ways, and as such, it makes sense that lasting reform will be made most possible by a focus on air quality, to continue the metaphor, as well as individual respiratory issues. That is, changing individual narratives (e.g., from neutralizations and false pride to redemption scripts) is an environmental–ecological task as much as it is an interpersonal one. Although crucial, targeting the justificatory narratives of individual deviants through a process of rehabilitative counseling may represent something of an individual pathology model. To be effective, this approach needs to be supplemented by sustained efforts to change public and cultural narratives that foster and support addiction, criminality, and domination.

This latter process is not unrelated to the work of recovery communities. Singer (1997), for instance, argued persuasively that the rehabilitation literature is too inward-looking and apolitical, with little mention of "how relapses could be prevented by investing the recovering persons in efforts to change the social and economic circumstances that promote addiction" (p. 298). Similarly, in what he has called the New Recovery Advocacy Movement, White (2001, p. 19) argued in favor of "turning personal stories into social action" and "turning recovery outwards." This movement involves a "shift in focus from mutual aid to a focus on creating pro-recovery community attitudes and policies and on expanding the range and quality of local recovery support resources" (White, 2001, p. 15). Advocacy in this framework is about recovering persons and their supporters "acquiring and using power to change the ecology of addiction and recovery" (White, 2001, p. 19).

LeBel (2001) eloquently made the case that a similar social movement, led by ex-convicts and their supporters, is necessary to reduce the stigma of persons coming out of prison (see also Maruna & LeBel, 2002). There are hundreds of mutual aid groups and formal reintegration organizations for ex-convicts across the United States and internationally. Almost all are focused on the individual or interpersonal level of helping released convicts (or ex-cons helping other ex-cons). Were these groups to, in addition, join voices around public issues such as voter disenfranchisement, employer discrimination, prison reform, parent education, racism, or social inequality, they could feasibly make a profound impact on the ecology of reentry and reintegration. Most important, they would introduce a voice into the public arena that was hitherto largely unheard.

The direct benefit of participation in such advocacy work for the ex-deviants themselves is unclear. Maruna (2001) and Singer (1997) argued that fighting the good fight on behalf of other people in recovery can be an empowering and satisfying role for former deviants and individuals in recovery. Yet, White (2001) underscored that advocacy itself should not be confused with mutual aid and is not alone an effective aid to personal recovery. "The history of recovery advocacy is strewn with the bodies of those who believed advocacy work would by itself keep them sober" (p. 19).

In any case, public advocacy work on the part of the recovery and treatment communities would have indirect benefits for recovering individuals through the destigmatization and shame management involved when large numbers of once-silenced group members come out of the closet. If Cressey (1963, p. 151) was right that offenders "become dishonest because of the words available to them," and reform has similar roots in "language labs" (White, 1996), then the more former addicts and offenders who tell their stories, the better. White (2001, p. 27) wrote, "It is only when we reach a critical mass of people in America who personally know someone in stable recovery that attitudes toward addiction and the possibility of recovery will change." In an imagined future in which the language of redemption is in the air, the process of personal reform would be less a personal one for counseling clients to grapple with than a communal effort of families, communities, and collective social will. As well, the shame to be managed will be collective rather than individual.

REFERENCES

Ahmed, E. (2001). Shame management: Regulating bullying. In E. Ahmed, N. Harris, J. Braithwaite, & V. Braithwaite (Eds.), *Shame management through reintegration* (pp. 211–311). Cambridge: University of Cambridge.

Alcoholics Anonymous. (1939). *Alcoholics Anonymous: The story of how many thousands of men and women have recovered from alcoholism.* New York: Author.

Antze, P. (1987). Symbolic action in Alcoholics Anonymous. In M. Douglas (Ed.), *Constructive drinking* (pp. 149–181). Cambridge: Cambridge University Press.

Bateson, G. (1971). The cybernetics of "self": A theory of alcoholism. *Psychiatry, 34*, 1–18.

Braithwaite, J., & Braithwaite, V. (2001). Shame, shame management and regulation. In E. Ahmed, N. Harris, J. Braithwaite, & V. Braithwaite (Eds.), *Shame management through reintegration* (pp. 3–69). Cambridge: University of Cambridge.

Brickman, P., Rabinowitz, V. C., Karuza, J., Coates, D., Cohn, E., & Kidder, L. (1982). Models of helping and coping. *American Psychologist, 37*, 368–384.

Bush, J., Glick, B., & Taymans, J. (1997). *Thinking for a change: Integrated cognitive behavior change program training manual.* Washington, DC: National Institute of Corrections.

Cain, C. (1991). Personal stories: Identity acquisition and self-understanding in Alcoholics Anonymous. *Ethos, 19*, 210–253.

Cressey, D. R. (1963). *Social psychological theory for using deviants to control deviation.* Paper presented at the conference on "The use of products of a social problem in coping with the problem," Norco, CA.

Diamond, J. (2000). *Narrative means to sober ends: Treating addiction and its aftermath.* New York: Guilford Press

Emmons, R., & King, L. A. (1988). Conflict among personal strivings: Immediate and long-term implications for psychological and physical well-being. *Journal of Personality and Social Psychology, 54,* 1040–1048.

Fox, K. (1999). Changing violent minds: Discursive correction and resistance in the cognitive treatment of offenders in treatment. *Social Problems, 46,* 88–103.

Frank, A. W. (1995). *The wounded storyteller.* Chicago: University of Chicago Press.

Frankl, V. E. (1984). *Man's search for meaning.* New York: Washington Square Press.

Garland, D. (1997). "Governmentality" and the problem of crime: Foucault, criminology, sociology. *Theoretical Criminology, 1,* 173–214.

Gibbs, J. C., Potter, G. B., & Goldstein, A. P. (1995). *The EQUIP Program: Teaching youth to think and act responsibly through a peer-helping approach.* Champaign, IL: Research Press.

Giddens, A. (1991). *Modernity and self-identity: Self and society in the late modern age.* Stanford, CA: Stanford University Press.

Goffman, E. (1961). *Asylums.* Garden City, NY: Anchor Books.

Hanninen, V., & Koski-Jannes, A. (1999). Narratives of recovery from addictive behaviors. *Addiction, 94,* 1837–1848.

Harris, N. (2001). Shaming and shame: Regulating drink-driving. In E. Ahmed, N. Harris, J. Braithwaite, & V. Braithwaite (Eds.), *Shame management through reintegration* (pp. 73–207). Cambridge: University of Cambridge.

Henry, S., & Milovanovic, D. (1996). *Constitutive criminology.* Thousand Oaks, CA: Sage.

Katz, J. (1988). *Seductions of crime.* New York: Basic Books.

Kurtz, E. (1979). *Not-God: A history of Alcoholics Anonymous.* Center City, MN: Hazelden.

Laub, J. (1983). Interview with Donald R. Cressey. In J. Laub (Ed.), *Criminology in the making* (pp. 131–165). Boston: Northeastern.

LeBel, T. (2001, Nov. 6–10). *Survive vs. thrive: Ex-offenders struggle to overcome stigma and lead conventional lives.* Paper presented at the American Society of Criminology conference, Atlanta, Georgia.

Lewis, H. B. (1971). *Shame and guilt in neurosis.* New York: International Universities Press.

Lofland, J. (1969). *Deviance and identity.* Englewood Cliffs, NJ: Prentice-Hall.

Maruna, S. (1997). Going straight: Desistance from crime and self-narratives of reform. *Narrative Study of Lives, 5,* 59–93.

Maruna, S. (2001). *Making good: How ex-convicts reform and reclaim their lives.* Washington, DC: American Psychological Association.

Maruna, S., & LeBel, T. (2002). Revisiting ex-prisoner re-entry: A new buzzword in search of a narrative. In S. Rex & M. Tonry (Eds.), *Reform and punishment* (pp. 158–180). Devon, UK: Willan.

May, G. (1988). *Addiction and grace*. San Francisco: Harper & Row.

McAdams, D. P. (1993). *The stories we live by: Personal myths and the making of the self*. New York: William Morrow.

McAdams, D. P. (1994). Can personality change? Levels of stability and growth in personality across the life span. In T. F. Heatherton & J. L. Weinberger (Eds.), *Can personality change?* (pp. 299–313). Washington, DC: American Psychological Association.

McAdams, D. P., Hart, H., & Maruna, S. (1998). The Anatomy of Generativity. In D. P. McAdams & E. de St. Aubin (Eds.), *Generativity and adult development* (pp. 7–43). Washington, DC: American Psychological Association.

McGovern, T. (1999). Language of disease and recovery: Concepts to be addressed in existing scales. *Conference summary: Studying spirituality and alcohol*. Washington, DC: NIAAA and the Fetzer Institute.

Monk, G., Winslade, J., Crocket, K., & Epston, D. (1996). *Narrative therapy in practice: The archaeology of hope*. San Francisco: Jossey-Bass.

Morgan, O. J. (1995). Recovery-sensitive counseling in the treatment of alcoholism. *Alcoholism Treatment Quarterly, 13*(4), 63–73.

Nathanson, D. L. (1992) *Shame and pride: Affect, sex and the birth of the self*. New York: W. W. Norton.

O'Reilly, E. B. (1997). *Sobering tales: Narratives of alcoholism and recovery*. Amherst: University of Massachusetts Press.

Parry, A., & Doan, R. E. (1994). *Story revisions: Narrative therapy in the postmodern world*. New York: Guilford Press.

Peteet, J. R. (1993). A closer look at the role of a spiritual approach in addictions treatment. *Journal of Substance Abuse Treatment, 10*, 263–267.

Ramsden, D. P. (2002). *The mature offender: Choosing crime?* Unpublished master's thesis, Institute of Criminology, University of Cambridge.

Rappaport, J. (1993). Narrative studies, personal stories and identity transformation in the mutual help context. *Journal of Applied Behavioral Science, 29*, 239–256.

Rogers, C. (1961). *On becoming a person*. Boston: Houghton Mifflin.

Ross, R. R., & Fabiano, E. A. (1983). *The cognitive model of crime and delinquency prevention and rehabilitation: Vol. 2. Intervention techniques*. Ottawa: Ministry of Correctional Services.

Rotenberg, M. (1987). *Re-biographing and deviance: Psychotherapeutic narrativism and the midrash*. London: Praeger.

Sarbin, T. (1986). The narrative as a root metaphor for psychology. In T. Sarbin (Ed.), *Narrative psychology: The storied nature of human conduct* (pp. 3–21). New York: Praeger.

Scheff, T. (1995). Shame and related emotions: Overview. *American Behavioral Scientist, 38*, 1053–1059.

Scully, D., & Marolla, J. (1984). Convicted rapists' vocabulary of motive: Excuses and justifications. *Social Problems, 31*, 530–544.

Sharp, B. D. (2000). *Changing criminal thinking: A treatment program*. Lanham, MD: American Correctional Association.

Sherman, L. W. (1993). Defiance, deterrence and irrelevance: A theory of the criminal sanction. *Journal of Research in Crime and Delinquency, 30,* 445–473.

Singer, J. A. (1997). *Message in a bottle: Stories of men and addiction*. New York: Free Press.

Sutherland, E., & Cressey, D. (1978). *Criminology* (10th ed.). New York: Lippincott.

Sykes, G. M., & Matza, D. (1957). Techniques of neutralization: A theory of delinquency. *American Sociological Review, 22,* 664–673.

Taylor, S. E. (1989). *Positive illusions*. New York: Basic Books.

Tedeschi, R. G., & Calhoun, L. G. (1995) *Trauma and transformation*. Thousand Oaks, CA: Sage.

Thune, C. E. (1977). Alcoholism and the archetypal past: A phenomenological perspective on Alcoholics Anonymous. *Journal of Studies on Alcohol, 38,* 75–88.

Tiebout, H. M. (1949). The act of surrender in alcoholism. *Quarterly Journal of Studies on Alcohol, 10,* 48–58.

Ward, T. (2000). Sexual offenders' cognitive distortions as implicit theories. *Aggression and Violent Behavior, 5,* 491–507.

White, W. L. (1996). *Pathways from the culture of addiction to the culture of recovery* (2nd ed.). Center City, MN: Hazelden.

White, W. L. (2001) *The rhetoric of recovery advocacy*. Unpublished manuscript. Available at http://wwwefavor.org/ADVOCACY.HTM

White, W. L., & Chaney, R. (1993). *Metaphors of transformation: Feminine and masculine*. Bloomington, IL: Lighthouse Institute.

Wurmser, L. (1994). *The mask of shame*. Northvale, NJ: Jason Arsonson.

8

THE CORE CONFLICTUAL RELATIONSHIP THEME APPROACH TO RELATIONAL NARRATIVES: INTERPERSONAL THEMES IN THE CONTEXT OF INTERGENERATIONAL COMMUNICATION OF TRAUMA

HADAS WISEMAN AND JACQUES P. BARBER

Patients seeking psychotherapy most frequently present the therapist with problems in interpersonal relationships, especially with significant people in their lives. Even when the so-called presenting problem does not appear initially as an interpersonal problem, such as feeling lack of motivation in university studies or bored at work, much of what is recounted is in the form of relational stories. Patients tell these relational narratives in psychotherapy both spontaneously and in response to the therapist's questions, referring to current as well as to past events in their lives. Individuals

This study was supported by the United States–Israel Binational Science Foundation (BSF Grant 94-00199). The authors acknowledge the invaluable help and input of Dr. Carol Foltz, University of Pennsylvania, and of Alon Raz, Idit Yam, Sharon Snir, Einat Metzl, Nurit Gur, and the research assistants of the Second-Generation Project, University of Haifa.

also tend to tell these interpersonal narratives outside of therapy. Consider the following story, recounted by a man in his 40s during an interview:

Shaul: When I was age 13 or 14, something like that . . . I was . . . also the one with the better technical skills in the house, to make small repairs, things like that and . . . the one that was always responsible for the working tools in the house, that was me, and I wanted to buy, I wanted them to buy me an electrical hand drill . . . and then my mother responded in a way that was very surprising, that is, then it seemed to me a very surprising response, later she explained to me why, but, she did not want to buy me an electrical drill, the noise, drives her crazy . . . *she did not tell me why the noise drives her crazy*, only much later, she said that during the Holocaust, she did forced labor, she worked in a factory that built airplanes, and they drilled, her job was to drill all day long in the tins. "This noise," she said, "I can NOT hear."

Interviewer: How much later did she tell you this?

Shaul: About two year later, not immediately. She said that the noise, that she does not want . . . she bought me the drill in the end, but this was different . . . everything I wanted, I got.

Interviewer: So there was here something different in that she refused in the beginning to get you the drill?

Shaul: Yes, because she said, "NO, I do NOT want a drill in the house, I do NOT want to hear this noise in the house." "But I want a drill, I need it for my working tools," . . . I insisted. I only later understood, I didn't really pay attention at that time, I would have done it much more calmly, but as a kid. . . .

Shaul told the interviewer about this memorable encounter with his mother in the context of our study on relational themes among sons and daughters of Holocaust survivors. In this chapter we present the way we applied the Core Conflictual Relationship Theme (CCRT) approach to study relational narratives told by descendants of parents who experienced extensive trauma. The CCRT framework was developed by Luborsky (1977) to understand central relationship patterns and issues that are manifested in relational narratives. How may a therapist listening to Shaul's hand drill story understand and work with this narrative? In the context of intergenerational communication of trauma, what can we learn from such narratives about the themes of silence, noise, and the experience of knowing-not-knowing the mother's Holocaust story ("why the noise drives her crazy")?

CORE CONFLICTUAL RELATIONSHIP
THEME FRAMEWORK

Among the various ways to understand and work with the stories patients tell in psychotherapy, the CCRT method (Luborsky & Crits-Christoph, 1998) is one of the influential frameworks within the psychodynamic approaches to narrative and psychotherapy (McLeod, 1997). Psychoanalytical or psychodynamic theorists and researchers such as Spence (1982), Luborsky (1984), Strupp and Binder (1984), and McAdams (1985) were among the first to point out the many ways in which sensitivity to narrative and storytelling can enhance the effectiveness of psychotherapy. The rise of the narrative perspective in psychotherapy, coupled with the developments of short-term psychotherapies (Omer, 1993), led Luborsky to offer a way of formulating a CCRT focus that was based on the patient's narratives. The narratives, called Relationship Episodes (REs), told by the patient about others, are often the stuff of stories that occur during psychotherapy sessions, as well as during many everyday conversations. The RE refers specifically to the patient's accounts of particular interactions that occurred between the patient and another person. These accounts have the quality of a story, with a beginning and end, and most often have the form of "this is what happened when I wanted him/her to . . . and he/she reacted . . . and as a result I felt. . . . " Rather than consider the patient's overall life story, the therapist listens for these specific interpersonal incidents to identify the CCRT in the patient's life.

In listening to such REs, three basic components can be identified and described: (a) wishes, needs or intentions (W); (b) experienced, anticipated, or fantasized responses from others (RO); and (c) anticipated or consequential responses of the self (RS), in the form of thought, emotion, behavior, or symptom (Luborsky, Barber, & Diguer, 1992). Thus, referring back to the RE that Shaul narrated, we can ask three basic questions in accordance with the three components of the CCRT: (a) What are his wishes and needs in relation to the other (in this case, his mother)? (b) How does the other/his mother actually respond, or how does he perceive her reaction (in response to his explicit or implicit wish)? (c) How does Shaul himself respond as a consequence of his mother's response? As we will demonstrate later, the answers to these three questions lead to the formulation of the three components of the narrator's CCRT.

The patient's overall CCRT is formulated on the basis of the specific components (W, RO, and RS) that occur most frequently across the narratives in which the patient tells about his or her relationships with others. The assumption is that these recurring themes capture the central relationship patterns or schemas that underlie a person's characteristic ways of relating to other people. These central relationship patterns are thought to be the product of highly ingrained patterns or schemas of relationships with important others. It is assumed that these relational schemas, which are initially constructed from emotionally laden interactions with parental figures in the earliest years of life, are carried forward into subsequent relationships (Bowlby, 1988).

In psychotherapy, the CCRT can be identified not only from the REs that the patient tells regarding interactions with meaningful others outside of therapy but also from REs that occur in therapy between the patient and therapist. According to Luborsky and Crits-Christoph (1998), identifying the CCRT components that play out in the session with the therapist provides a reliable way of formulating the transference. Freud (1912/1958) originally assumed that a central relationship pattern is formed in the early relationship with the parents; once formed, it is constantly "reprinted afresh" in the person's subsequent close relationships, including the one with the therapist. In fact, certain ideas are pervasive across narratives in therapy sessions, and this lends the greatest support to the concept of a pattern or schema that serves as a template, like the "transference template."

CORE CONFLICTUAL RELATIONSHIP THEME-FOCUSED THERAPY

In CCRT-focused therapy, the therapist listens to the relational narratives that the patient tells about past and current interactions with important people in the patient's life. Therapists may often need to help patients tell better stories to facilitate an important goal: that patients come to a clearer understanding about what is happening in their interpersonal interactions. Book (1998) provided insightful suggestions to therapists on how to help patients develop narratives, such as asking the patient explicit questions like, "What were you hoping would happen in this situation?" "What did you want from this person?" "What did you say or do, then what happened?" After extracting the W, RO, and RS from each RE, the therapist summarizes the most frequent of these elements across the set of narratives, with the highest frequency combination defining the CCRT in the case formulation. The CCRT provides the basis for the interpretive work in the context of a supportive therapist–patient relationship. The therapist listens for and responds to narratives concerning the relationship triad: current relationships, family of origin, and the therapist. The goals of supportive–expressive psychotherapy (SE) include an increased understanding of problematic interpersonal patterns, as well as mastery over these cycles. These two outcomes are believed to lead to change in symptoms because the problematic cycles maintain symptoms (Siqueland & Barber, 2002).

RAP INTERVIEWS AS A SOURCE OF
RELATIONAL NARRATIVES

Initially, the CCRT was identified only from relational narratives told spontaneously in psychotherapy sessions. Later on, Luborsky (1990) developed a specialized interview, called the Relationship Anecdotes Paradigm (RAP), designed to elicit narratives to identify the CCRT components in the same way as the narratives drawn from psychotherapy sessions. This method of interviewing enabled researchers to study narratives outside of the psychotherapy sessions and to study narratives in individuals who were not in psychotherapy, as we did in our study of second-generation Holocaust survivors.

The instructions for administration of the RAP interview are as follows: "Please tell me some incidents or events, each about an interaction between yourself in relation to another person. . . . " The accounts should be about *specific* incidents, not just amalgams of several incidents. For each specific incident, the interviewee is asked to tell when it occurred, with whom, some of what the other person said or did, some of what the interviewee said or did, and what happened in the end. The RAP instructions indicate that the event in the narrative "has to be about a specific event that was personally important or a problem to you in some way" (Luborsky, 1998, p. 110). The total time for an RAP interview, in which the interviewee is usually asked to tell 10 of these incidents (REs), is about 30 to 50 minutes.

Barber, Luborsky, Crits-Christoph, and Diguer (1995) showed that the CCRTs obtained from the RAP interviews conducted before therapy started were quite similar to the ones obtained by independent judges from early therapy sessions. This finding suggests that, in studying relational narratives obtained from RAP interviews, we are simulating, to some extent, the kind of relational narratives that may be told in psychotherapy. In what follows we present the relational narratives that sons and daughters of Holocaust survivors told during RAP interviews; we do this to demonstrate the application of the CCRT framework to understanding interpersonal themes and patterns among this high-risk group. In addition, we explore the way intergenerational communication of trauma emerges as a central theme in these relational narratives.

RELATIONSHIP NARRATIVES TOLD BY
SECOND-GENERATION HOLOCAUST SURVIVORS

In developing this research project on offspring of Holocaust survivors, also referred to as the second generation, we were inspired by the position of the late Hillel Klein (1980), an analyst whose work and writings were influential in the understanding of the survivors and their children: "Research has shown that we can no longer speak of the transmission of psychopathology from one generation to the next, but rather of the transmission of common motifs, mythologies, issues, sensitivities within families and between the generations" (p. 553).

We chose to focus on common *interpersonal themes* and patterns manifested by the second generation of Holocaust survivors in adulthood. Our major assumption was that the questions that needed to be asked about the transmission of trauma were the ones within the realm of the relational world of the second generation (Bar-On et al., 1998; Sagi, Grossmann, Joels, Scharf, & Van IJzendoorn, 1999; Wiseman, Barber, Raz, Yam, Foltz, & Snir, 2002).

In previous research on nonclinical samples of the second generation, it has been reported that "when the participants were debriefed of the findings that showed that they scored in the normal range, they indicated that they *did* suffer from emotional difficulties, which they ascribed to their being offspring of Holocaust survivors, yet the questionnaire was irrelevant to their specific problems" (Blumenthal, 1981, cited in Rieck, 1994, p. 650). Our contention was that by studying the interpersonal themes using the CCRT method we will be able to reveal such difficulties and sensitivities as experienced by the second generation. Thinking over vivid examples of the narratives told to us by second-generation patients, clinical case studies we have read (Wardi, 1992), stories in books written about the experience of the second generation (Grossman, 1986; Semel, 1985), and movies (*Because of That War*; Ben-Dor-Niv, 1988), we suggested that the CCRT method would be a unique way to remain close to the narrators' personal experiences and would be highly relevant to clinical practice.

The relational narratives, told by sons and daughters of mothers who were survivors of Nazi concentration camps, were collected as part of our study on interpersonal patterns in a nonclinical sample of second-generation Holocaust survivors (for information on the process of recruitment and details on the sample, see Wiseman et al., 2002). Judges that were trained in the CCRT method rated these narratives. The judges described the main wishes, responses from other, and responses of self using their own words (i.e., tailor-made method) and using the set of standard categories developed for research purposes (Barber, Crits-Christoph, & Luborsky, 1998). In what follows, the relational narratives of two women are presented together with the judges' CCRT tailor-made descriptors and formulation.

The Thirst Story

In the RAP interview, Hanna, in her early 40s, married, and a mother of four children, told the following RE with mother:

Hanna: I remember once, I was a little girl, don't remember how old, 8, 9, 10, and *I was very thirsty* in the kitchen and my mother was busy with something, and *she did not want to give me a drink.* And, I stood there and made all the possible faces, with all the "poor me" in the world in order that she will give me water. I imagine that in the end she gave me (water), but I remember that I stood and I did like this (moves her lips to demonstrate to the interviewer) *with my mouth,* in order *that she will understand that I am very thirsty.* I presume that in the end, she did give me (to drink), but it is interesting that I don't remember that, but instead I remember the part of standing there, asking for it, and I remember that *she got mad at me,* I don't remember the part that she brought me the glass of water.

Interviewer: Do you remember how you felt in this situation with mother?

Hanna: *I don't remember being hurt,* or something like that. I just simply really wanted to drink, maybe *I even wanted more to annoy her* in that I stood there, and maybe *I wanted to pull for a madder response from her.* I don't . . . don't remember myself as pitiful. I remember *I always wanted to stand on my own* and I never dare to do so with my mother. There is no such thing as to say NO or something like that, that nowadays kids say. But that I would say to my mother NO, *that word never came out of my mouth,* never with my mother.

Analysis of Narrative of the Thirst Story

Analysis of the thirst story using CCRT follows.

- *Wishes*: Hanna's primary wishes are to get from her mother what she wants and needs, to get attention and to be responded to by her mother. Her secondary wishes are to annoy her mother, to defy her and to assert herself.
- *Responses from other*: Her mother is perceived as rejecting, not understanding Hanna, and being annoyed and irritable.
- *Responses of self*: Hanna feels not responded to, ignored, and as a result, she tries to annoy her mother on purpose.

In a way that is perhaps symbolic to their relationship, the narrative begins with a busy mother and a thirsty daughter. This opening defines the major themes that are played out in Hanna's recollection of the interaction between herself and her mother. Hanna wanted a connection, a response, and to be attended to; however, Hanna perceived the response of her mother to this wish as ignoring and later being annoyed with Hanna. In response, Hanna intensified her attempt to get what she wanted (to have her mother give her a drink of water), even to the point of desiring conflict with her mother, if only to have some contact between them. Hanna stated that she was *not hurt* and that she did not feel pitiful. The meaning she seems to give this interaction centers around the themes of power, autonomy, and separation more than the themes of intimacy, relatedness, and closeness.

The Guilt Story

Sarah, in her early 40s, is married and has three children. She told of an episode that appears to be at first rather ordinary but then evolves into a narrative that seems to point to deeper meanings concerning her experience with her mother.

> *Sarah:* My mother was really all these years a homemaker. We didn't really have heart to heart conversations or things like that. *Mother was always very closed*, did not tell, had great difficulty to talk about the . . . all this area, mother was really a child in the Holocaust. And it . . . *bothered her a lot, for example, that I am not neat, but I told her, you clean up after me all the time, how do you want me to . . . you don't give me the opportunity, you say do this, and you immediately run and do it yourself.* So it turned out that she once got from the Germans, she got an additional portion of food near her bed, there in the (concentration) camp, she found another . . . she found some, I don't know, some kind of piece of cloth and put it on some piece of wood, there they had some box instead of a table, and she put it like a table cloth and she also found a flower and put it . . . and for this she got from the Germans a reward, another portion of food. It could be, I always thought to myself, that maybe it imprinted on her, that this issue of being organized and clean is so very important for her. *I thought maybe this is a part that influenced her,* to be tidy and everything in its place, "balabosta A+" [balabosta is a Yiddish word for perfect and competent homemaker]. Something that I can't say for myself.

> *Interviewer:* What does this leave you with, with what kind of feeling, that mother tells you that you are so messy, and you tell her you actually don't allow me to. . . .

> *Sarah:* You see, *I had for many years feelings of guilt toward my mother,* in all kinds of ways, that I can NOT live her world. It is hard for me, it is not me that lives her world.

And she really, it is hard to explain this. She does tell many times about her childhood, how she used to run and was very mischievous . . . mother until not long ago was very active and went and came and ran, nothing was difficult for her. Yes, I know for a long time I had feelings of guilt toward my mother, that I don't do enough and I don't listen to what she tells me to do, but I learned to overcome it, because I can NOT live all the time with this kind of feeling, of guilt. I am not guilty for what happened to her, *it is not my fault*. It took me really a lot of time to get free of it, I am not sure that I am free of it totally, that is the truth, because every time I think what a difficult life she had and how difficult it was for her and how much she suffered it really is a very unpleasant feeling, that if you don't do what she asks, or if you are hurting her in a certain thing, it is very hard for her after this. You feel that you are hurting the . . . I don't know how to explain it. *She is very vulnerable, and it is difficult for me with this vulnerability.*

Interviewer: *So you are like walking on eggshells.*

Sarah: Exactly. It took me many years to talk about this feeling that everything I do I feel some kind of feeling of guilt toward my mother. Maybe I didn't do enough for her, maybe I hurt her, but there comes a time that you really feel that I need to make a stop (to draw the line).

Analysis of Narrative of the Guilt Story

Analysis of the guilt story using CCRT follows.

- *Wishes:* Sarah's primary wishes are to be free of the burden of guilt, to create boundaries, to be independent. Her secondary wishes are to please her mother and to avoid conflict. The conflict is between the wish to appease and to make the other feel good, versus the wish to be independent and assertive.
- *Responses from other:* Her mother is perceived as critical, confusing, making demands out of her own needs (she demands neatness compulsively), and vulnerable. She is perceived as not accepting Sarah's independence and experienced by Sarah as demanding identification with her.
- *Responses of self:* Sarah feels guilty toward her mother, she avoids conflict with her, is cautious, and does not express anger. She attempts to make partial boundaries in her interaction with her mother, but feels that she is not completely successful in doing so and is left feeling ambivalent.

In this RE, Sarah's response of avoiding conflict with the mother appears to be related to her feelings of guilt. In trying to make sense of her experience with her mother, whose behavior she finds confusing (both demanding that Sarah tidy things up and at the same time doing the work herself), Sarah made a connection between her mother's behavior and one of the very few stories that her mother told her about her experiences during the Holocaust. Sarah held onto this rare fragment from her mother's story about her experience in the concentration camp. This is an example of how the parent's trauma is inevitably present in the home, even when it is not discussed directly (Bar-On, 1995; Krell, 1979). Because Sarah's mother rarely discussed her traumatic experiences and much is left undiscussable (Bar-On, 1999), this leaves much room for the daughter's fantasies about her mother's experiences, and the various influences these experiences may have had on her mother. This unknown part of the mother's past and the thoughts about it ("every time I think . . . how much she suffered") left the daughter feeling guilty. Sarah's experience of her mother as vulnerable made it too dangerous to oppose her mother, and out of identification with the mother's suffering, she was afraid to let her down and add to her suffering. This dynamic between the survivors and their children is further explored in our analysis of the communication patterns as expressed in the relationship narratives.

INTERGENERATIONAL COMMUNICATION OF TRAUMA: SILENCE, NOISE, AND KNOWING-NOT-KNOWING

What was the experience like for the child who sensed in the air that there had been a horrifying experience that he or she was not told about and that was not discussed between the adults and children? Not only did our participants grow up with parents who were faced with the almost unbearable possibility of telling their children about what they went through during the Holocaust, but they were also raised in a time when survivors were not encouraged to discuss their experiences. In the 1950s, the period when our participants grew up, the Holocaust was met with silence by the Israeli society at large (Bar-On, 1995; Shapira, 1997).

In studying interpersonal patterns among second-generation Holocaust survivors, we suggested that the way the parents communicated their own traumatic Holocaust experiences while their children were growing up was highly relevant to the interpersonal themes that can be found among the second generation (Wiseman et al., 2002). After we completed the first stage of analyzing the relational narratives that we collected, using the CCRT framework as the basis for identifying its three components, our next step was to examine the narratives in a discovery-oriented manner. A major theme that emerged from this qualitative analysis, which we felt was only hinted at with the CCRT framework, referred broadly to the intergenerational communication of trauma.

In this further analysis of the relationship narratives, we became aware that the "wordless" interpersonal space was somehow expressed in the narratives of the second generation concerning their survivor mothers. Occasionally it was the major theme of the story (this was usually the exception), but most times it had a presence that could only be detected after reading the narrative again and again. It was as if the narrator was telling the story without paying attention to the communication difficulties that played out in the narrated relationship episode. Indeed, not saying in words, not telling, not expressing, and not knowing seemed to be a given in the story.

Returning to Hanna's thirst story, we identified a theme we called *without words*. In recounting this episode, Hanna demonstrated to the interviewer the way she made faces at her mother. Focusing on the communication theme, what is most idiosyncratic in this story of thirst is the way Hanna expressed her need without words, with her mouth, and with facial expressions, as if she did not have a voice to express her needs. Instead, it appears that the nonverbal channel was the only one available to her concerning her need to be taken care of and nurtured by her mother. Memories of wanting help and wanting to be nurtured have prevailed in the narratives told about encounters with parents during childhood (Thorne, 1995). Hanna, however, could not voice her need, and wanted her mother to respond and to understand her, so she spoke "sign language," which was expressed with her mouth. When asked about her feelings, Hanna denied feeling hurt and said she even wanted to annoy her mother on purpose. This wish to annoy her mother is followed by speaking about her wish to assert herself with her mother, a central wish in the narratives of the second generation. However, examining the communication theme further, it is interesting that while talking about how she did not dare to say no to her mother, she returned to the mouth—"that I would say NO to my mother NO, that word never came out of my mouth, never with my mother." Hanna does not have the words to say what she needs and is unable to say no to what does not suit her in relation to her mother.

In recounting this remembered encounter from childhood, Hanna, unlike Sarah, did not mention the Holocaust in relation to her mother. However, one could speculate about an association between this story of thirst and the terrible experiences of thirst, hunger, and other basic deprivations that Hanna's mother experienced in the concentration camp. Hanna might have been feeling as thirsty as a person who, because of extreme thirst, cannot utter a word. Moreover, she seemed to be feeling helpless and without a voice or the ability to fulfill her most basic needs, as a person who is at the mercy of others. Hanna's way of communicating her needs for connection and independence seemed to represent not only the idiosyncratic way these needs were expressed but also the dynamics involved in these core relational conflicts. Not having the words and not voicing her needs are part of the complex relational scheme that governs her interactions with her mother, and possibly with others. As to the way Hanna's mother communicated with her, we know little from this story.

Going back to the story about the hand drill, we can see that Shaul, unlike Hanna, told a story in which he knew exactly what he wanted from his mother (a drill), and he voiced his request out loud and insisted on getting what he wanted. He was surprised by his mother's unexpected refusal to get him the drill, because he was used to getting what he wanted from his mother. Shaul's mother said no to him but did not tell him why the noise drove her crazy. In other words, it is his mother who did not communicate fully her own response to his request. On the one hand, Shaul sounded frustrated in *not knowing why* his mother could not stand the noise. On the other hand, after realizing that what he wanted was related to his mother's traumatic memories from the labor camp, he appeared, in retrospect, to feel guilty that he had insisted on the drill. Thus, although Shaul's story related that he is in control and achieving his goals, his mother's Holocaust trauma left him feeling somewhat guilty and embarrassed by his insistence in light of his mother's painful memories, of which she tells him only later.

The drill also appears to have a metaphorical meaning. From a psychodynamic perspective, the wish for a drill can be viewed as a symbol of Shaul's wishes for independence and manhood. Yet the noise of the drill seems to stand in sharp contrast to his mother's silence about her traumatic experiences during the Holocaust. Earlier in the interview, Shaul explained that "mother did not mention the Holocaust, on the contrary she tried to repress these things." The drill story may stand out to Shaul as an outstanding event, later leading to his mother telling him about her war time experience that is directly related to the noise of the drill. Shaul did not give much detail concerning the context in which she later told him. He also did not ponder on why she did not explain it to him immediately. However, there seems to be some closure to the story, because he later understood his mother's surprising response. In spite of this, his feelings of guilt and embarrassment seem to suggest that perhaps he should have known without even being told. The theme of guilt in the narratives of the second generation appears to be related to the dynamics identified in Shaul's narrative: not being told, yet knowing somehow that there is something very painful in the parent's traumatic past that the son or daughter must be cautious not to touch.

The Wedding Story: We Did Not Know, She Did Not Tell

Zvi, in his late 30s, is married and has three children. In the interview he told of an episode with his mother that took place at his wedding (when he was in his early 20s).

Zvi: At our wedding, yes, my mother was all the years in bad terms with her family. I don't know the reasons, in principle, I don't get into all these things . . . but when it came to my wedding, we did it in a Wedding Hall. Mother is totally anti-religious . . . she doesn't observe Yom Kippur [the holiest day of the Jewish Calendar] . . . we didn't even have a Bar-Mitzvah [Jewish religious ceremony for boys when they reach 13, usually also observed by nonreligious Jews], nothing. When she understood that the wedding will be in a Hall, and there will be a Rabbi to perform the ceremony and everything, it was very difficult for her. When we arrived at the wedding hall, I saw her . . . I understood that she had taken a number of tranquilizer pills, and she was very much "out of it." I was very, very worried that there will be some kind of blow up with somebody, that things will get out of hand. The part with the Rabbi we managed to overcome, the part with her family we also managed to get over, up to the point of the music, which was actually relatively soft compared to what one hears these days, it bothered her. She went over to the band and shouted at them to lower the volume of the music. They tried to explain to her that it is impossible to play the music quietly. Until we managed to calm her down, but she was in such a state that it was not possible to talk to her.

Interviewer: Do you remember your feelings . . . ? (asking for the RS)

Zvi: I was terribly hurt that she isn't at wedding. The minute she was on pills, and all that, I understood that she is not with us at all. And the part that all the time I had to be afraid and worry, and watch and look out to see what she is doing, in order that nothing will happen, that there will not be some kind of explosion that will destroy for us the whole "simcha" [expression for a happy event like a wedding]. So I was very angry. . . . I didn't understand. Until this very day I don't understand the. . . .

Interviewer: What was it for you that she will be with you at the wedding?

Zvi: That she will be happy with us, that she will enjoy, that she will react appropriately, and will be with the whole family. I thought it would be an opening for some kind of togetherness with the whole family, but it didn't happen. . . . We didn't know anything about the Holocaust, we did not know about the whole connection. . . . She wrote a diary and she did not translate it into Hebrew, she left it in her mother tongue. Only when I was 18, at the request of my eldest niece (the oldest granddaughter), she did translate it for the first time into Hebrew. Only then did we understand and know what she went through. Until then we did not know anything, she did not tell us anything. We only knew that she was in the Ghetto.

Anaylysis of Narrative of the Wedding Story

In Zvi's sad story about his wedding night, his mother was described as disconnected from the event and from Zvi, who felt her pill-taking disrupted her ability to take part and be connected to him and the others around her. Because of his mother's unpredictable behavior, Zvi was anxious for things to go smoothly. The music, which is part of the expression of joy and entertainment in this event, was too noisy and unbearable for her. Zvi wanted his mother to feel happy and connected, but he was unable to get through to her, and there is a sense of a communication breakdown. In his mother, the wedding may have aroused certain associations that made it painful for her. Feelings of sadness and grief about the loss of loved ones not there to share the joy are often connected with such family events. For Holocaust survivors, such feelings of grief are amplified by the trauma of their massive losses.

Metaphorically speaking, the noise of the music in Zvi's wedding was unbearable for his mother, as was the noise of the drill for Shaul's mother. Both men try to understand their mothers' surprising responses in light of their Holocaust experiences. In Shaul's case, he described a very concrete connection between his mother's specific response to his request and her experiences with drilling during the Holocaust. Although he did not express much affect while relating that connection, he alluded to his feelings of guilt about not knowing the connection. In Zvi's case there are more feelings expressed, and as is evident from other parts of his interview, he felt more directly affected by his mother's trauma. What we found to be striking in reexamining Zvi's story was that after describing his mother's extreme detachment during the wedding, he spontaneously continued to tell the interviewer about his mother's diary. The mother did not translate the diary until her granddaughter asked her to. Up to this point, his mother's story, which was written in her language, remained unreadable and untold. His mother's detachment during the wedding and her miscommunication with the band recalls the language barrier between the mother's language of the past and her son, who does not know her language.

In each of the narratives that we presented in this chapter, there was some form of distressed and distorted communication. Hanna, as a child of 8 or 10, tried to get her mother to know that she was thirsty without using words. Shaul, at the age of 13, asserted his need for a drill, but his mother did not tell him why she would not comply with this desire; however, he found out later that the noise of the drill was related to her traumatic Holocaust experiences. Zvi, in his early 20s, could not make contact with his mother on his wedding day, and he was unable to understand her detachment on a day in which he desired togetherness and happiness. These distressed and strained modes of communication can be viewed in relation to these mothers' traumatic experiences. Our participants grew up feeling that there were "secrets" they were not allowed to know or that their mothers dared not tell them.

The silent style of communication, whereby from early on the child had a nonverbal awareness of the parent's trauma yet this awareness was surrounded with silence and a lack of factual information and emotional sharing of experiences, led to a sense of "knowing-not-knowing." Growing up to the music of knowing-not-knowing seemed to leave the sons and daughters of the second generation with a certain degree of unfinished business that was carried into their interpersonal adult life (Wiseman et al., 2002).

WORKING WITH RELATIONAL NARRATIVES IN PSYCHOTHERAPY

The CCRT framework is used in Luborsky's (1984; see also Barber & Crits-Christoph, 1995) supportive–expressive (SE) psychodynamic approach to short-term psychotherapy (Book, 1998) and is a major method used in psychotherapy research (Barber & Crits-Christoph, 1993; Connolly, Crits-Christoph, Barber, & Luborsky, 2000). According to Crits-Christoph and Connolly (1998), the most important difference between Freudian psychoanalysis and SE therapy is the explicit connection of recent versions of the SE model to the interpersonal school within the psychodynamic movement. This is characterized by a shift away from drives and instinctual wishes, with greater emphasis placed on motivations arising from interpersonal transactions.

One of the strengths of the CCRT method is that it provides a way to formulate the main issue that needs to be addressed in time-limited SE therapy. Furthermore, it provides therapists with a way of knowing what needs to be interpreted (Crits-Christoph, Cooper, & Luborsky, 1988). The main expressive (i.e., exploratory or interpretative) technique of SE therapy is the interpretation of the patient's maladaptive interpersonal themes (i.e., wish and response patterns). The SE model postulates that through self-understanding of the maladaptive CCRT patterns, patients are able to gain new, more adaptive ways of interacting with others, leading to eventual symptom alleviation. Barber, Crits-Christoph, and Luborsky (1996) have also shown that when SE expressive techniques are competently delivered early in treatment, patients' depression is more likely to decrease during the rest of therapy.

Much of the therapy work involves patients becoming aware and taking responsibility for self-defeating patterns (Siqueland & Barber, 2002). The therapist works with the patient to understand whether the expected response of other and response of self is still necessary or useful. What are most likely to change are the patients' responses of self—either because they become clearer about what they want, or they understand how others' interactions affect them. This understanding may either lead to change in the interactions themselves or to change in how patients perceive themselves related to the interactions. Responses of the self have both affective and behavioral components. Patients come to either feel differently, behave differently, or both. Patients begin to differentiate themselves from others' perceptions or question others' perceptions if it conflicts with their own experience. They learn to hold on to what they know or understand of themselves in the face of others' reactions. Research in SE treatment has suggested that wishes do not change significantly with treatment, maybe because some of the most common wishes are fundamental to the human experience (wishes to be close, to be accepted) or maybe because the therapies studied were relatively brief. However, responses of self do change, as well as perceived responses of other (Crits-Christoph & Luborsky, 1998).

CONCLUSION

The application of the CCRT framework to the study of the relational themes and interpersonal sensitivities prevalent among second-generation Holocaust survivors that was described in this chapter is clearly relevant to psychotherapists working with such second-generation adults who seek psychotherapy. For example, it is possible that the nature of the transference that will develop may include the components of the CCRT that were identified in the relational narratives with the parents. Specifically, the transference relationship may be characterized by the client's wish to be assertive (W), his or her perception of the therapist as controlling (RO), and the client feeling that in response he or she must avoid conflict (RS) with the therapist. The therapist's awareness, perceptiveness, and ability to listen and identify such relational themes can facilitate the understanding of intrapersonal and interpersonal in-session processes. Moreover, the therapist needs to pay special attention to the tendency of second-generation Holocaust survivors to avoid confrontation, because it may be played out with the therapist in a manner similar to the processes involved in "withdrawal alliance ruptures" (Safran & Muran, 2000, p. 141).

The communication aspects of the relational themes described in our study shed additional light on the intergenerational communication patterns that have been explicated regarding families of survivors of various trauma, such as descendants of Japanese American internment camps (Nagata, 1998), Dutch war sailors and resistance veterans (Op den Velde, 1998), and Vietnam War veterans (Ancharoff, Munroe, & Fisher, 1998). These studies suggest that the quality of familial communication (both verbal and nonverbal) about the parents' traumatic experiences may have major consequences for the inner and interpersonal life of their children (see Danieli, 1998).

The conflicts of the survivors of trauma themselves, between the wish to forget and the need to tell their stories (Herman, 1997), seem to provide the background music of both silence and noise in the lives of the sons and daughters growing up in such families. In working with such patients, therapists have to be especially attuned to what Rogers et al. (1999) referred to as the unsaid, unsayable, and the unspeakable. These authors' insight on the ways to interpret such discourse in interview data is also relevant to discourse in psychotherapy. As they put it, "The roles of figure and ground are reversed, so that what is unsaid, unsayable, and unspeakable emerge as figures to the ground formed by what is spoken, or the actual words of the transcript" (p. 92).

We suggest that therapists working with patients that grew up in families that had experienced extensive trauma need to be aware that such patients may experience difficulties in expressing their wishes in a direct verbal manner. This kind of interaction, where the patient has difficulty expressing his or her emotions verbally and directly, may play itself out in both individual psychotherapy and group psychotherapy with the members of the group. When these kinds of processes occur, the therapist's awareness of knowing-not-knowing (Wiseman et al., 2002) processes and their verbal and nonverbal expressions may enable the therapist to participate with the patient in a different kind of dialogue. In this kind of open dialogue, the therapist will help the client to make the nonverbal into verbal and to shift from not-knowing to knowing. In this way the client will experience a corrective emotional experience in his or her relational world.

REFERENCES

Ancharoff, M. R., Munroe, J. F., & Fisher, L. (1998). The legacy of combat trauma: Clinical implications of intergenerational transmission. In Y. Danieli (Ed.), *International handbook of multigenerational legacies of trauma* (pp. 257–279). New York: Plenum Press.

Barber, J. P., & Crits-Christoph, P. (1993). Advances in measures of psychodynamic formulations. *Journal of Consulting and Clinical Psychology, 61*, 574–585.

Barber, J. P., & Crits-Christoph, P. (1995). (Eds.). *Dynamic therapies for psychiatric disorders (Axis 1)*. New York: Basic Books.

Barber, J. P., Crits-Christoph, P., & Luborsky, L. (1996). Effects of therapist adherence and competence on patient outcome in brief dynamic therapy. *Journal of Consulting and Clinical Psychology, 64*, 619–622.

Barber, J. P., Crits-Christoph, P., & Luborsky, L. (1998). A guide to the CCRT standard categories and their classification. In L. Luborsky & P. Crits-Christoph (Eds.), *Understanding transference: The CCRT method* (pp. 43–54). New York: Basic Books.

Barber, J. P., Luborsky, L., Crits-Christoph, P., & Diguer, L. (1995). A comparison of core conflictual relationship themes before psychotherapy and during early sessions. *Journal of Consulting and Clinical Psychology, 63*, 145–148.

Bar-On, D. (1995). *Fear and hope: Three generations of five Israeli families of Holocaust survivors*. Cambridge, MA: Harvard University Press.

Bar-On, D. (1999). *The indescribable and undiscussable: Reconstructing human discourse after trauma*. Budapest: Central European University Press.

Bar-On, D., Eland, J., Kleber, R. J., Krell, R., Moore, Y., Sagi, A., et al. (1998). Multigenerational perspectives on coping with the holocaust experience: An attachment perspective for understanding the developmental sequelae of trauma across generations. *International Journal of Behavioral Development, 22*(2), 315–338.

Ben-Dor-Niv, D. (Director/Writer). (1988). *Because of that war* [film]. Israel: Manor Production Inc., Israel Motion Pictures.

Book, H. E. (1998). *How to practice brief dynamic psychotherapy: The CCRT method*. Washington, DC: American Psychological Association.

Bowlby, J. (1988). *A secure base*. New York: Basic Books.

Connolly, M. B., Crits-Christoph, P., Barber, J. P., & Luborsky, L. (2000). Transference patterns in the therapeutic relationship in supportive–expressive psychotherapy for depression. *Psychotherapy Research, 10*, 356–372.

Crits-Christoph, P., & Connolly, M. B. (1998). Empirical basis of supportive–expressive psychodynamic psychotherapy. In R. F. Bornstein & J. M. Masling (Eds.), *Empirical studies of the therapeutic hour. Empirical studies of psychoanalytic theories* (Vol. 8, pp. 109–151). Washington, DC: American Psychological Association.

Crits-Christoph, P., Cooper, A., & Luborsky, L. (1988). The accuracy of therapists' interpretations and the outcome of dynamic psychotherapy. *Journal of Consulting and Clinical Psychology, 56*, 490–495.

Crits-Cristoph, P., & Luborsky, L. (1998). Changes in CCRT pervasiveness during psychotherapy. In L. Luborsky & P. Crits-Cristoph (Eds.), *Understanding transference: The CCRT method* (pp. 151–173). Washington, DC: American Psychological Association.

Danieli, Y. (Ed.). (1998). *International handbook of multigenerational legacies of trauma*. New York: Plenum Press.

Freud, S. (1958). The dynamics of transference. In J. Strachey (Ed. and Trans.), *The standard edition to the complete psychological works of Sigmund Freud* (Vol. 12, pp. 99–108). London: Hogarth Press. (Original work published 1912)

Grossman, D. (1986). *See under love*. Tel Aviv: Hakkibutz Hameuchad.

Herman, J. (1997). *Trauma and recovery*. New York: Basic Books.

Klein, H. (1980). The survivors search of meaning and identity. In *Proceedings of the Fourth Yad Vashem International Historical Conference: The Nazi Concentration Camps* (pp. 543–553). Jerusalem: Yad Vashem.

Krell, R. (1979). Holocaust families: The survivors and their children. *Comprehensive Psychiatry, 20*, 560–568.

Luborsky, L. (1977). Measuring a pervasive psychic structure in psychotherapy: The Core Conflictual Relationship Theme. In N. Freedman & S. Grand (Eds.), *Communicative structures and psychic structures* (pp. 367–395). New York: Plenum Press.

Luborsky, L. (1984). *Principles of psychoanalytic psychotherapy: A manual for supportive–expressive (SE) treatment*. New York: Basic Books.

Luborsky, L. (1998). The Relationship Anecdotes Paradigm (RAP) interview as a versatile source of narratives. In L. Luborsky, & P. Crits-Christoph (Eds.), *Understanding transference: The core conflictual relationship theme method* (pp. 109–120). New York: Basic Books.

Luborsky, L., Barber, J. P., & Diguer, L. (1992). The meaning of narratives told during psychotherapy: The fruits of a new observation unit. *Psychotherapy Research, 2*, 277–290.

Luborsky, L., & Crits-Christoph, P. (Eds.). (1998). *Understanding transference: The core conflictual relationship theme method* (2nd ed.). Washington, DC: American Psychiatric Association.

McAdams, D. P. (1985). *Power, intimacy, and the life story: Personological inquiries into identity*. New York: Guilford Press.

McLeod, J. (1997). *Narrative and psychotherapy*. London: Sage.

Nagata, D. K. (1998). Intergenerational effects of the Japanese American internment. In Y. Danieli (Ed.), *International handbook of multigenerational legacies of trauma* (pp. 125–141). New York: Plenum Press.

Omer, H. (1993). Short-term psychotherapy and the rise of the life-sketch. *Psychotherapy, 30*, 668–673.

Op den Velde, W. (1998). Children of Dutch war sailors and civilian resistance veterans. In Y. Danieli (Ed.), *International handbook of multigenerational legacies of trauma* (pp. 147–163). New York: Plenum Press.

Rieck, M. (1994). The psychological state of Holocaust survivors offspring: An epidemiological and psychodiagnostic study. *International Journal of Behavioral Development, 17*, 649–667.

Rogers, A. G., Casey, M. E., Ekert, J., Holland, J., Nakkula, V., & Steinberg, N. (1999). An interpretive poetics of languages of the unsayable. In R. Josselson & A. Lieblich (Eds.), *Making meaning of narratives: The narrative study of lives* (Vol. 6, pp. 77–106). Thousand Oaks, CA: Sage.

Safran, J. D., & Muran, J. C. (2000). *Negotiating the therapeutic alliance: A relational treatment guide*. New York: Guilford Press.

Sagi, A., Grossmann, K. E., Joels, T., Scharf, M., & Van IJzendoorn, M. H. (April, 1999). *The Holocaust child survivors study: Attachment across generations, Part I: Some theoretical and methodological considerations*. Paper presented at the Society for Research in Child Development Biennial Meeting, Albuquerque, NM.

Semel, N. (1985). *Glass hat*. Tel Aviv: Poalim Library.

Shapira, A. (1997). *New Jews old Jews*. Tel Aviv: Am Oved.

Siqueland, L., & Barber, J. P. (2002). Supportive–expressive psychotherapy. In J. J. Magnavita (Ed.), *Comprehensive handbook of psychotherapy* (Vol. 1, pp. 183–205). New York: John Wiley & Sons.

Spence, D. P. (1982). *Narrative truth and historical truth: Meaning and interpretation in psychoanalysis*. New York: Norton.

Strupp, H. H., & Binder, J. L. (1984). *Psychotherapy in a new key: A guide to time-limited dynamic psychotherapy*. New York: Basic Books.

Thorne, A. (1995). Developmental truths in memories of childhood and adolescence. *Journal of Personality, 63*, 139–163.

Wardi, D. (1992). *Memorial candles: Children of the Holocaust*. London: Routledge.

Wiseman, H., Barber, J. P., Raz, A., Yam, I., Foltz, C., & Snir, S. (2002). Parental communication of Holocaust experiences and interpersonal patterns of offspring of Holocaust survivors. *International Journal of Behavioral Development, 26*(4), 371–381.

9

THE PLACE OF PSYCHOTHERAPY IN THE LIFE STORIES OF WOMEN IN HOUSEHOLDS WITHOUT MEN

AMIA LIEBLICH

A vast corpus of research debates what is and is not effective in psychotherapy. Patients or former patients fill out questionnaires about their experience, but much less has been investigated about how the experience of psychotherapy gets integrated into a person's life history. Furthermore, when people are asked direct questions regarding their experience in therapy, defensive processes may lead to idealized or highly critical responses. But how do people relate to their therapy in normal discourse when *not asked* about it?

This chapter presents the role of therapists, or therapy and its evaluation, from the point of view of women living in households without men, as expressed in their personal narratives. It is based on spontaneous references that women made to their experience in psychotherapy within the framework of a life story research interview and attempts to describe and analyze the place and nature of therapy in these women's storied lives.

Life stories that included such data were obtained in a research study of 36 women who live in unconventional families, loosely defined as a household without a man in permanent residence—in other words, women who are single, single parents, lesbian mothers, divorced, widows, or in commuting couples where the spouses do not reside together on a full-time basis. All the participants were middle-class Israeli Jewish women with a minimum of high school education. All but two were working outside of their homes (one is a retired teacher, the other a young woman currently supported by her son's father). In essence, these women can be defined as well-functioning individuals.

I interviewed each of the women individually, and presented my purpose as "collecting stories for a book about the 'new familiy' in Israel"—which was indeed my aim (Lieblich, 2002). The participants were asked to describe or define their present family status and tell the story about how they had reached this situation. Although no question was ever asked about the narrator's experience in psychotherapy, reading the transcriptions without predetermined categories, I became aware of the frequent reference to therapy or counseling in the narratives and the major role it played in the lives of some of these women. The individual narratives naturally covered the entire life span and contained many events, processes, and significant others. Featuring among them quite prominently were therapists, counselors, therapy groups, and the experience of psychotherapy. Only 7 of the recorded 36 life stories do not refer at all to the subject of psychotherapy or a similar process. In other words, about 80% of the interviewees, all well-functioning adults, have used some help from mental health professionals during the course of their lives. This help was significant enough to be remembered and presented in their condensed life stories, as narrated within the two to three hours of a research interview.

Therapy from the vantage point of these women is studied from several perspectives, starting with a content analysis, which revealed four major categories of utterances concerning therapy, followed by examination of the women's evaluations of their experience in therapy. Three cases of complex and long involvement in therapy are presented next, and finally, the chapter focuses on the place of therapy or support groups in the women's narratives.

FOUR ISSUES REQUIRING PSYCHOLOGICAL HELP

Approximately 60 sentences or paragraphs referring to therapy were present in the 36 interviews. Most of the 29 women who referred to therapy in their stories mentioned it more than once in their narratives. Rough categorization of these sections (see Lieblich, Tuval-Mashiach, & Zilber, 1998, pp. 112–140, on categorical-content analysis), some of them single sentences and some of them descriptions taking several pages, produced the following outcome:

1. The majority of references to therapy (21) relate to the experiences of motherhood (the decision to become a mother, transition to motherhood, etc.) and child raising. They refer primarily to seeking help or advice for their children rather than for themselves.
2. An almost similar number of references to therapy (19) concern personal development or identity issues of the woman herself. Some participants described a long therapy process, even to the present, and others focused on therapy during times of transition and turmoil in the past.
3. Couple relationships were the next frequent subject for psychological consultation (11), usually with family therapists. This topic came up at great length when past relationships that had failed were narrated.
4. The least frequently mentioned issue in this context was relationships with parents (7), mostly narrated as part of the past.

Other issues mentioned in the context of therapy were extremely rare.

As these content categories indicate, the kind of therapy most of the narrators experienced is broadly oriented toward various personal or developmental dilemmas and problems of living. In Israel, psychotherapy is still widely practiced in an intensive, supportive, and expressive framework. Whether using a dynamic or a humanistic–existential perspectives, most therapy in Israel is not symptom-oriented, as has been recently the case in the United States, where, according to Yalom (2002), psychotherapy is sometimes "deformed by economic pressures and impoverished by radically abbreviated training programs" (p. xv). Although a description of the cultural setting of Israeli mental health services is beyond the scope of this chapter, suffice it to say that public psychological services in Israel offer long-term individual or family therapy when needed. In addition, many middle-class individuals use private therapy for their problems and have long-term relationships with their therapists.

Another conclusion implied by the previous grouping of issues is that the central theme of therapy as constructed in the participants' narratives is the present and absent relationships in their lives. In other words, the participants weave therapy into their stories predominantly within the relational realm, thus accentuating the relational concerns that are conceptualized as important to women generally (Gilligan, 1982; Josselson, 1992; Miller, 1976, 1986). The emergence of this conclusion from the narrators' references to their therapy is nonetheless illuminating because of their immense emphasis on autonomy and agency in their lives, which is perhaps the most striking characteristic of this group of women (Lieblich, 2002).

Following are elaborations and demonstrations of the four content categories.

Therapy in the Context of Mothering

A wide span of ideas, opinions, and experiences expressed by the participants related to psychotherapy in the context of motherhood. Many explanations can be proposed for this phenomenon. Because all the mothers interviewed in the study did not have a full-time father with whom to emotionally share the responsibility of child raising, they seem to cosult the therapist on issues that in two-parent families would be resolved between the parents. In that sense, they seem to use their therapists as a substitute for missing partners.

Moreover, in a society that is still highly traditional in its family orientation (see Fogiel-Bijaoui, 1999), the women studied live more or less outside the norm. Some of them have consciously paved the road for alternative life styles and have few models to follow. Although sexual life and preference may be kept private, having a child, or even being pregnant, is immediately visible. Motherhood leans on public services—for example, baby clinics and childcare facilities. Unwed mothers may meet social criticism and may have to defend their choices. Divorced and widowed mothers may need therapy to help their children to cope with their losses.

Whatever the mother's life circumstances, going to a counselor or a therapist for the sake of the child may be an easier starting point, or "a cover," for the woman's more self-oriented need to consult a therapist. (Israel is a very child-focused society, and if people are perceived as dedicated to their children, their own shortcomings or deviations from the norm might be excused. All the lesbian mothers told me, for example, that once they had a child, they felt welcomed and accepted even in highly conservative communities.)

The following quotations represent these contents. First and foremost, several participants attributed tremendous importance to the professional input regarding their *decision to mother*. As Rina told me:

> As I was getting to become 40, I kept looking for a meaningful relationship with a man, but in order not to be under so much pressure with the biological clock ticking, I decided to try simultaneously to get pregnant from artificial insemination. This is something I realized after a long time and many hours in my therapy: There needn't be a correlation between finding a partner and having a child. My therapist has always encouraged me to mother and to try artificial insemination from the sperm bank.

After failing to become pregnant, another research participant, Lisa, a single woman, adopted a baby when she was 47. She said,

When I was going through the fertility treatments, I went to this social worker for conversations. . . . Suddenly she threw this new word into the room: "adoption"! I said I don't object even to this, I am willing to consider anything. I always knew that if I won't conceive a child naturally, I will look for one in the gutters, wherever people throw infants away (crying). I was certain that whatever happens, I would raise a child somehow. If only I could mother all the poor babies of the world!

So, to make a long story short, the social worker took out a book from her shelf, a book by a lawyer who wrote about adoption abroad, and she said, "Why don't you call him?" This was a crucial moment, I suddenly realized my time has run out, and so I made this phone call, and the next day I met this lawyer and this was it.

These narrators constructed their therapists, who were in most cases women, as sharing and understanding their deep needs to mother. At the same time the therapists are portrayed as highly liberal, legitimizing, and empowering the patients' choices and liberating [them] from traditional roles and life styles.

Two of the interviewees spoke about their decision to attempt to become pregnant after having a dream and analyzing it in therapy. One of them concluded her account of this therapy session by saying,

And so I realized that I was looking for a child, ready for a child. This therapist was actually the godmother! And she can certainly be proud of her godchild, as I told her many times since.

Once the child is born, mothers whose lifestyles are considered out of the norm in Israeli society often need some special counseling. Anne, a single mother of a 3-year-old boy (from artificial insemination), said,

Recently Yoram has started to ask me about his father. I expected this, since he is so well developed, and I went to a psychologist for several conversations regarding the matter. How and when do I tell him? As a result of our conversations, I understood that different answers are suitable for different ages, and in fact I will have to explain this again and again as he grows up. We decided that when he asked me where his father was, I would say that he did not have one. "Mommy didn't marry, because she didn't find an appropriate man, but she wanted you very very much, so she had you alone. You have no father, but you have a mother and a grandfather and a grandmother, and we all love you dearly." Indeed I talked to him exactly like this, and he seemed to be satisfied. This therapist also gave me a children's book to read to Yoram, it is all about alternative families, a very fine book.

When children of these "new families" grow older, other typical issues arise. The narratives abound with stories about the special needs of adopted children, learning disabilities, adolescence issues, and so forth, about which the mothers sought therapy for guidance and support.

Most of the stories conveyed the therapist as supportive of the mother's actions or the mother as willingly following the therapist's advice. Some of the narratives, however, presented a conflict between the two, in which the mother finally prevails, as exemplified in the following report of Dora, a single mother of a 13-year-old boy:

> Long time ago I told the boy that I had not married and I wanted a child very very much, so I decided to take it upon myself alone, and that his father was actually someone I had once been in touch with, for about a year. . . . There was a time he was very interested in meeting his father, but I used to tell him: "No, he is not a father. A father is someone who raises you, someone who supports you, who educates you. This man is a biological father only, that's a difference." I told him that when he grows up, in another year, another year, he might be ready to meet him. Maybe when he will be 18, as in cases of opening the adoption file.
>
> But you see, Gal was in therapy all these years, because of all kinds of learning difficulties. I wanted another person to be in the picture, someone who may be able to steer him, to be with him. . . . In fact I went to see that same therapist myself for a while. Later I stopped, but Gal has continued. At some stage this psycholgist told me: "Your son has to get to know his father, since he has a problem with his identity." He was sort of leading me towards allowing this meeting to take place. But I absolutely refused. I didn't want to allow it. First of all, because I think that he would not have been a good father. He would not do us any good! And besides, I would have been feeling as if this so-called father was taking advantage of me once more.

We see that in spite of the prevalent tendency among these new family women to seek counseling, they are highly confident in their intuitions, "knowing what was best" for their familes, and sometimes they used their parental authority and judgment to overrule professional advice.

Therapy and Self-Development

Issues of self development and problems concerning identity are central in the experience of all. In her follow-up research of American women, Josselson (1996) noticed of the 30 college-educted interviewees she followed from college to age 43, 18 had some experience of therapy by the time they were in their early 40s. They used therapy in their search for identity, to gain insight about their lives, and to find courage to make changes in them. This process may be even more essential for individuals whose life course deviates from the normative one, as in this study. Such deviations produce double effects: doubts and dilemmas concerning self-acceptance and conflicts with significant others about one's chosen life course—another relational issue.

Among the lesbians in the study group, the transition into, and struggle with, homosexual identity was always accompanied by some kind of therapy. A clear example of this can be taken from the story of Tammy, as she gradually realized that she was a lesbian:

> My anxiety didn't appear as long as this affair continued, but immediately after its termination. And let me tell you, it was an immense fear. I was 20 years old, and I sank deeply into some kind of darkness, in all respects. In fact there was a long period in which I was sort of asleep, in deep slumber, and had absolutely no sexual experiences of any sort. I would come and go like . . . as if life were utterly meaningless.
>
> And then, at the university, I started to see a therapist, and my treatment made it possible to open a crack in the wall which I built around myself. Somehow my treatment opened it, opened me, my identity, with all the terrible fears and anxieties I had inside. After a while, it enabled me to get to know Joan, and become her lover.
>
> At the same time, however, I also got involved with a man, and I remember the morning after, being really in panic, being physically so weak and alarmed, and running to this therapist to understand all this. . . . What was happening to me? Today I am still in therapy. I do have these anxiety attacks from time to time, but much more rarely. My therapy helped me to accept myself as a lesbian, and now I am more free to work on my professional identity.

Another quotation from Hana, a celibate woman, concerning her identity:

> All these years I didn't have any meaningful intimate relationship with a man or a woman. I used to think that they don't want me, and I felt rejected. Then, after years of therapy I realized that in fact I don't like anyone enough to develop such a relationship. I noticed how I am looking at other people . . . nobody attracts me really. My therapist helped me see that there is something inside me which would not let anyone come close to me.

Therapy is also referred to in the context of coping with the absence of relationships or loneliness, as reported by Liora, a divorced woman:

> In my therapy I did much work on the subjects of loneliness and aloneness. For many years I walked around with a big hole in my heart. I didn't believe it could be filled. When I brought it up in therapy, the response was: This is a hole, your wound, you have to accept it as such. Yet today I can say that I don't feel this hole as much as I used to. I filled it—not with my children, not with my career, but simply with me. I have finally become an independent woman.

Several women depicted their psychotherapy as "conversations with themselves," as part of their ongoing development or their attempts to reach integration in their lives. Like Rivka, a 70-year-old single woman:

> Normally I am quite good in deciphering myself. But in recent years I went back to therapy to really understand myself better. So many memories come back about my parents, my childhood. I am asking these basic questions: What am I, where did it all come from. Also about death and dying, you know. I think a lot about my sister's death, and that I am next in line. I used to be such a closed person, keeping all my feelings deep inside. Now they come out in therapy.

It is obvious in most of these quotations, whether we use the term *transference* or not, that the therapist her- or himself becomes a highly significant person in the participants' relational world.

Therapy in the Context of Couple Relationships

Seeking therapy appeared almost always in the participants' stories about their failing couple relationships. Despite what may seem similar experiences, the nuances of the narratives vary and attest to the rich variety of experiences in this context.

When our interview took place, Judy was in the process of couple therapy together with her son's father, following their recent separation. She said,

> We have not given up yet, we go to counselling together. This counsellor, she asks me: "Why did you do that, and when did this happen for the first time. . . . " And all I can say is: "How can I tell you, it is so difficult to be accurate, I feel like a person after a car accident. I hurt here, and there, everywhere."
>
> I still have very deep feelings for my partner, as well as much anger. I need to continue in this therapy process for myself, to see if I go back to him, and if not—to really be able to get out of this relationship for good, so that I will not look back upon this period of my life with pain and regret as I do now.

Naomi, a recently divorced woman, told me the following:

> At some stage I asked him to go together to a family therapist. After two or three sessions, the therapist asked to see Ben [her ex-husband] alone. Following this single session, the therapist told me that he saw no point in continuing the therapy. Today I understand that Ben revealed his affair to him, but was not ready to tell me about it. So . . . I am terribly angry at this therapist. Maybe if we continued to go to therapy together, something would have come out of it.

Similar stories in several other cases imply that the woman was willing to invest more effort in saving the couple but the men—both ex-husbands and therapists—failed to cooperate. This is, of course, the woman's own construction of the situation. For example, Ruth described,

> There was this stage, before the divorce, when I convinced my ex-husband to go to a marriage counsellor with me. At that time I already felt so bad about the marriage.
>
> We had a number of sessions together with this therapist, and then also separately. After the therapist saw my ex-husband for the third time, he told him not to come anymore. He realized that he wasn't ready to change or to invest in this marriage in any form.

Only in the case of Rachel was family therapy reported as having helped in preserving a relationship. Rachel and Dina went to a counselor when they decided to live together as a lesbian couple.

> You see, this kind of relationship stands or falls on the trust between us. I knew that Dina had many parallel relationships before the two of us fell in love. I wanted to be sure that everything would be clean between us from now on. Then we started to discuss the kind of family we might have, we faced many problems. I wanted to start a family right away, while Dina still had her doubts. At this stage we went to a family counselor for several conversations and that was it, we settled our conflicts and decided to go for it.

Relationship With Parents as a Subject for Therapy

The women who related to this topic usually referred to it as something that had happened in the past. Ella gave an extreme example:

> My mother was a depressed woman, real clinical depression, which eventually led to her suicide when I was 22. During my adolescence I suffered a lot from this. In high school I went to my teacher and told her that I needed some help. She referred me to the school counselor, who was actually a good therapist. I sat with her for perhaps 10 sessions, and talked all the time about my mother. The end of this treatment came about when I realized that all the problems were hers, and not mine, that I was really okay. I went home to my father and told him: "Mom is sick, how long will you ignore it! Will you take her to a psychiatrist?" While I, myself, stopped therapy then.

The death of a parent is another event that may lead to therapy, as accounted by Anat:

> And then when my mother died I was in turmoil for many weeks. My grandmother outlived my mother, and I was very resentful towards her. Not only because it was un-natural for her to live while my mother,

her daughter, died. . . . But I felt that she didn't care enough. I went back to therapy to sort out my feelings and actually managed to say good-bye to my mother and also come to terms with my grandmother. We had a very good relationship until she also died.

To sum up the content analysis, when all the former sections are taken into account, it becomes apparent that the narrators paint a picture of a dense relational world, which forms both the context and the subject of their experiences in therapy. Above and beyond the expression of the narrators' meaningful relationships with their therapists, they use the interpersonal realm of therapy mainly to work through their experiences in relation to their children, partners, and parents. Even the quotes that were categorized as therapy and self-development most frequently deal with relational issues—for example, Am I attracted to women or men? How do I accept loneliness? In other words, the narrator's identity and well-being are constructed and judged through her past and present relationships or dialogues, which take place in the context of conversations with a therapist.

THE NARRATORS' EVALUATION OF THERAPY

Being in therapy is a volitional act, and continuing to engage in it may be taken as a proof of its worth in the eyes of the client. Nevertheless, this is not always the case in retrospective accounts. We should consider the narrators' evaluations of their therapy in the context of their intense need for autonomy, which is manifested in their unconventional life choices and of their emphasis on their ability to cope with their problems by themselves, which is a major theme in their life stories. Some ambivalence toward therapy is, therefore, to be expected.

An example of a positive evaluation of therapy appears in Shiri's narrative and represents the major message of the participants in the study:

All these years I was in therapy on and off. It is a psycho-dynamic treatment, with a woman I highly appreciate. She helped me with my lesbianism, with having a child, as well as with many problems at work. I really believe in therapy. I think it is one of the most important things that I have done for myself in my life.

Several women expressed skepticism about the worth of therapy, however, as for example in the case of Esther, when she talked about the mourning period for her husband Yoni:

After my husband died, a psychologist told me that there is this theory that if you had a good relationship with your deceased husband, like if there were no unfinished business left between you, there is a rather fast process of mourning, separation, and recovery. I would soon be able to form other relationships, she predicted. It was sort of nice to be given such a theory, since it made me less guilty when I started to see other men. I even could see it as a compliment for my relationship with Yoni. But, if you ask me, I don't think that psychologists can help one after such a loss, they are not any better than a good friend.

Only three women expressed direct criticism of their therapists. This happened mostly in the context of couples therapy, when the therapist was unable to bring about any improvement in the relationship. As Naomi said, "I am terribly angry at this therapist. Maybe if we continued to go to therapy together, something would have come out of it."

Some more complex attitudes toward therapists will be demonstrated in the next section.

Therapy as a Life Engagement

Therapists played an unusually large role in the life stories of three of the participants of the study. Not only were these women in a long process of therapy—as were some other narrators—but they constructed their therapists as having a major role in their personal development and in their making crucial life transitions. In these stories, therapists were sometimes portrayed as supporters, and at other times, as antagonists.

Dalia, a lesbian single mother, is a woman who has been in therapy with the same female therapist on and off since her adolescence, for the past 20 years of her life. The therapist helped her, among ther things, to reach some harmony with her parents, to accept her lesbian identity (which Dalia conceptualized as "becoming a free person"), to make up her mind about getting pregnant, and to develop her educational stance with regard to her daughter. Dalia also credited her therapist with providing guidance about her ongoing academic studies and her professional identity. Following is one of the sections in which she described the place of her therapist in her life:

> I have this very same therapist for a very long time. We grew up together, you may say. Sometimes I come to her only once a month, it depends on my condition. But it is good to know that there is someone who knows me and my past so well, and can immediately understand what I am talking about. I often feel that my daughter, and our very fine relationship, is the culmination of all that I have achieved in these years of therapy. . . . No matter how often I see her, I feel that my contact with my therapist is alive all the time. I know that in the future I will need to discuss new issues with her. I feel that . . . it is immodest to stop my therapy, like some kind of pride on my side, as if saying: "Now I am fine, and that's it. I have all the answers! I can manage by myself!" Life brings us all kinds of surprises, or better to say "challenges."

I am not dependent on my therapist, I could have sustained myself without her. But she is already part of my life, you see. Talking to her is a way to see things, and to make things better.

Hana is a woman who has two children, fathered by a gay man who acts as an equally active parent but lives separately. When I asked Hana to tell me her life story, she felt perplexed about where to begin. After a few moments of thinking, she said, "Well, when I was about 20 I saw a therapist." This therapist was recommended by her mother after she complained about feelings of mild depression. The therapist helped her comprehend her needs and experiences as a child. She was extremely helpful in Hana's search for an understanding of her difficulties in forming relationships. She helped Hana to construct a narrative of herself as a woman with a mild neurological condition that had made her resent physical contacts rather than as a woman who had been rejected by men (see quotations from Hana earlier). About 45 minutes later in the interview, when the story about Hana's childhood seemed to be exhausted, I asked another question: "And how did you come to have such a family?" Hana repeated exactly the same sentence: "When I was about 20, I saw a therapist." This can be taken, obviously, as a strong indicator for the place of therapy in her development. As we will see, however, the input of therapy was not always been accepted by Hana.

The initial role of Hana's therapy is portrayed as helping her to overcome some of her stereotypical thoughts about families and about herself:

> Before treatment I thought that having children outside of marriage was completely illegitimate. I used to see this as much too problematic. I would never have considered it for myself. It actually started in the framework of my therapy. My therapist helped me change my views in many other respects as well.

As a result of her gradual self-understanding and empowerment through therapy, Hana reached a crucial stage of asserting her own will against her therapist. As phrased by her narrative:

> All these years we were talking about couple relationships. I was sure that something was wrong with me, because I didn't find love, and I didn't become part of a couple. I felt that I had no sex-appeal whatsoever. Gradually, however, I realized that I don't really want to be in a couple relationship. The question then came up: What do I want? And it became crystal clear to me that I want to have children. This was a great discovery! Furthermore, I knew that I didn't want to wait and wait and eventually be an old mother. I didn't want to start my family when I'll be 40. . . .
> I remember my therapist saying, "Very well, if you want chidren so intensely, and you want them now, let us explore this. Let us talk about

why do you want children, what do they mean for you, and why now." And you know what? I ran away (laughing). I said to her: "That's it, this is my red line. I will return to therapy when I am a mother." Indeed I left therapy and didn't return till my second boy was 1-year-old. You know why? Because I didn't want to talk about pregnancy etcetra, I wanted to do it! I didn't feel the need to explore my wishes, to clarify them, because I had decided this is what I wanted. And I refused to allow anything to spoil it for me.

It is very clear from the narrative that Hana's personal development, which was probably partly a result of her long-term psychotherapy, finally resulted in her ability to reach what *she experienced* as an independent decision, to be self-assertive and reject the suggestion of "interference" or "delay" by her therapist. She still needed to frame her decision in terms of being in opposition to her therapist, demonstrating the impact of her therapist as an internalized counter-voice she had to overcome. From the point of view of her therapist, she might have been seen as impulsive or acting out. This chapter, however, tries to remain on the phenomenological level of the narrators' experiences as told. It is significant that the relationship between Hana and her therapist withstood the break, and after several years she briefly returned to therapy to work out some of her issues concerning motherhood.

In the case of Nili, a major disagreement over her own wishes versus the direction advocated by her therapist led to the termination of Nili's long treatment. As in Hana's case, however, Nili's ability to assert her own will and implement her independent decisions grew out of many years of support from her therapist. Nili constructed her narrative as a tale of a married woman, who discovered her need for independence at mid-life. When Nili started to think about leaving her husband, whom she had married at a very young age, she encountered the opposition of her therapist.

> I was in therapy for many years. In the beginning, I didn't feel that I was really helped by the process, but I continued just the same. I felt some unrest in my life, I knew that I was not satisfied, but I didn't know what was what. I didn't exactly know what to expect from therapy. Gradually, in therapy I became aware that my life was much more interesting and exciting outside my home and family, than at home. Many people in my life were more significant for me than my husband. I was sharing my life, my most meaningful thoughts and feelings, with others, whereas my husband, who should be my closest friend, was becoming less and less relevant to me.
>
> When we discussed this in therapy, my therapist actually reassured me, she tried to calm me down. . . .
>
> But the situation between me and my husband became very frustrating to me, and I started to tell her that I was considering separating from him, that I wanted a divorce. At this stage she vehemently objected

to what I was leading to. She told me that she was unable to understand my decision, since I had a "prince" at home. (She had met us as a couple once, and this gave her the opportunity to meet my husband.) She said that he was a good man, and provided so well for the family—which was all true but not enough for me! Furthermore, she drew such a terrible picture for me about my future as a divorced woman, as if I was certainly going to fall into a black pit of sorts. Yes, I think she acted completely out of her own projections, and not as a professional should. . . .

I remember that I confronted her and asked if taking such a strong stand against her client is what a good therapist should do. At the end, I felt that I had to leave her. First I left her, and then I prepared myself to leave my husband. I was sure that this was the right thing for me to do.

As in the case of adult children who are able to separate from their parents, the autonomous actions of Hana and Nili may be conceived as the outcomes of their long and successful relationships with their therapists, which finally empowered them to act in their best interest by themselves. Although other interpretations of this twist of events may be proposed, the one provided is closest to the narrative as a whole and loyal to the narrators' own self-images.

Support Groups in the Lives of the Participants

About half of the women interviewed mentioned belonging to a therapy or support group at a certain stage of their lives. Many of them described participation in the group for a long period of time, especially during important transitions. They attributed a significant influence to these groups on their lives. The leaders or therapists who might have been involved in the groups were rarely mentioned, and perhaps some of those were indeed leaderless groups, but the group as a whole appeared as an important element in the women's narratives.

All the lesbian women who participated in the study belonged, at least for some time, to a lesbian support group. They talked a lot about the importance of the community—which is manifested as a network of support groups—for their lives, especially during important turning points such as coming out of the closet or making the decision to become mothers. All of the mothers among them mentioned belonging to groups for lesbian mothers, which they valued a great deal.

Mothers who have adopted children also tend to have belonged to support groups. Such was the case of Noa:

I followed my intuition, but I participated in many groups for adopting parents, which helped me. Sometimes it was for adopting parents, including fathers, sometimes for adoptions abroad, and sometimes for single adopting mothers, like myself. I used the groups to reinforce my intuition, in other words I often discovered that what I was doing was correct. But I took an idea, or even one sentence, from each one of these groups and I remember them fondly.

It is evident that these groups served as a source for new norms and expectations for the new family women. Moreover, groups often provided the narrators with the opportunity to shift from the position of help recipient to that of a help provider, a greatly empowering experience that does not happen in individual therapy.

Diane is an interesting case: an ultra-orthodox woman who is a single mother of three children (from artificial insemination), an extremely courageous life course decision within her community. Diane did not mention any therapist in her life story but referred to two groups of women who supported her during her difficult transition: a group of single women who intended to mother, which she found in the local paper, and the other a virtual group on the Internet. About the second she said,

> This was even more meaningful for me. It included also single women who had already had kids, some by adoption and some through the donors' bank. It was very encouraging to hear their stories and see the pictures of their children on the net. The fact that these women were sort of strangers made it much easier for me to disclose my feelings. This group was of utmost importance to me during the difficult stage of telling my parents about my intentions. I still belong to this group, and have recently encouraged several younger women to become mothers.

Ella provided another interesting example when she described how her women's support group sustained her after the sudden death of her mother. Her moving description closed with the following sentences: "I will always remember this. They made me feel better, that I was not so alone in the world."

Although several narrators presented belonging to a support group as a remedy for loneliness, some women considered themselves too individualistic or unique to be aided by such groups. When I had the impression that Dora was quite lonely with her two boys (one from her former marriage and the second from artificial insemination) and perplexed about her family situation, I inquired if she had considered joining a group for single mothers. Her response was,

> People often proposed all kinds of groups that I might join, but I have always refused. I didn't want to . . . because I think we are all very different. It is very superficial to throw all of us into the same basket, so to speak, of "single mothers." Each one of us has completely different life. I have a friend who is also a single mother, but her daughter has very warm and supportive grandparents, which makes it all so much

easier for them. So how can you compare our lots? My aloneness is totally different than hers.

CONCLUSION

Spontaneous references to therapy in the narratives presented in this chapter demonstrate the prevalence and significance of psychotherapy in the lives of modern, well-functioning women who live in households without men. Therapy gets integrated into the narrators' life stories primarily as a means to cope with relational problems of various sorts, as a positive experience leading to personal empowerment, and as an accessible service in the women's environment. Support groups are described as having similar functions, while also serving as a source for new norms and expectations for these new family women. Moreover, groups provide the narrators with the empowering opportunity to shift from the position of help recipient to that of provider of help and support to others.

On the whole, the narratives collected for this study indicate that the participants are deeply concerned with their relational world and use the therapeutic setting—which is interpersonal in its essence—predominantly to understand their relationships and improve them. Given what is known about the psychology of women, it is not surprising that relationships or their absence play a central role in the participants' narratives of their therapy experiences. Relating to men and women alike, in his recent book of advice for therapists, Yalom (2002) suggested, "Keep in mind that our patients generally come to see us because of their lack of success in developing and maintaining gratifying interpersonal relationships" (p. 23). In fact, however, people may use therapy also for overcoming symptoms and undesirable habits, for self-actualization and obtaining achievements, for improving their self-image, and other ego-centered goals—issues that are almost entirely missing in the discourse of the women in this study about their experience of therapy.

Having chosen—or been fated—to live relational lives that deviate from the traditional majority norms or roles, these participants were deeply mindful about their often innovative interpersonal relationships. Because a permanent adult partner is often missing in the lives of these women in the new family, they tend to use their therapists as partners, who may be taking the role of the absent significant other in their and their children's lives in terms of helping them through difficult family decisions and transitions or effecting their norms and values about mothering. Members of support groups, either real or virtual, can also be conceived as substituting for missing family members and for the often highly unsympathetic parents or siblings of the narrators, thus gaining significance in the narrators' lives.

The mere frequency of reports about therapy among the research participants—in about 80% of the cases—speaks for itself. This high rate is, however, difficult to evaluate, not only because of the small size of the studied group for reaching quantitative conclusions. Unsolicited reports about therapy in life stories are extremely rare as topics in professional literature. In Josselson's follow-up of adult women in the United States (1996), she reports 60% have been involved in therapy. In her words, "A passage through psychotherapy has become a rather common rite of passage" (p. 253). According to Helson (personal communication, April 2002) about 75% of the Mills sample of women (Helson, Stewart, & Ostrove, 1995; Roberts & Helson, 1997) had some sort of psychotherapy in their lives by age 61. These women were, however, older than the majority of the women I studied and had a longer time span over which to have had therapy. Moreover, at several points of Helson's longitudinal project the participants were directly asked whether they had had therapy. It is probably because of their particular family situation, which classified them as highly deviant within an exceedingly traditional and family-oriented society, that my group of participants consumed therapy more than the others.

Above and beyond its individual significance, however, psychotherapy for these women can be conceived as contributing to social change and reform. In the vast majority of the cases the process of therapy is not portrayed by the narrators as serving society—in making women adjust to traditional oppressive roles and life styles—as early feminists claimed most therapists do (Chesler, 1972). On the contrary, the therapists (in most cases women) were predominantly depicted as highly liberal people who empowered their clients to make radical changes and innovations in their lives or to live in harmony within their unusual family life circumstances. As a result, evaluation of therapy within these narratives has been, for the most part, clearly positive. In general, the role of therapy in the studied life narratives illuminates how therapy is situated and interwoven in the lives of well-adjusted adults and how it has much more to do with understanding the self in its relationships and cultural expectations than it does with overcoming symptoms or other pathological states in which therapy is usually framed in the psychological literature.

REFERENCES

Chesler, P. (1972). *Women and madness*. New York: Doubleday.

Fogiel-Bijaoui, S. (1999). Families in Israel: Between familism and post-modernism. In D. Izraeli, A. Friedman, H. Dahan-Kalev, S. Fogiel-Bijaoui, H. Herzog, M. Hasan, et al (Eds.), *Sex, gender, politics—Women in Israel* (pp. 107–166). Tel Aviv: Kibbutz Hameuchad.

Gilligan, C. (1982). *In a different voice*. Cambridge, MA: Harvard University Press.

Helson, R., Stewart, A. J., & Ostrove, J. (1995). Identity in three cohorts of midlife women. *Journal of Personality and Social Psychology, 74*, 1093–1108.

Josselson, R. (1992). *The space between us—Exploring the dimensions of human relationships*. San Francisco: Jossey-Bass.

Josselson, R. (1996). *Revising herself: The story of women's identity from college to midlife*. New York: Oxford University Press.

Lieblich, A. (2002). *Women in the "new family."* Tel Aviv: Schocken.

Lieblich, A., Tuval-Mashiach R., & Zilber, T. (1998). *Narrative research: Reading, analysis and interpretation*. Thousand Oaks, CA: Sage

Miller, J. B. (1976). *Toward a new psychology of women*. Boston: Beacon Press.

Miller, J. B. (1986). What do we mean by relationships? *Work in Progress, Stone Center Working Paper Series, 33*. Wellesley, MA: Stone Center.

Roberts, B. W., & Helson, R. (1997). Changes in culture, changes in personality: The influence of individualism in a longitudinal study of women. *Journal of Personality and Social Psychology, 72*, 641–651.

Yalom, I. D. (2002). *The gift of therapy*. New York: HarperCollins.

10

A LOVE STORY: SELF-DEFINING MEMORIES IN COUPLES THERAPY

JEFFERSON A. SINGER

Linda Harwood let Emily, the cat, into the kitchen and then let me in as well. She said that my hair looked different, "shorter," but I thought that she had changed little in the seven years since I had last seen her. Now 78 years old, her round, broad face, with silver hair to the tip of her shoulders and parted on the side, was still dominated by owl-size glasses, her alert and intelligent eyes looking straight out. Her voice had the whisper of her New England seacoast upbringing, almost faintly English in its intonation.

When Linda and her late husband, Charles, would talk about their home in our couples sessions, it was a moment of clear coming together— of an almost conspiratorial pride in what they had pulled off. Standing in the living room, with the Long Island Sound as the front yard and Spruce Island a rowboat's quick pull away, I knew that this place, built 40 years ago by Charles's own hands, stood as a symbol of their best years together. As Linda led me to an armchair and took her seat beside me, underneath a large framed photograph of two granddaughters in a studio pose, I noticed Charles's handiwork on cabinets with carved silhouettes of sandpipers and, down the hall, below the bathroom sink, seahorses as well. In the middle of the narrow hallway between the living room and the bathroom, an open spiral staircase, much like you would see on a ship's deck, rose to the second floor. Catching me admiring the staircase, Linda said, "He could do anything with his hands. Woodwork, wiring, plumbing. He had the mind of an engineer—always looking for puzzles to work out and solve."

In a photograph in the hallway, I could see Charles's face and Linda's, surrounded by their two children and their granddaughters. It was not the Charles that I had known. There was no mistaking his professorial bearing, the high forehead, the narrow gaze, head tilted upward, bearing a smile but hoarding the slightest reserve. All this seemed familiar, but it was the flesh that filled out his face, the weight on his bones that struck a chord of difference. The Charles I had known had weighed no more than 100 pounds. When he had called me in February of 1995, he had told me without qualification that he was dying of cancer. He had had cancer of the larynx, mouth, and jaw, dating back to the early 1990s, but a carcinoma in the pleura of the lung had recently metastasized. His body had grown too weak to tolerate any more chemotherapy and the remainder of his life was now measured out in months. He said this with an engineer's matter-of-factness but indicated that there was one loose end that he wanted to address: "I do not want to die with this large gulf that exists between my wife and me. After all that has happened, I want us to be able to feel like husband and wife again."

Realizing that I had probably stared at the photograph in silence a moment too long, I turned to Linda and reminded her of why I had called and the purpose of my visit. I wanted to write about a memory that they had shared with me several times in their couples work and one that ultimately I had explored with them as a means to close the rift between them. Before we talked about that memory, I wanted to be sure that my old scribbled notes from our sessions were accurate about the details of their lives and marriage. We settled into our conversation as she took me back to the first years of their relationship.

BACKGROUND OF THEIR MARRIAGE

Linda began,

We met at a USO dance in May of '46. I liked him from the first. He had an air of intelligence and wit. I found that very attractive. We were married that September. That first night he had three drinks. My father had done his bit of drinking and I told Charles that if he wanted to see me again, he better not be a drinker. After that, I didn't see him drink in my presence for years and years.

For Linda, who had grown up in rather sheltered circumstances, Charles's travels in the Navy during World War II and his polymath mind brought the hint of something exotic and exciting to her life. Linda's father had died when she was only 13, leaving her mother to take over his stone monument business. Linda had to help in every facet of the work, and soon she became the bookkeeper for her mother, whose own education had ended in the primary grades. Linda had little time for socializing during her teenage years, and her mother had done nothing to prepare her for the intimacies that occur between a husband and a wife. When Charles approached her on their wedding night, she became sick to her stomach. She felt in love and wanted to make love, but "emotionally, it didn't work." Charles was very understanding, and over time, they were able to consummate their marriage and find a rhythm to their love making.

Despite this progress, it became clear after many years of trying that they would not be able to conceive a child. They eventually adopted two children and loved them as their own flesh and blood. Their efforts to be affectionate and involved parents were in stark contrast to Charles's upbringing in the suburbs of Hartford. "His parents were cold as the wind outdoors today." Even years after her marriage, Linda could only call her mother-in-law, "Mrs. Harwood."

There are two striking facts about Charles's childhood. The most remarkable is his claim (which Linda verified with his mother) that he barely spoke until he was 13 years old. At first his parents thought he was deaf, and then perhaps mentally retarded, but all tests and his subsequent school record revealed a perfectly healthy and unusually intelligent (in fact rather gifted) child. Although there was not a formal diagnosis at the time, Charles suffered from what is now called selective mutism (American Psychiatric Association, 1994), a functional lack of speech that is not traceable to any form of medical condition. In retrospect, Charles wondered if the coldness of his home had led him to develop an inner resentment that expressed itself in willful silence. Once his mother realized his intelligence, she pushed him to achieve academically, which only made him pull more tightly into his shell of silence.

His release came when he applied for and received a full scholarship to a boarding school in Massachusetts. He left home at age 13, and only after he had arrived at school did his teachers realize his virtual muteness. Soon an English teacher took Charles under his wing and slowly coaxed him to speak. The two of them decided that they would set the goal of Charles entering a public speaking contest and this would be his public debut in the world of words. On the day of the contest, silent Charles rose to speak for the first time in front of his now wordless classmates. The first words of his speech were "My cat. . . . " The novelty of hearing his mouth discharge these syllables in front of his classmates so tickled him that he repeated them again and again, "My cat, my cat, my cat" as his classmates clapped and shouted. Winning the contest, he went on to become someone who was gifted with words, as a teacher, as a writer, and a conversationalist the rest of his life.

The other striking fact was that the same teacher who in one sense saved Charles also scarred him as well. As their relationship deepened, the teacher pressed Charles for physical contact. To encourage Charles to reciprocate, he would share alcohol with him and the two would drink and be intimate together. This relationship, based on a confusing mixture of kindness, alcohol, and exploitation, lasted for quite some time, although Charles never pinpointed exactly how long. One certain legacy, however, was Charles's love of Scotch whiskey, a taste he continued to cultivate in secret for the first 15 years of his marriage to Linda.

In those early years of their marriage, Charles returned to school after the Navy, earned a graduate degree in physics, and, after teaching in high school for a while, became a college professor at a local community college. They built their home over a four-year period, having found a vacant lot among the tiny summer cottages that were the only structures on Jenning Point in those days. Linda had known of the Point since childhood, when her father, still healthy and the center of her world, had rented a cottage for the family for several summers in a row. It was a coincidence that Charles's family had also spent some summers near by, but the choice to build a year-round home there seemed a natural one. When they were not working on the home, they took small trips together to Canada and later on to Ireland and England. They loved to travel together, planning, bargaining, and making small purchases to add to the home.

THE SELF-DEFINING MEMORY:
THE CAR RIDE HOME FROM THE HOSPITAL

As Linda raised the two children and Charles worked at the college, his late nights began to increase. He was teaching an additional class at an evening session in Hartford, but this commitment could not explain why he would get home at 2:00 or 3:00 in the morning. His breath smelled of whiskey and there was no longer any hiding from her that he was drinking. His great capacity for silence began to return, and he would stonily withdraw from her when the topic of drinking was raised. Betrayed and mortified by this secret habit, which was now becoming increasingly obvious to her, the children, and soon others in the community, she often expressed her resentment by withdrawing from him in bed. She could not stand the smell of his breath or the meanness that overcame him when he drank. Although there was never a moment of physical violence between them, the mutual anger and frustration drove a deep and bitter divide between them.

With the type of full-blown alcoholism that Charles displayed at this time, the next set of events was fairly predictable. Unable to moderate his drinking, his body requiring more and more alcohol simply to function at equilibrium, Charles started to show the effects at work. Year after year, his family, his employer, his physician, and various psychiatrists all stepped in to support Charles's forays into treatment programs and recovery. Meanwhile Charles did the best he could to keep drinking. From the late 1960s to the late 1970s, he went through 23 inpatient programs for alcoholism. Forced to leave his college position, and thereafter subsequent public school teaching positions, he was out of work for much of this period. Linda had attended a teachers' college before she had met Charles and took up a teaching position to support the family. Finally, after receiving a couple of DWIs and facing the possibility of jail, he asked to go to a long-term treatment facility. Linda saw the difference in his eyes and knew that, for the first time, he genuinely had given up and wanted to stop. He stayed at the facility for 18 months, and it was the longest period of sobriety that he had in more than 40 years.

Although the psychiatrist wanted him to stay even longer, Charles felt that he was ready to leave. During his time there Linda and he had made many strides in repairing some of the damage to their relationship. They had met weekly in couples therapy, and after 6 months, Charles had begun to have weekend visits home. They had resumed their intimate relationship for the first time in several years, and Linda had allowed herself a glimmer of optimism about the future. Right before his discharge, Charles had felt some resentment toward her because she had initially agreed with the psychiatrist that he should continue his stay. She was afraid that this time would end like all the others and did not want to take this risk. However, Charles was well enough to have regained some of his lifelong stubbornness. He told her that if she did not support his decision, he would not come home to her. He might even move in with a female patient he had met there. Fuming at this threat, she still relented and agreed to have him leave against the psychiatrist's orders. Linda had reached the moment in her narrative that was to become a central focus of our couples work.

> It was the day he was to come home. He was going to drive. He was starting to be stand-offish. Still feeling like I had taken the doctor's side. I don't know what possessed me because I'm not the type who would normally cuddle up to him when he drove. But I must have felt happy that he was coming home and I wanted him to know that. So I slid over across the seat and reached my hand to his. He pulled away. I pulled back then too. We rode in silence after that. From that point in 1978 right to when Charles called you in 1995, 17 years later, we were never physically intimate again. Oh, we slept in the same bed

every night, but we never held hands, hugged, kissed. I would have wanted to, but he seemed to have completely shut down. Out of pride, and anger, I suppose. . . . I did not pursue the matter either.

What struck me as I heard the memory again for the first time in seven years was that I had not remembered who had reached out to the other and who had withdrawn the hand. It did not seem to matter. They both knew how to build a wall that kept the emotion and words inside each of them, while the space between them kept its formal shape. They both assured me that they did not once in those subsequent 17 years talk about the cessation of their physical intimacy.

In preparing myself to talk more with Linda about the couples work we did, and how we referred to the memory, I recalled one more twist to their story. In 1984, the same year Linda's mother died, the same year she had a breast removed due to her own cancer, Charles started drinking and took up with another woman. He left their home for the first time in the marriage and lived with a lover. Inexplicably, he would still come back sober to the house each weekend and they would have Sunday dinner together. There seemed to be an understanding that he could not drink and live with her. After several months, for the first and only time in the marriage, she told him that she would divorce him if he did not seek treatment and return home. By the middle of 1985, he entered the hospital for six weeks. He returned to his home with Linda, gave up the lover, and remained sober for the last 10 years of his life. Their marriage resumed its uneasy truce, propped up by their mutual talent for New England stoicism and forbearance. They focused, as they always had, on the children, and now the grandchildren. Although their own relationship held little for each of them, they worked as an efficient team in reaching out as parents, as members of the Unitarian Church that they had grown to love, and as friends and neighbors.

As a couples therapist, I have seen great variations in marriages over the years, and I do not hold any marriage to one template. For some couples, the loyal partnership spanning 49 years, which the Harwoods had achieved, would have been sufficient. They seldom bickered, never raised their voices. Charles continued to fix everything around the house and comply with every request that Linda made for help. They ate their meals together and took their afternoon tea with the sunsets over Spruce Island. It might have been enough to preserve this peace as a hard-won victory after all the decades of destructive illness and estrangement.

This question certainly went through my mind more than once as I got to know Linda and Charles in the early meetings of our work. It was soon clear to me that for Charles, facing the last months of his life, his familiar stubbornness would not allow this separate peace to be enough. In our third session, when Charles spoke about the memory of the car ride home from the hospital in therapy, he made it clear why he wanted more.

> There was a moment on that ride, when if I hadn't been too pig-headed, still always keeping that I-know-best attitude, I could have seen that our marriage, our real full marriage, and Linda's love for me, was there, but I didn't. We pulled back and we haven't pulled together, not in that *way*, since. It was a stupid waste and I don't want that to go on, not with the time I have left.

Charles wanted nothing less than for Linda and him to be an intimate couple again. It did not matter that they were both in their 70s (see Zeiss, Zeiss, & Davies, 1999, for a discussion of older adults' sexuality), and it did not matter that he was physically compromised by his cancer. Whatever they could manage was good enough for him: If they could make love, that would exceed his wildest hopes, but he would settle for holding hands, hugs, kisses—anything that would bring the wall down between them.

SELF-DEFINING MEMORIES: THE USE OF MEMORY IN INDIVIDUAL AND COUPLES THERAPY

The divide, as represented in the memory of the car ride, seemed like a formidable boundary indeed. When I first heard this memory, it immediately struck me as a particular type of memory—what I have called in the past a self-defining memory (Singer, 1995; Singer & Salovey, 1993). A self-defining memory is a highly significant personal memory that expresses central themes or conflicts of one's sense of identity. It is a memory that can be characterized by the following properties. It evokes *strong emotion*, not merely at the time of its occurrence but in its current recollection. It is *vivid* in the mind's eye, filled with sensory detail, like a snapshot or video clip. We return to this memory *repeatedly*. It becomes a familiar touchstone in our consciousness that we consciously retrieve in certain situations or that returns to us unbidden (Salaman, 1970/1982). It is representative of other memories that share its plotline, emotions, and themes. Although it is the most central one in our collection, it is highly *linked* to related memories. Finally, self-defining memories revolve around the most important *concerns and conflicts* in our lives: unrequited loves, sibling rivalries, our greatest successes and failures, our moments of insights, and our severest disillusionments.

In my work as a therapist, I have often relied on clients' self-defining memories as important sources of dialogue and interpretation in individual therapy (Singer & Blagov, in press-a, in press-b; Singer & Salovey, 1996; Singer & Singer, 1992, 1994). work with Linda and Charles was the first time that I made a conscious effort to work with a couple through a shared self-defining memory. Over the past two decades, there has been a gathering literature in the social and clinical fields about the importance of shared memories to couples. As social psychology began to incorporate a concern with autobiographical memory into its models of social cognition and interpersonal processes (Ross & Conway, 1986), it inevitably asked questions about how couples shared or differed in their memories about important relationship events (Ross & Holmberg, 1990). Initially, this work looked at questions of accuracy and gender difference (females were more accurate and detailed in recollection, whereas males were more likely to revise and embellish their accounts), but more recently has turned to looking at how current relationship status affects the structure and content of these relationship memories (Holmberg & Veroff, 1996).

In particular, Holmberg and Veroff have looked at the degree to which married couples' shared memories conform to *cultural*, *subcultural* (ethnically or socioeconomically influenced), and *individual* scripts. They define *script* as "a knowledge structure that contains information about how things develop over time" (Holmberg & Veroff, 1996, p. 349). The formal definition of a script as a knowledge structure may be traced to the seminal work of Tomkins (1979) and the early cognitive science studies of Abelson (1981; Schank & Abelson, 1977). In a looser sense, dramaturgical models of relationships find their roots in the transactional theorizing of Eric Berne (1968), who wrote about the roles individuals inhabit in each others' lives and the games they play out with each other through relationship patterns.

Holmberg and Veroff (1996) suggested that cultural scripts are communicated through mass media, folk tales, places of worship, schools, and any other vehicles of cultural transmission. Couples may feel the influence of these cultural scripts on the recall of each phase of their relationship, from courtship to wedding to domestic life and child rearing. Cultural scripts provide narrative templates that prescribe specific roles for each partner, the sequence of actions, and their timing in the course of the relationship.

Subcultural scripts also prescribe patterns for couples' recollections, but these patterns are heavily shaped by the couples' ethnic, religious, and social class memberships. The courtship script for a traditional couple from India that came together through an arranged marriage will differ radically from a young couple in the United States who were under no formal proscriptions as to whom they might date and marry. These divergent scripts overlay the ways in which couples recall and retell their courtship experience.

Finally, individual scripts express the more specific personal beliefs and values of a given couple. Their unique concerns or ideological preferences influence the content and tone of memories recalled by the couple and provide the narratives a specificity that expresses the couple's personal, as opposed to cultural, identity. Across all three levels, Holmberg and Veroff emphasized how these scripts strongly shape how events in the couples' lives are recalled and also to a large extent *what* events are recalled. Couples' memories are not veridical accounts of their life experiences but rather emerge from reconstructive efforts, influenced by the transforming power of overlearned scripts in the retrieval process.

Narrative family and couples therapists (e.g., White & Epston, 1990) have extended these ideas to suggest that relationship patterns (not just memories of them) are constructed or constitutive texts (Zimmerman & Dickerson, 1996, p. 13) that express the meaning systems and power dynamics of particular cultures. According to Zimmerman and Dickerson, as couples tell their stories, the narrative structures and language they use invoke problems that are social constructions based in how their culture has modeled negative social roles and unhealthy intimate relationships. The solution to these problematic narrative scripts, as White and Epston suggested, is to help clients "externalize the problem" (p. 38) by seeing these narratives as outside themselves and capable of being controlled, modified, or discarded.

> We make the general assumption that persons experience problems, for which they frequently seek therapy, when the narratives in which they are "storying" their experience, and/or in which they are having their experience "storied" by others, do not sufficiently represent their lived experience, and that, in these circumstances, there will be significant aspects of their lived experience that contradict these dominant narratives.
>
> ... If we accept the assumptions made above ... we could also assume that, when persons seek therapy, an acceptable outcome would be the identification or generation of alternative stories that enable them to perform new meanings, bringing with them desired possibilities—new meanings that persons will experience as more helpful, satisfying, and open-ended. (White & Epston, 1990, p. 15)

This approach operates at Veroff and Holmberg's cultural script level. It emphasizes how individuals can liberate themselves from confining and often pathologizing cultural scripts that impose a textual rigidity on relationships. At the other extreme, and representing a tradition dating back to the beginning of the previous century, Adlerian therapists highlight the linkage of memories recounted in therapy to the expression of highly idiosyncratic and personally relevant life styles (Adler, 1927; Ansbacher, 1973; Bruhn, 1990). In this view, memories are most expressive of individual scripts, serving as projective devices that convey insight into individuals' current themes and interests, which have been woven into putative accounts of past events. In contrast to the heavy cultural determinacy favored by the narrative therapy school, Adlerians see these memories as indicative of an individual's basic convictions (Belove, 1980, pp. 191–192):

These convictions include expectations about life, expectations about people, the self and others as well as guiding intentions or conclusions about what it takes to live in a world so understood. This framework of basic convictions, expectations, and intentions is referred to as a person's unique, self-created style of life.

Belove applied this perspective to a sample of couples that recounted their first meetings (what he called "first encounters of the close kind" or FECK). Belove's contention is that these FECK narratives provided by couples convey their current relationship style or dynamics.

> Like early recollections and myths FECK stories seem to condense the main themes of a relationship into a kind of metaphor *a deux*. The expectations and remembrances of a marriage are captured in a living story, actively remembered, as if the partners were saying to themselves and each other, "For as far back as we can remember this is how things were between us and this is probably how they will be." (Belove, 1980, p. 197)

My use of a self-defining memory in my couples work with Linda and Charles was probably much closer to an Adlerian perspective than the social constructionist work of narrative therapists. Certainly, cultural and subcultural influences surfaced in the memory. When their effort at intimacy failed, they may have felt the oppressive weight of a cultural script that told them that sobriety should lead to happiness and a more intimate marriage. Similarly, their frosty distance from each other resonated with a subcultural script of New England reserve, Yankee stubbornness, and Protestant repressiveness about sexual matters. However, the self-defining memory approach, in sympathy with the Adlerian tradition, sees the memory as a compelling expression of the *unique* shared identity that this couple had forged out of their long-standing relationship. The memory provided a textual metaphor that allowed them to read in a quick and emotionally resonant way who they were with each other and how they interacted as a couple.

My working premise about self-defining memories is that their role as a touchstone for identity makes them relatively fixed in the personality. However, as developmental changes take place in the life course, the meaning or emotional significance of the memory can shift, increasing or diminishing its importance to the self. In series of studies (Moffit & Singer, 1994; Singer, 1990), I was able to demonstrate that the affective intensity of self-defining memories was a function of their relevance to the success or failure of ongoing goals that individuals valued in their current lives. A reordering of a personal goal hierarchy could be expected to influence the weight or salience of particular self-defining memories for an individual or couple, although the content or narrative detail of the memory might show little change.

In Linda and Charles's case, Charles's press toward intimacy in the last days of their marriage brought the memory of their car ride to the forefront of their shared memories. Its commentary on their failed effort at intimacy sounded a warning alarm that these new efforts were indeed risky and doomed to failure. At the same time, their repeated return to this exact memory suggested a kind of repetition compulsion, or unconscious need to return to this experience, perhaps in the hopes of overcoming and mastering its unresolved conflict (Freud, 1920/1973; Singer & Salovey, 1993, p. 43).

APPLYING THE CRITERIA OF SELF-DEFINING MEMORIES TO LINDA AND CHARLES'S MEMORY

To prepare for any intervention with the couple based on this car ride memory, I started by looking more systematically at the exact nature of the self-defining qualities of the memory. I began with what is a significant and perhaps hopeful aspect of their shared recollection. Unlike the couples in the Ross and Holmberg study, Linda and Charles were in agreement about the details of the memory, and even more, about its emotional significance in their marriage. It was the great stopping point—the moment of withdrawal that had yet to be repaired.

Indeed, there could be no question about the *emotional power* that this memory held for the couple. The pain registered in each of their faces, averted from the other's glance, barely able to look at me, signaled how much enduring emotion remained for them in recollecting this brief moment of their lives. Perhaps nothing was more indicative of its self-defining nature than the *repetitive way* in which they returned to this memory within the first few sessions. One of them would say, "That day we left the hospital . . . " and the other would nod, and complete the thought. By my own notes, I counted six times that they referred to this memory in our first three meetings. The memory had also retained a powerful *vividness*; they knew the exact date that it happened. They could describe in detail the moment when they pulled apart and the icy silence that filled the car for the remainder of the drive.

It was *linked in their minds* not so much to other specific memories but to blended memories of the multiple times earlier in the marriage when Linda had pulled back from Charles in resentment at his drinking, or to the times since the car ride when Charles had withdrawn from any tentative gesture that Linda might have made. It was linked to the hovering silence that had choked off intimate communication about sex or gentleness or forgiveness in the last four decades of their marriage.

Finally, the walls that they laid down in the car ride rested on foundations laid deep in the soil of *unresolved conflicts* carried over from their own families. For Linda, the loss of her father at 13 was an irreparable hole. Sitting with me in her home, talking now about his death some 65 years earlier, she still choked up. "I lost that sense of security. He made me feel safe. He could fix everything. I was daddy's girl, his princess. I don't think you ever get over it." Linda told me that she and her mother learned to endure. They took control and kept on, pushing the pain back to a discreet place that did not interfere with what needed to be done day to day.

Before Charles's hospitalization in 1977, Linda had given up any hope of having her husband back. He too had been someone who could "fix anything," but the years of alcoholism had worn away her trust in him. The loss of her father had returned as Charles slipped away. When he recovered during this extended treatment, she had gingerly let herself believe that she might regain her sense of security again. As they drove home, she let herself make that vulnerable reach from her side of the car. His rebuff shocked her to her familiar senses: *Losses never heal and this gap will not close*. She resumed her dignified solitude with Charles and directed her love toward her children.

From Charles's part, authorities—his parents, his teacher, doctors, psychiatrists—all had tried to shape his life and tell him when to speak, when to achieve, when to drink, and when not to. Slowly, over time, he had acceded to his wife's authority as well. His drinking had given her more and more control. Now when he had finally taken a significant step to impose some healthy structure on his own life, she had sided (at least initially) with the authorities again. In all his life, his two greatest weapons against the rigid withholding forces of power he had faced were silence and drinking. Having nearly followed drinking to its ultimate conclusion and now determined to abandon it, he had only silence left. *Fearful of having his nascent sense of free will crushed, he pulled back in muteness*.

There he sat, frightened of ever letting go of his fragile self; there she sat, having lost a piece of her self at age 13, determined not to do so again. There they both sat, separate from each other. And this is how they both sat in my office, wondering what to do to break this impasse.

USING THE COUPLE'S SELF-DEFINING MEMORY
AS A VEHICLE OF CHANGE

Because Linda and Charles had no trouble recalling and tagging this memory as a pivotal and self-defining moment in their marriage, the next question was simply, how could therapy make use of this memory to promote change in the relationship? In White and Epston's words (1990, p. 15), what might be done to assist this couple in the "generation of alternate stories?"

In my previous work with self-defining memories in individual psychotherapy, I had often relied on transference interpretations that identified the same interpersonal pattern captured by a memory as now manifest in the psychotherapeutic relationship. This vivifying of the memory through an actual relationship in the present was a powerful tool to help modify attitudes and behaviors that had appeared frozen when only glimpsed through repetitive retelling of the memory narrative. As the therapeutic relationship evolved to a stronger and healthier ground, the memory increasingly served as a touchstone for the way things "used to be" but did not have to be any longer.

In couples work, where transference is not the key agent of change, the therapist is more likely to use more active suggestions and interventions. In my work with Linda and Charles, which, given Charles's health, needed to be as active and focused as possible, I chose to use some gestalt techniques of reenactment and role-playing around their memory. My goal was to help them view the memory from a different angle and to provide them with an alternate ending that would open up new ways of thinking and feeling about their relationship and its current possibilities.

Let me return to my visit with Linda at her home on the Sound. When she finished recounting the memory for me, I asked if she remembered that I asked them to replay the memory for me but to take each other's part. She said that she did and that it had helped, but that the sessions before had readied them for that moment. In the meetings before, they had clarified the issues intellectually. Linda knew that Charles wanted them to grow closer again, that he wanted to be forgiven for his secrets and betrayals. She resented that he might ask this depth of good will from her. Was it not just another form of selfishness, a way that he could die with all the pieces to the puzzle in place, his life finally tied up neatly?

On the other hand, she acknowledged that she was frightened of reaching out to him, that opening up to him, while on the verge of losing him, might be devastating for her. But, she recognized, to lose him, without having him again, would seem like a final and unchangeable loss that she might continually regret. As she worked at articulating these questions and doubts, Charles remained constant in his desire to be close and more loving. Yet, just as he hid from her with alcoholism and silence, he now found ways of using the fatigue and discomfort from his illness to forestall their efforts at closeness. I would give them homework assignments of watching a video while holding hands or trying a gentle backrub for each other, but even these small goals proved difficult for him. He was able to see this pattern of resistance and connect it to his earlier methods of passive retaliation. As they each acknowledged their fears and their inadvertent ways of sabotaging their goal of intimacy, they would raise the memory of the car ride again.

In the fifth session, Linda entered the meeting in a state of guarded anger. In the waiting room at the hospital, Charles's ex-lover had briefly passed by. This old wound had been stirred up and it was hard for Linda to turn her attention to their goal of coming together.

As Linda and I recalled this meeting, I told her, "You still managed to do this work, though your anger was right there." With some wisdom, she said, "Perhaps that's why I could." That day I asked them to shift their chairs closer, more in a parallel position, approximating the front seat of the car. Once again, I asked them to tell me the memory of the day Charles left the hospital. I told them to close their eyes to envision the moment more clearly. Linda spoke first and set the scene of Charles at the wheel and her beside him. I asked the time of day, the speed of the car, the view from the window. Now it was time for Linda to make her move. At this moment, I asked them to switch roles—for Linda to imagine that she was Charles and Charles, Linda.

In what was growing increasingly more common as the months of his illness progressed, Charles spoke first and tried to imagine Linda's thoughts at that moment,

> I am so scared that he will hurt me again. I am so scared that I will trust him and he will disappoint me. I am scared that he will think he does not need me or want me any more.

Linda hesitated a bit to tell Charles's thoughts, but finally replied,

> O.K., I am thinking that Linda still does not trust me, that she doesn't think I am ready. I want her to know that I am better, that I can be a responsible person.

I then asked her to imagine Charles's thoughts as she reached over to his hand, "Charles is thinking—I mean I'm thinking—that she is going too fast. I'm not ready." At this point the real Charles did indeed reach over and take Linda's hand. She returned this gesture by squeezing his hand and allowing it to remain in hers.

Linda then asked that we move ahead in time, that we go to the point in 1984 when he told her that he did not love her and walked out. How could we rewrite that moment? Charles lowered his head and expressed his remorse. She warned him again of her fear of being hurt. He accepted this, but told her it was different now. Linda said how new this was to her and how she was not sure what to do with this. Although the session ended shortly after this, I felt that there was now an opening in each wall. They were looking more honestly at each other, looking with more accepting eyes and with more understanding. The anger remained (how could it could ever fully leave?), but it was tempered by other feelings, ones that were both much older (their first affection that had never fully dissipated) and newer (a fresh determination to give to each other in these waning hours).

SUBSEQUENT SESSIONS AFTER
THE MEMORY INTERVENTION

The following sessions gathered momentum. They began to take their homework more seriously, expressing more frequent signs of physical connection. In their third month of therapy, they ended a session with an embrace and brief kiss. Charles's health had stabilized and he had rallied enough that they planned a final trip in June to Norway. It would be a challenge for him, but he wanted this last time with her. He wanted to build a new set of memories that would leave a happier legacy.

There was one last way that they made good use of the car ride memory. In a meeting in April, their fourth month with me, they discussed Charles's anger at his doctor, who refused to pursue any additional chemotherapy. She had tried to defend the doctor's position and he had withdrawn in a sulk. They quickly saw the pattern outlined from the car ride memory now projected on to the current situation and took action through communication to preempt any distance that might develop. The memory had given them a tangible script and metaphor that could either spiral them into repetitive dysfunction or guide them toward more satisfying resolutions. Although it took practice, they were learning to take the latter course.

In the last block of sessions, they achieved three important goals. Linda was able to speak more and more openly about her fears, anger, and moments of happiness. Charles supported her opening up, and thanked her for willingness to do so. At the same time, she asked him to speak up and make his wishes known about his estate, his funeral, and his burial. She wanted him to help her manage the difficult times ahead; it mattered to her that he not withdraw and passively hand the control over to her. In a moment of some meaning for them, they confirmed that he would have the burial plot beside her intended plot. After all they had been through, they would lie next to each other in the end. Their third goal was to plan and carry off their trip to Norway. It seemed a far-flung hope that Charles could manage such an excursion, but he remained stubbornly determined to make it work.

And in fact, they did go. They made it to Lapland, rode the train from Oslo to Bergen, shared a reindeer banquet. They were very enthusiastic and proud of the trip, although Charles needed a great deal of rest and assistance throughout the two weeks. From June to September, I saw them every few weeks, but Charles's condition worsened considerably and he began heavy doses of morphine that often made him sleepy and weak.

By October, Charles could no longer come in to meet me, and Linda asked to have her son and daughter come to speak with me. I sat with Linda and her children and we talked about the plans for the funeral, memorial service, obituary, will, and cremation. Charles would have been pleased at how carefully the details were now in place. But even more, his son talked about the change that he had seen in his parents, a gentleness that they had shown to each other in the last few months. He spoke briefly about how he had talked with his father about these changes and his father's continued remorse for his earlier years. Linda heard this and realized that there were still more words they needed to say and resolved to talk more with Charles in the next few days.

Two weeks later, late in October 1995, Charles died in a hospice bed in the living room of the Jennings Point house, his family at his bedside. For every day of his illness, Linda had slept in the bed beside him. Only on this last day, when the hospice staff moved him to the living room, did she sleep alone in the bedroom at the top of the spiral staircase he had built for her.

A LOVE STORY

We had finished our interview, talking right through lunch time without so much as a break for a glass of water. I felt tired, but Linda somehow looked serene. I expressed my gratitude for her helping me to revisit her story, and I also hoped that we had not stirred up too many painful thoughts for her. Linda smiled and looked directly at me again.

> My life has gone on, though there isn't a day I don't miss Charles. There is a fullness that his death, the way he died, gave to me. I understand now in a way that I never could before, that love is what matters—not what we could have had—not the beauty of this home— but rather the spirit that built it.
>
> In the Episcopal religion in which I was raised, there was so much emphasis on the life after, on what we would become in the next life. I suppose I am pretty much a Yankee cynic about such things. In the Unitarian faith that I have embraced, we don't spend much time on eternity, we look at what we have and what we can do right now. The other day our minister, who is a former Catholic, celebrated with her woman partner the adoption of a young girl from China. All the members shared in the ceremony at the meeting house. When the prayers were finished, the minister and her partner turned to walk down the aisle holding the hands of their daughter between them. Their faces were radiant with happiness.

As I drove off from Linda's house that day, I thought about the complexity of her marriage to Charles—his drinking and betrayals, their bitter distances, the physical isolation that they lived with so long, and at the same time, their loyalty, their mutual commitment to their children and grandchildren, and their tentative willingness to come back to each other before his death. One could see Linda's determination to find a message of love in this story as a kind of denial of the pain she had suffered or a justification of the "wasted years" of their marriage. My acceptance of this version of her story could be my collusion in her self-justification or my own rationalization to find value in the therapeutic work we did together.

Over time, I have come to see the merit in all of these explanations of Linda's parting words to me, but I see the greatest merit in recognizing that they did indeed come back to each other and recommit to their marriage. To acknowledge this accomplishment is to see their relationship as a love story, but certainly not the simple romance of a fairy tale or teenage magazine. Love is often bundled with human weakness, resentment, and regret. It coexists with our ability to hurt, and because of the extreme vulnerability it exposes, can shift with the slightest provocation to cruelty or attack. It is neither always pretty nor always constant, but it can endure and it can harness its power to be a catalyst of change. And if we dismiss its ability to allow us at certain critical moments to transcend our own ample limitations as humans, we do so at our own risk. This may not offer the Hallmark tidiness that we would like to find in a love story, but it is the message that Linda and Charles ultimately extracted from their memory of the car ride home. By finally clasping hands, they acknowledged their mutual commitment and let the final journey of their marriage end in peace.

CONCLUSION

In this chapter, I extend my work on self-defining memories and their role in psychotherapy (e.g., Singer & Blagov, in press-a, in press-b; Singer & Singer, 1992, 1994) to consideration of a couple's shared memory. Just as individuals may possess self-defining memories that serve as a metaphor of an enduring concern or conflict in their lives, couples may also share a memory narrative that expresses an important theme of their relationship. In the case presented, the couple was in agreement about the details of the memory and their telling of it varied little from partner to partner. As the work by Ross and Holmberg (1990) suggested, variation in how a shared memory is recounted by each partner would also be a potential source of information about the partners' perceptions of each other and their relationship.

Thorne (2000) has suggested that personal memory telling may reveal different aspects of personality development, including levels of ego strength or maturity, motives of agency and communion, and willingness to present a particular portrayal of the self to the world. Similarly, the systematic study of couples' memories may reveal critical aspects of their relationship, including their attachment style, their characteristic portrayals of each other, and the way they portray their relationship to the world. Finally, as illustrated, using couples' memories as the basis for role-playing and other dynamic exercises may assist in reframing the particular meanings attached to these memories. Such exercises may encourage partners to make new or renewed efforts to seek different endings to familiar relationship patterns. The power of shared memories to invoke strong emotional responses in the couple can mire them in repetitive conflict, but it can also be harnessed to promote creative and committed change.

REFERENCES

Abelson, R. P. (1981). Psychological status of the script concept. *American Psychologist, 36,* 715–729.

Adler, A. (1927). *Understanding human nature.* New York: Greenberg.

American Psychiatric Association. (1994). *Diagnostic and statistical manual of mental disorders* (4th ed.). Washington, DC: Author.

Ansbacher, H. L. (1973). Adler's interpretation of early recollections: Historical account. *Journal of Individual Psychology, 29,* 135–145.

Belove, L. (1980). First encounters of the close kinds (FECK): The use of the story of the first interaction as an early recollection of a marriage. *Individual Psychologist, 36,* 191–208.

Berne, E. (1968). *Games people play: The psychology of human relationships.* New York: Penguin Books.

Bruhn, A. R. (1990). *Earliest childhood memories, Vol. 1: Theory and application to clinical practice.* New York: Praeger.

Freud, S. (1973). Beyond the pleasure principle. In J. Strachey (Ed.), *The complete works of Sigmund Freud, standard edition* (vol. 17). London: Hogarth. (Original published 1920)

Holmberg, D., & Veroff, J. (1996). Rewriting relationship memories: The effects of courtship and wedding scripts. In G. J. O. Fletcher & J. Fitness (Eds.), *Knowledge structures in close relationships: A social psychological approach* (pp. 345–365). Mahwah, NJ: Erlbaum.

Moffitt, K. H., & Singer, J. A. (1994). Continuity in the life story: Self-defining memories, affect, and approach/avoidance personal strivings. *Journal of Personality, 62,* 21–43.

Ross, M., & Conway, M. (1986). Remembering one's own past: The construction of personal histories. In R. M. Sorrentino & E. T. Higgins (Eds.), *Handbook of motivation and cognition: Foundations of social behavior* (pp. 122–144). New York: Guilford Press.

Ross, M., & Holmberg, D. (1990). Recounting the past: Gender differences in the recall of events in the history of a close relationship. In J. M. Olson & M. P. Zanna (Eds.), *Self-inference processes: The Ontario Symposium* (Vol. 6, pp. 135–152). Hillside, NJ: Erlbaum.

Salaman, E. (1982). A collection of moments. In U. Neisser (Ed.), *Memory observed* (pp. 49–63). San Francisco: Freeman. (Original published 1970)

Schank, R. C., & Abelson, R. P. (1977). *Scripts, plans, goals and understanding: An inquiry into human knowledge structures.* Potomac, MD: Erlbaum.

Singer, J. A. (1990). Affective responses to autobiographical memory and their relationship to long-term goals. *Journal of Personality, 58,* 535–563.

Singer, J. A. (1995). Seeing one's self: Locating narrative memory in a framework of personality. *Journal of Personality, 63,* 429–457.

Singer, J. A., & Blagov, P. S. (in press-a). The integrative function of narrative processing: Autobiographical memory, self-defining memories and the life story of identity. In D. R. Beike, J. M. Lampinen, & D. A. Behrend (Eds.), *The self and memory.* New York: Psychology Press.

Singer, J. A., & Blagov, P. S. (in press-b). Self-defining memories, narrative identity and psychotherapy: A conceptual model, empirical investigation, and case report. In L. E. Angus & J. McLeod, *Handbook of narrative and psychotherapy: practice, theory, and research.* Thousand Oaks, CA: Sage.

Singer, J. A., & Salovey, P. (1993). *The remembered self: Emotion and memory in personality.* New York: Free Press.

Singer, J. A., & Salovey, P. (1996). Motivated memory: Self-defining memories, goals, and affect regulation. In L. L. Martin & A. Tesser (Eds.), *Striving and feeling: Interactions among goals, affect, and self-regulation* (pp. 229–250). Hillsdale, NJ: Erlbaum.

Singer, J. A., & Singer, J. L. (1992). Transference in psychotherapy and daily life: Implications of current memory and social cognition research. In J. W. Barron, M. N. Eagle, & D. L. Wolitzky (Eds.), *Interface of psychoanalysis and psychology* (pp. 516–538). Washington, DC: American Psychological Association.

Singer, J. A., & Singer, J. L. (1994). Social–cognitive and narrative perspectives on transference. In J. M. Masling & R. F. Bornstein (Eds.), *Empirical perspectives on object relations theory. Empirical studies of psychoanalytic theories* (Vol. 5, pp. 157–193). Washington, DC: American Psychological Association.

Thorne, A. (2000). Personal memory telling and personality development. *Personality and Social Psychology Review, 4,* 45–56.

Tomkins, S. S. (1979). Script theory: Differential magnification of affects. In H. E. Howe & R. A. Dienstbier (Eds.), *Nebraska symposium on motivation* (Vol. 26, pp. 201–236). Lincoln: University of Nebraska Press.

White, M., & Epston, D. (1990). *Narrative means to therapeutic ends.* New York: W. W. Norton.

Zeiss, A. M., Zeiss, R. A., & Davies, H. (1999). Assessment of sexual function and dysfunction in older adults. In P. A. Lichtenberg (Ed.), *Handbook of assessment in clinical gerontology. Wiley series on adulthood and aging* (pp. 270–296). New York: John Wiley.

Zimmerman, J. L., & Dickerson, V. C. (1996). *If problems talked: Narrative therapy in action.* New York: Guilford Press.

AUTHOR INDEX

Numbers in italics refer to listings in reference sections.

Abelson, R. P., 196, *206, 207*
Adler, A., 197, *206*
Ahmed, E., 131, *146*
Ainsworth, M. D. S., 94, *107*
Alon, N., *5*
Amir, N., 89, *107*
Ancharoff, M. R., 167, *168*
Angus, L., 24, *24*
Ansbacher, H. L., 197, *206*
Anttonen, A., 78, *86*
Antze, P., 139, *146*
Argyris, D., *107*
Aristotle, 56, *64*
Attanucci, J., *107*

Bakhtin, M. M., 22, *24*, 119, 120,
    126
Balamoutsou, S., 23, *26*
Barber, J. P., 7, 153, 154, 155, 156,
    165, 166, *168, 169, 170*
Bardige, B., *107*
Bar-On, D., 121, *126*, 156, 160, *168*
Bateson, G., 133, 144, *146*
Bavelas, J. B., 105, *107*
Belove, L., 197, 198, *206*
Ben-Dor-Niv, D., 156, *168*
Benjamin, W., 16, *25*
Berne, E., 196, *206*
Binder, J. L., 153, *170*
Bion, W. R., 122, 123n, 124, *126*
Blagov, P. S., 195, 205, *207*
Bluck, S., 114, *126*
Bohart, A. C., 19, *25*
Bollas, C., 113, 123n, *126*
Book, H. E., 154, 165, *168*
Boothe, B., 23, *25*
Bowlby, J., 154, *168*
Braithwaite, J., 130, 134, 136, 140, 143,
    146
Braithwaite, V., 130, 134, 136, 140,
    143, *146*
Brickman, P., 142, 143, *146*
Brown, L. M., 91n, *107*

Bruhn, A. R., 197, *206*
Bruner, J., 5, 8, 16, 22, *25*
Bucci, W., 14, 24, *25*
Burbridge, J. A., 105, *109*
Bush, J., 133, *146*

Cain, C., 129, 138, *146*
Calhoun, L. G., 131, *149*
Caruth, C., 91, *108*
Casey, M. E., 91, *109*, 127, *170*
Chaney, R., 140, 141, *149*
Chesler, P., 186, *187*
Chu, J. A., 90, 106, *108*
Coates, D., *146*
Coates, L., 105, *107*
Cohn, E., *146*
Cohn, N., 34, *47*
Comte-Sponville, A., 30, *47*
Connolly, M. B., 165, *168*
Conway, M., 196, *206*
Cooper, A., 166, *169*
Cornforth, S., 23, *25*
Corradi, C., 52, *64*
Crenshaw, K., 50, *64*
Cressey, D. R., 132, 135, 146, *146,
    149*
Crits-Christoph, P., 14, *26*, 153, 154,
    155, 156, 165, 166, *168, 169*
Crocket, K., 13, *26*, 138, *148*
Cushman, P., 12, 18, *25*

da Venza Tillmanns, M., 13, *25*
Danieli, Y., 167, *169*
Davies, H., 195, *208*
Davies, J. M., 89, 90, 106, *108*
de Lauretis, T., 75, 75n, *86*
Diamond, J., 131, *147*
Dickens, C., 111, *126*
Dickerson, V. C., 197, *208*
Diguer, L., 153, 155, *168, 169*
Doan, R. E., 13, *26*, 138, *148*
Dwivedi, K. N., 22, *25*

Ekert, J., 91, *109*, *127*, *170*
Eland, J., *168*
Elshtain, J. B., 78, 86
Emmons, R., 144, *147*
Epston, D., 4, 9, 13, 22, 24, 25, 26, 27,
    138, *148*, 197, 201, *207*
Erikson, K., 102, *108*
Etter-Lewis, G., 50, *64*

Fabiano, E. A., 133, 142, *148*
Fine, M., 49, *64*
Fisher, L., 167, *168*
Fitzpatrick, J., 102, *108*
Foa, E. B., 89, *107*
Fogiel-Bijaoui, S., 174, *187*
Foltz, C., 156, *170*
Fonagy, P., 122, 123, *127*
Forrest, M. S., 37, *48*
Forward, S., 35, *48*
Fox, K., 134, *147*
Frank, A. W., 138, 140, *147*
Frankfurt, M., 23, *26*
Frankl, V. E., 106, 143, *147*
Frawley, M. G., 90, *108*
Freshman, M. S., 89, *107*
Freud, S., 3, 8, 89, 94, 95n, 105,
    108, 154, *169*, 199,
    206
Frieze, I., 94, *108*
Frye, N., 51, *64*

Garland, D., 134, *147*
Gee, J. P., 24, *25*
Gergely, G., 123n, *126*
Gergen, K. J., 16, 20, *25*
Gibbs, J. C., 133, *147*
Giddens, A., 12, *25*, 131, *147*
Gilford, P., 18, *25*
Gilligan, C., 91n, *107*, 173, *188*
Glenn, E. N., 50, *64*
Glick, B., 133, *146*
Goffman, E., 135, *147*
Goldstein, A. P., 133, *147*
Gordon, T., 68, 69, 84, *86*
Grand, S., 90, *108*
Greenspan, H., 121, *126*
Grossman, D., 156, *169*
Grossmann, K. E., 156, *170*
Guinzburg, C., 34, *48*

Habermas, T., 114, *126*
Hamilton, G., 51, *64*
Hanninen, V., 141, 142, *147*
Hardtke, K., 24, *24*
Harney, P. A., 91, *108*
Harris, N., 131, 133, *147*
Hart, H., 142, *148*
Harvey, M. A., 91, *108*
Helson, R., 187, *188*
Henry, S., 138, *147*
Herman, J., 106, 107, *108*, 121, *126*, 167,
    169
Holland, J., 91, 86, *109*, *127*, *170*
Holmberg, D., 196, 197, 205, 206, *207*
Howe, D., 17, *25*

Ibsen, H., 4

Jackson, S., 70, *86*
James, H., 4
Joels, T., 156, *170*
Johnson, T., 105, *107*
Johnston, K., *107*
Josselson, R., 4, 6, 7, 8, 9, 173, 176,
    188

Karuza, J., *146*
Katz, J., 135, *147*
Keskinen, S., 6
Ketcham, K., 92, *108*
Khan, M., 125n, *126*
Kidder, L., *146*
King, L. A., 144, *147*
Kirkwood, C., 70, *86*
Kleber, R. J., *168*
Klein, H., 123n, 155, *169*
Kleinman, A., 23, *25*
Koenen, K., 91, *108*
Komulainen, K., 72, 75, 75n, 77, *86*
Koski-Jannes, A., 141, 142, *147*
Krell, R., 160, *168*, *169*
Krook, D., 56, 62, *64*
Krumer-Nevo, M., 5, 6, 49, 50, 52, 59,
    64, 65
Kurtz, E., 143, 144, *147*

Lahav, R., 13, *25*
Lahelma, E., *86*

Langellier, K. M., 22, *26*
Langer, L. L., 102, 103, 105, *108*
Laub, D., 91, *108*
Laub, J., 132, *147*
LeBel, T., 145, *147*
Levitt, H., 24, *24*
Lewis, H. B., 131, *147*
Lieblich, A., 4, 7, 8, 9, 172, 173, *188*
Linde, C., 112, 124, *126*
Lofland, J., 140, *147*
Loftus, E., 92, *108*
Luborsky, L., 14, *26*, 153, 154, 155, 156,
    165, 166, *168*, *169*
Lynch, G. A., 13, *26*
Lynch, G., 23, *26*

MacIntyre, A., 119, *126*
Madigan, S., 19, 20, 21, *26*
Marcus, S., 4, 8
Marolla, J., 131, *148*
Maruna, S., 7, 138, 141, 142, 143, 145,
    147, *148*
Matza, D., 132, 133, *149*
May, G., 144, *148*
McAdams, D. P., 4, 18, 8, 9, *26*, 105,
    108, 130, 138, 142, *148*, 153,
    169
McDougall, J., 113n, 122, *126*
McFarlane, A. C., 94, *109*
McGovern, T., 144, *148*
McLeod, J., 5, 12, 13, 14, 18, 22, 23, *26*,
    153, *169*
Miller, A., 35, *48*
Miller, J. B., 90, *108*, 173, *188*
Milovanovic, D., 138, *147*
Mishler, E. G., 91, *108*
Moffitt, K. H., 198, *206*
Monk, G., 13, *26*, 138, *148*
Moore, Y., *168*
Morgan, O. J., 138, 143, *148*
Munroe, J. F., 167, *168*
Muran, J. C., 167, *170*

Nagata, D. K., 167, *169*
Nakkula, V., *109*, *127*, *170*
Nevo, R., 56, 59, 60, *65*
Niemi-Kiesiläinen, J., 68, *86*
Nousiainen, K., 68, *86*
Novick, R., 52, *65*

O'Reilly, E. B., 129, 130, 131, 139, 140,
    142, *148*
Ochberg, R. L., 68, *87*
Ogden, T., 125n, *126*
Omer, H., 5, 51, 65, 153, *169*
Ong, W. J., 17, *26*
Op den Velde, W., 167, *170*
Ostrove, J., 186, *188*
Overing, J., 22, *26*

Parry, A., 13, *26*, 138, *148*
Pasupathi, M., 105, *108*
Peavy, R. V., 12, 13, *26*
Penn, P., 23, *26*
Pennebaker, J. W., 22, *26*, 89, 105, *109*
Perttu, S., 69, *87*
Peteet, J. R., 142, *148*
Polanyi, L., 23, *26*
Polatnick, M. R., 50, *65*
Potter, G. B., 133, *147*
Prokhovnik, R., 78, *87*
Proust, M., 4

Rabinowitz, V. C., *146*
Ramsden, D. P., 7, 135, *148*
Rappaport, J., 129, 138, *148*
Rapport, N., 22, *26*
Raz, A., 156, *170*
Rennie, D. L., 19, *27*
Rieck, M., 156, *170*
Riessman, C. K., 23, *27*
Roberts, B. W., 186, *188*
Rogers, A. G., 91, 91n, 101, *109*, 121,
    127, 167, *170*
Rogers, C., 140, *148*
Ronkainen, S., 68, 69, *87*
Rosenfeld, J. M., 52, *65*
Rosenthal, G., 52, *65*
Ross, M., 196, 205, 206, *207*
Ross, R. R., 133, 142, *148*
Rotenberg, M., 139, 140, *148*
Roth, P., 121, *127*
Russell, R. L., 23, *27*
Ruuskanen, M., 70, *87*

Safran, J. D., 167, *170*
Sagi, A., 156, 168, *170*
Salaman, E., 195, *207*

Salovey, P., 195, 199, *207*
Sarbin, T. R., 16, *22*, *27*, 130, *148*
Schafer, R., 4, 9, 51, 60, *65*
Schank, R. C., 196, *207*
Scharf, M., 156, *170*
Scheff, T., 140, *148*
Schon, D. A., 52, *65*
Schuster, S., 13, *27*
Schutz, A., 119, *127*
Scott, J., 69, *87*
Scully, D., 131, *148*
Seagal, J. D., 89, *109*
Seidman, I. E., *109*
Semel, N., 156, *170*
Shapira, A., 160, *170*
Shapiro, F., 37, *48*
Sharp, B. D., 134, *148*
Shay, J., 102, *109*
Sheinberg, N., *109*, *127*
Sherman, L. W., 134, *149*
Singer, J. A., 8, 131, 133, 135, 140, 144,
        145, *149*, 195, 198, 199, 205,
        206, *207*
Singer, J. L., 195, 205, *207*
Siqueland, L., 154, 166, *170*
Snir, S., 156, *170*
Sollie, D. L., 102, *108*
Sorsoli, L., 6, 105, *109*
Speedy, J., 13, *27*
Spence, D. P., 124, 125, *127*, 153,
        170
Stafford, J., 89, *107*
Steinberg, N., *170*
Stewart, A. J., 186, *188*
Stiles, W. B., 22, *27*
Stiver, I. P., 90, *108*
Strupp, H. H., 153, *170*
Sutherland, E., 135, *149*
Suzuki, J., 105, *109*
Sykes, G. M., 132, 133, *149*
Sykes, I. J., 52, *65*

Target, M., 122, 123, *127*
Taylor, S. E., 131, 138, 143, *149*

Taymans, J., 133, *146*
Tedeschi, R. G., 131, *149*
Thorne, A., 161, *170*, 205, *207*
Thune, C. E., 130, 139, *149*
Tiebout, H. M., 143, 144, *149*
Tomkins, S. S., 196, *207*
Tuval-Mashiach, R., 172, *188*

Van den Berg, J. H., 11, *27*
van der Kolk, B. A., 92, 94, 95, 105, *109*
Van IJzendoorn, M. H., 156, *170*
Veroff, J., 196, 197, *206*
von Wyl, A., 23, *25*

Ward, T., 131, *149*
Wardi, D., 156, *170*
Watson, J. S., 123n, *126*
Wepfer, R., 23, *25*
Werbner, P., 86, *87*
White, M., 4, 9, 13, 19, *22*, 24, *25*, *27*,
        197, 201, *207*
White, W. L., 131, 132, 133, 138, 139,
        140, 141, 143, 145, 146, *149*
Whitebrook, M., 67, 72, *87*
Wigren, J., 90, *109*
Willi, J., 13, *27*
Wilson, B., 130
Winnicott, D. W., 123, 123n, 124, 125n,
        127
Winslade, J., 13, *26*, 138, *148*
Wiseman, H., 7, 156, 160, 165, 167, *170*
Wurmser, L., 131, *149*

Yalom, I. D., 173, 186, *188*
Yam, I., 156, *170*
Yuval-Davis, N., 86, *87*

Zeiss, A. M., 195, *208*
Zeiss, R. A., 195, *208*
Zilber, T., 172, *188*
Zimmerman, J. L., 197, *208*

SUBJECT INDEX

Abandonment, feelings of, 96, 98–99
Abstract individualism, 68, 69–70, 71,
    77, 85, 86
Abuse, domestic. *See also* Abuse, sexual;
    Childhood trauma; Therapy, of
    abused women
    toward children, 35–36, 55, 61, 71,
        90, 92
    toward spouse, 54, 59
Abuse, sexual. *See also* Abuse, domestic;
    Childhood trauma; Therapy, of
    abused women
    of children, 6, 92, 95, 101
    feelings of distrust, 101
Acknowledgment, in demonic narrative,
    32–33, 42, 46
Addiction, 131, 133. *See also* Alcoholism;
    Substance abuse
Adoption, 175, 191
Agency, and fate, 50
Alcoholics Anonymous, 7, 113, 129–130
    and identity transformation, 139
    prototypical narratives of, 141, 142
    and vulnerability theme, 144
Alcoholism, 111, 113, 115, 120, 131,
    139, 191–192, 194. *See also*
    Substance abuse
Audience, for narratives, 105
Autobiographical reconstruction, 130
Autobiography, 6–7, 15. *See also* Narra-
    tive, of one's life; Self-narrative

Behavior, abusive. *See* Abuse, domestic;
    Therapy, of abused women
Behavioral reenactments, 92, 93–94,
    96n
Birth story, 22
Buddhism, 30

Cambridge Hospital, 90
Childhood. *See also* Childhood trauma;
    Abuse, domestic
    truth of, 35–36

Childhood trauma, narrative and, 89–
    107. *See also* Abuse, domestic;
    Abuse, sexual; Therapy, of
    abused women
    abandonment, feelings of, 96, 98–99
    behavioral reenactments, 92, 93–94,
        96n
    disclosure of, 6, 7, 89–90, 92, 96n,
        106–107
    and future relationships, 93, 94–96,
        97, 101, 102, 107
    life stories, 92–105
    repetition of, 90, 92, 96n
    silence and, 7, 92, 95, 97, 100
    and telling, 103, 104, 105, 107
    traumatic symptoms, 106
    vulnerability, feelings of, 96, 97, 103
Chronic depressive personality, life story,
    19–22
Citizenship, 69
    women's, 77–78
Coherence
    in narrative, 4, 7, 122, 124–125
    in redemption narratives, 144
Communication
    listener involvement, 105, 106
    struggles with, 98–101, 167
Confession, in demonic narrative, 32–33,
    34, 42, 45, 46
Confrontation, identity, 134
Constructive fatalism, 38
Constructivism, 16
Content analysis, 172
Continuity, 75, 77
Core Conflictual Relationship Theme
    (CCRT) approach, 7, 151–167.
    See also Holocaust survivor
    narratives
    framework of, 153–154
    maladaptive themes, 166
    and relational narratives, 154–155
    Relationship Anecdotes Paradigm
        (RAP), 155
    Relationship Episodes (REs), 153,
        154

Core Conflictual Relationship Theme
(CCRT) approach, *continued*
responses from other, 153, 157, 159,
167
responses of self, 153, 157, 159, 166
therapist–patient relationship,
154–155
wishes, 153, 157, 159, 166
Counseling, 6, 17. *See also* Therapy
philosophical, 13
as "wounded healer," 140, 142
Couples therapy, 7, 8, 178–179, 182,
189–206
conflicts, unresolved, 200
cultural scripts, 196, 197, 198
life stories, 178–179, 182, 190–205
memories, use of shared, 195–199,
205–206
Criminality, 132–133145
Culture
and couples therapy, 196, 197, 198
and marriage, 80
and narrative, 5, 15, 21, 22
and sociodynamic therapy, 13
and therapy, 5, 15–19

Death, 94, 179–180, 185
Defect, shameful, 56–57, 58
Demonic narrative, 5, 29–47. *See also*
Tragic narrative
assumptions of, 30–33, 42
dualism within, 29–30, 43
eradication process, 47
life story, 41–47
major sequence of, 37
negative internalized parental voice,
34, 35
pschyodemonic narrative, 33–37
and skepticism, 34
vs. tragic, 38, 39, 40
Denial, 133
Depression, 42–43, 46, 131, 166, 182. *See*
Chronic depressive personality
Deviant affect-mirroring, 123n
Deviant behavior, 132. *See also* Redemption narratives; Self-narrative
confrontation, 134
false pride, 133, 135
rebelling against authority, 134
redemption themes for, 141–142

responsibility acceptance, 133–135
verbalizations and, 132–133
Disclosure, and recovery, 6, 89–92, 96n,
106–107
Domestic abuse. *See* Abuse, domestic;
Abuse, sexual; Childhood
trauma; Therapy, of abused
women

Ecological therapy, 13
Embeddedness, redemption theme of, 144
Emotions. *See also* Suffering
of abandonment, 96, 98–99
and abstract individualism, 69, 77,
85, 86
difficulty expressing, 98–100
grief, 164
love, 8, 20
needs of abuse victims, 97
pity, 39
self-interpretation of, 122, 123
and victimhold, 70, 78–83, 86
Environment
personal relationship with, 51
Epic form, 119–120, 121, 124
Equality and gender, 68–69
Evaluation, by therapy participants, 172
Evil, in demonic narrative, 30–31, 34, 36
Exorcism, in demonic narrative, 32, 34

Fatalism, constructive, 38
Fate, and tragedy, 6, 51–52, 62–63, 64
and agency, 50
defined, 38
Feminism, 187. *See also* Women's issues
and citizenship and motherhood, 78
and social inequality, 50
"First encounters of the close kind"
(FECK), 198
Flaw, fatal. *See* Defect, shameful

Gender. *See* Therapy, of abused women;
Women's issues
and equality, 68–69
Guilt, 159–161

Habitual narrative, 23
Hero, concept of, 6, 51

Heroines, tragic, 50. *See also* Women's
    issues
    and fate, 6, 62–63
    impossible choices of, 6, 60, 61–62
    ironic reversal of fortune, 6, 59, 60
    responsibility of, 63
Holocaust survivor narratives, 7, 167.
    See also Core Conflictual
    Relationship Theme (CCRT)
    approach
    hand drill story, 152, 162, 164,
      165
    interpersonal themes of, 151, 156,
      160
    guilt story, 158–160
    life stories, 152, 155–160
    silence of, 7, 161–162, 165
    thirst story, 156–158, 161
    transmission between generations, 7,
      156, 161, 167
    trauma of loss, 164
    wedding story, 163–165
Homosexuality, 177, 179, 180, 181–182,
    184
Hubris, and tragic narrative, 38–39

Identity. *See also* Narrative; Narrative, of
    one's life; Self-narrative
    defined, 139
    loss, 135
    and narrative, 77, 138
    and shame, 131
    and therapy, 4, 173
    and therapy, 176–178, 181, 182
    transformation, 138–139
Illiteracy, 53–54, 57–59
Independence narratives, 75, 76–77
Imprisonment, 134
    and identity loss, 135
    life stories, 135–138
    recovery advocacy, 145–146
    and shame management, 136–137
    stigmatism of, 136–137, 145–146
Insight, achievement of, 33
Interviews, 104
    Relationship Anecdotes Paradigm
    (RAP), 155

Key rhetoric, 72

Lesbians. *See* Homosexuality
Life stories. *See also* Narrative; Narrative,
    of one's life; Self-narrative
    of abused childhood, 92–105
    of abused women, 72–77, 78–84
    of alcoholism, 111–126
    of chronic depressive personality,
      19–22
    and couples therapy, 178–179, 182,
      190–205
    in demonic narrative, 41–47
    guilt story, 158–160
    hand drill story, 152, 162, 164, 165
    of Holocaust survivor children, 152,
      155–160
    and identity, 130
    of motherhood, 174, 175, 176
    narrating one's own life, 111–121
    narrator vs. protagonist, 112
    of parental relationships, 179–180
    of prison inmates, 135–138
    of self-development, 177–178
    thirst story, 156–158, 161
    in tragic narrative, 52–62
    wedding story, 163–165
Listener involvement, 105, 106
Love, 8, 20

Macronarrative, 23, 24
Manic defenses, 123, 124
Memories
    and reenacting, 92–95, 105
    self-defining, 8, 195, 198, 197–
      205
    shared, 195–199, 205–206
    of silence, 101–102
    use in therapy, 195–199
Meta-narrative, tragedy as, 49–64. *See
    also* Tragedy; Tragic narrative
    agency and fate, 50
    and impossible choice, 60–62
    life story, 52–62
Motherhood, 7, 77–78, 85. *See also*
    Women's Issues
    and adoption, 175
    life stories, 174, 175, 176
    and therapy, 173, 174–176
Mutism, 191
Mutual dependency. *See* Vulnerability
Myths, personal, 131

Narrative, 3–4. *See also* Childhood trauma, narrative and; Core Conflictual Relationship Theme (CCRT) approach; Couples therapy; Demonic narrative; Life stories; Narrative, of one's life; Redemption narratives; Self-narrative; Storytelling; Therapy; Therapy, of abused women; Tragedy; Tragic narrative
  concept of, 14–15
  demonic, 5, 29–37
  identity, 4, 67–68, 72, 75, 77, 138
  of independence, 75, 76–77, 85–86
  master, 5, 117–119
  oral, 16–19
  personal dimension of, 15
  relational, 154–155
  reconstruction, 141
  structure models, 14
  and therapy, 3–5, 13, 15, 22, 23–24, 140, 186–187
  in traditional, modern, and postmodern periods (exhibit), 18
  tragic, 5, 30
  types of, 23
Narrative, of one's life, 6–7, 15, 111–126
  ambiguity of, 123
  coherence in, 7, 122, 124–125
  control of, 116
  epic form, 119–120, 121, 124
  external vs. internal, 121–122
  genre mode, 119
  learning to construct, 116
  life story, 111–121
  narrator vs. protagonist, 112, 120
  novelistic form, 121
  psychic reality, 122–125
  reconstruction, 138–141
  redemption narratives, 141
  therapeutic, 118, 120
"Narrative feeding," 123n
Narrative in traditional, modern, and postmodern periods (exhibit), 18
Narrative structure models, 14
Narrative therapy, 3–5, 13, 15, 22, 23–24
Narrators, and therapy evaluation, 180–186
Neutralization theory, 132–133
New Recovery Movement, 145
Normotic trait, 113, 113n, 123n

Oedipus Rex, 39, 40, 58, 62
Oral narrative, 16–19
  vs. media, 16, 17–18
  types of, 16
"Other," concept of in tragic narrative, 39

Parents and parenting. *See also* Core Conflictual Relationship Theme (CCRT) approach; Motherhood
  central relationship pattern, 154
  death of, 94, 179–180, 185
  interpersonal themes of Holocaust survivors, 151, 156, 160
  life stories with, 179–180
  relationships with, 179–180
  therapy over, 173
Personality, 138
Personal story, 23
Philosophy
  Eastern, 30
  Western, 30
Philosophical counseling, 13
Postmodernism, 13–14, 16
Postpsychological therapy, 12–15, 22
  defined, 13
  and postmodernism, 13–14
Poststructuralism, 16
Poverty, 51. *See also* Women's issues
  and women, 50
Pride, false, 133, 135
Prisons. *See* Imprisonment
Psychic reality, 122–125
Psychodemonic narrative, 33–37, 42
Psychotherapy. *See* Therapy
Punishment, 34
Purification, in demonic narrative, 33, 34

Recovery. *See also* Redemption narratives; Shame management
  and disclosure, 6, 89–92, 96n, 106–107
  narrative and, 138–141
  advocacy for, 145–146
Redemption narratives, 7. *See also* Deviant behavior; Narrative, of one's life; Self-narrative
  coherence, 144
  components of, 141

embeddedness, 144
reparation, 142
tragic optimism, 153
vulnerability in, 143–144
Rehabilitation. *See* Recovery; Redemption narratives; Shame management
Relationship Anecdotes Paradigm (RAP), 155
Relationship Episodes (REs), 160. *See also* Core Conflictual Relationships. *See also* Core Conflictual Relationship Theme (CCRT) approach; Couples therapy; Motherhood; Parents and parenting
struggles with communication, 98–101
and therapy, 7–8, 173
Relationship Theme (CCRT) approach
components of, 153, 154
defined, 153
Religion, and therapy, 11, 14
Remembering
and reenacting, 92–95, 105
and self-defining memories, 8, 195, 198, 197–205
Rhetoric, key, 72

Science, and therapy, 12
Self. *See also* Identity; Self-development; Self-narrative
concept of, 14, 15
destruction, 45
new vs. old, 75
Self-defining memories, 8, 192, 198, 197–200
characteristics of, 195
as vehicle of change, 200–203
Self-development
life stories, 177–178
and therapy, 176–178, 182
Self-destruction, 45
Self-narrative, 7, 129–146. *See also* Narrative, of one's life; Redemption narratives
identity transformation, 138–139
life stories, 135–138
management of shame, 131, 140

reconstruction of, 138, 139–141
responsibility acceptance, 133–135
Sexual abuse. *See* Abuse, sexual
Shame. *See also* Shame management
and identity, 131
shameful defect, 56–57
defined, 131
vs. guilt, 131
Shame management, 7, 132–133. *See also* Deviant behavior; Narrative, of one's life; Redemption narratives; Shame; Self-narrative
defenses of, 131
defined, 130
of the incarcerated, 136
and self-narrative, 131, 140
Silence, 6, 7
conspiracy of, 36
by Holocaust survivors, 160–162
in memories, 101–102
of others, 97
safety in, 100
Silencing, 23
Social constructionism, 16, 118
Sociocultural therapy, 15–19
and loss of oral tradition, 16–17, 21
Sociodynamic therapy, 13
Storytelling, 15–16, 19. *See also* Narrative
"analog" story, 140
rhythm of, 24
social nature of, 22
transformative power of, 138
"Subordinated woman," 75, 75n, 77, 84
Substance abuse, 7, 131, 133
Suffering, 7, 30–31
as redemptive, 143
and tragic narrative, 38, 42
Support groups, 184–186
Supportive–expressive (SE) psychotherapy, 154
vs. Freudian psychoanalysis, 165
maladaptive themes, 166
time-limited, 165–166
Survivors, 167. *See also* Holocaust survivor narratives

Therapy, 4, 11–24. *See also* Narrative; Self-narrative; Therapy, of abused women

Therapy, *continued*
  ecological, 13
  history of, 5
  as life engagement, 181–184
  life stories of, 72–77, 78–84
  vs. literature, 4
  and narrative, 4–5, 13, 15, 22, 23–
    24, 140, 186–187
  narrators' evaluation of, 180–186
  postpsychological, 12–15, 19, 21–22
  and religion, 11, 14
  social significance of, 12
  sociodynamic, 13
  supportive–expressive (SE), 154,
    166
  and tragedy, 51–52
Therapy, of abused women, 6, 67–86. *See
    also* Childhood trauma; Narra-
    tive; Therapy; Women's issues
  and abstract individualism, 68, 69–
    70, 71, 77, 85, 86
  agency and, 68, 70, 72, 75
  continuity, 75, 77, 85
  dichotomy of individual, 83
  and emotions, 70, 78–83, 86
  expectations of, 69–70
  Finnish ethnographic study, 71–72
  gendered norms, 6, 68–69, 85
  "independence narratives" of, 75,
    76–77, 85–86
  key rhetoric in, 72
  life stories, 72–77, 78–84
  motherhood and, 7, 77–78, 85
  narrative identity and, 67–68, 72,
    75, 77
  "subordinated woman", 75, 75n, 77,
    84
  victimhold, 78–79, 86
Therapy groups. *See* Support groups
Tragedy, 5–6, 49–64. *See also* Heroines,
    tragic; Tragic narrative; Women's
    issues
  and fate, 6, 50, 51–52, 62–63, 64
  vs. demonic, 38, 39, 40
  fate and, 6, 50, 62–63, 64
  impossible choices in, 6, 60, 61–62
  ironic reversal of fortune, 6, 59, 60
  life story, 52–62
  linear time of, 60
  as meta-narrative, 50, 64
  and psychotherapy, 51–52

  shameful defect in, 56–57
  tragic character, defined, 51
Tragic narrative, 5, 30. *See also* Narra-
    tive; Tragedy
  assumptions of, 38–40
  and Buddhism, 30
  classical, 38
  concept of "other," 39
  and hubris, 38–39
  life story, 41–47
  and suffering, 38
  and Western philosophers, 30
Tragic optimism, 153
Trauma, 91. *See also* Childhood trauma

Verbalizations, and deviant behavior,
    132–133
Victims of Violence (VOV), 90
Vietnam War, 167
Violence, 68–70, 82, 84–85. *See also*
    Childhood trauma, narrative
    and; Therapy, of abused
    women
  and forgiving, 83
Voice. *See also* Narrative
  internalized parental, 34
  in narrative, 22–23
Vulnerability, 159
  feelings of, 96, 97, 103
  in redemption narratives, 143–
    144

Women's issues, 49–64. *See also* Couples
    therapy; Feminism; Heroines,
    tragic; Motherhood; Therapy;
    Therapy, of abused women
  abstract individualism, 68, 69–70,
    71, 77, 85, 86
  and couple relationships, 173,
    178–179
  economic independence, 68
  gendered norms, 68–69, 85
  and households without men,
    171–187
  life stories, 52–62, 72–77, 78–84,
    174, 175, 176, 178–179
  mother–daughter relationship,
    61–62
  narrative identity, 67–68, 72, 75

and self-development, 176–178
and social inequality, 5–6, 50, 64
spousal abuse, 59, 68
"subordinated woman," 75, 75n, 77, 84
support groups for, 184–186

victimhold, of abused women, 78–80
"Wounded healers," 140, 142

"Yachdav" (Together) program, 52

ABOUT THE EDITORS

Amia Lieblich is a professor of psychology at the Hebrew University of Jerusalem. Her books have presented an oral history of Israeli society and deal with war, military service, prisoners of war, and the kibbutz. Her psychobiography of the Israeli female author Dvora Baron, *Conversations With Dvora*, was published in 1998, and a recent psychobiography of the Israeli female poet Lea Goldberg, *Learning About Lea*, was published in 2003. She also published, together with two of her students (Rivka Tuval-Mashiach and Tamar Zilber), *Narrative Research: Reading, Analysis and Interpretation*, a book that presents her approach to narrative research. She has taught graduate courses on life stories and their use in research.

Dan P. McAdams is the Charles Deering McCormick Professor of Teaching Excellence, professor of human development and psychology, and director of the Foley Center for the Study of Lives at Northwestern University. A fellow of the American Psychological Association (APA) and recipient of the 1989 Henry A. Murray Award, he has published widely on the topics of identity and the self, intimacy, generativity and adult development, and the role of narrative and life stories in personality and developmental psychology. He is the author of *The Stories We Live By* and *The Person: An Integrated Introduction to Personality Psychology* and is editor (with Ed de St. Aubin) of *Generativity and Adult Development: How and Why We Care for the Next Generation* (APA, 1998) and (with Ed de St. Aubin and Tae-Chang Kim) of *The Generative Society: Caring for Future Generations* (APA, 2004).

Ruthellen Josselson is professor of psychology at the Hebrew University of Jerusalem and is on the faculty of the Fielding Graduate Institute. Recipient of the 1994 Henry A. Murray Award from the American Psychological

Association and of a Fulbright Research Fellowship for 1989 to 1990, she has also been a visiting professor at the Harvard Graduate School of Education. She is the author of *Revising Herself: The Story of Women's Identity From College to Midlife* (1996), which received the Delta Kappa Gamma International Educators' Award, and *The Space Between Us: Exploring Dimensions of Human Relationships* (1992). With Terri Apter, she coauthored *Best Friends: The Pleasures and Perils of Girls' and Women's Friendships* (1998). She has also published many scholarly articles on narrative and life-history research. She is a practicing psychotherapist and offers workshops in group psychotherapy.